AF740364

Counseling Adults with Autism

Counseling Adults with Autism is a practical guide for counselors, psychologists, and other mental health professionals looking to improve their confidence and competence in counseling adults diagnosed with mild to moderate autism spectrum disorder (ASD). Organized into 11 chapters based on key areas for guiding assessment and treatment planning for this population, this book highlights evidence-based practices and therapeutic interventions through case examples to demonstrate how assessment and treatment can be applied. Replete with insights from a variety of disciplinary approaches, this is a comprehensive and accessible resource for practitioners looking to support and empower clients struggling with social and behavioral challenges.

Ali Cunningham Abbott, PhD, LMHC, QS, is a licensed mental health counselor in private practice and assistant professor at Lynn University. She has over 10 years of experience counseling clients with autism and their family members, and previously served as the Assistant Director of Florida Atlantic University's Center for Autism and Related Disabilities.

Counseling Adults with Autism

A Comprehensive Toolkit

Ali Cunningham Abbott

Routledge
Taylor & Francis Group
NEW YORK AND LONDON

First published 2020
by Routledge
52 Vanderbilt Avenue, New York, NY 10017

and by Routledge
2 Park Square, Milton Park, Abingdon, Oxon, OX14 4RN

Routledge is an imprint of the Taylor & Francis Group, an informa business

© 2020 Taylor & Francis

The right of Ali Cunningham Abbott to be identified as author of this work has been asserted by her in accordance with sections 77 and 78 of the Copyright, Designs and Patents Act 1988.

All rights reserved. No part of this book may be reprinted or reproduced or utilized in any form or by any electronic, mechanical, or other means, now known or hereafter invented, including photocopying and recording, or in any information storage or retrieval system, without permission in writing from the publishers.

Cover image: "Facing the Future," ©Joseph Michael Vidal, 2010.

Trademark notice: Product or corporate names may be trademarks or registered trademarks, and are used only for identification and explanation without intent to infringe.

Library of Congress Cataloging-in-Publication Data
Names: Cunningham Abbott, Ali, author.
Title: Counseling adults with autism : a comprehensive toolkit / Ali Cunningham Abbott, PhD, LMHC.
Description: New York, NY : Routledge, 2019. | Includes bibliographical references and index.
Identifiers: LCCN 2019004673 (print) | LCCN 2019006843 (ebook) | ISBN 9780429506055 (eBook) | ISBN 9781138584389 (hardback) | ISBN 9781138584396 (pbk.) | ISBN 9780429506055 (ebk)
Subjects: LCSH: Autism spectrum disorders–Treatment.
Classification: LCC RC553.A88 (ebook) | LCC RC553.A88 C87 2019 (print) | DDC 616.85/882–dc23
LC record available at https://lccn.loc.gov/2019004673

ISBN: 978-1-138-58438-9 (hbk)
ISBN: 978-1-138-58439-6 (pbk)
ISBN: 978-0-429-50605-5 (ebk)

Typeset in Bembo
by Wearset Ltd, Boldon, Tyne and Wear

Contents

Acknowledgments

The professional and personal relationships in my life are the key ingredients that contributed to my completion of this book. The most important part of my work as a counselor has been the relationships I've cultivated with former and current clients and their families. My passion for the field of mental health counseling was invigorated and sustained by the people I've had the pleasure of offering services to over the last decade. These clients have invited me into their lives in intimate ways which allowed me to gain the experience and expertise in my chosen career. I've been honored to work alongside autistic adults, their parents, partners, children, job coaches and more who shared many of the goals identified in this book. They are the reason I've been able to write this book.

My professional relationships with colleagues over the years have helped support and challenge me to grow in ways I could not have imagined. I acknowledge those who have directly contributed to this work in more detail in the Introduction. But it's worth restating that I could not have accomplished this with the same level of expertise nor in the timeframe without the efforts put forth by Alison, Elisa, and Ryan. You are wonderful professionals, women, and friends.

I certainly did not set out to write a book early in my career, but with the encouragement of my peers in counseling, the autism community, and academia, I was able to accomplish something I hadn't initially considered. My colleagues are consummate clinicians, researchers and educators who I respect and admire for their commitment to this work. The leadership at Lynn University, specifically Debbie Ainbinder, my program chair and Katrina Carter-Tellison, academic dean, have supported my efforts in so many ways. Their support allowed me to fit writing a book into my teaching and service efforts over the last year.

Over the last decade, my family relationships have been invaluable to my professional success that eventually led to the publication of this book. While seeking my doctoral degree, my interest in assessing treatment outcomes for adults with autism was born. During this same time, my mother was diagnosed with cancer, suffered through months of treatment and eventually died. It is still the biggest personal challenge I've ever faced. But from her sad and untimely death grew a relationship between my father, sister, brother-in-law, aunt, and cousins that has never been closer. Both my dad, Bill, and sister, Christina, have supported my career through logistic and emotional support over the last ten years. From copyediting feedback (thanks, Dad) to talking me through writing blocks and imposter syndrome, they directly and indirectly played roles in helping me complete this book.

Five years ago, I met my loving husband Kevin. It is true, even if cliché, to say that I absolutely could not have done this without him. He knows how to support me in ways that I'd never experienced before he came into my life. Throughout the process of writing this book, Kevin helped serve in the vital role of reminding me when I took on too much and encouraging me when I needed an extra push. If he wasn't such an egalitarian, empathic, and emboldening partner, I certainly would not have been able to do this. He coached me through several tearful conversations and supported my hours-long writing sessions as we made the biggest transition in our family. This year we welcomed our son, Jad, into the world. Birthing both a child and book in the same year was an ambitious goal. I could not have done it and enjoyed the new journey of motherhood as much as I have without my husband. My dad also played a vital role as he offered to be with Jad at any opportunity possible while I wrote. These men in my life have made the process of simultaneously becoming both a mother and author that much sweeter. Jad, thank you for being a calm and loving cherub of a baby. I'm so looking forward to sharing this life with you and watching you grow.

Introduction

This book is designed as a practical guide for counselors, psychologists and other mental health professionals. I hope it will help provide effective counseling and psychotherapy to adults diagnosed with autism spectrum disorder (ASD). In an effort to build a comprehensive network to enhance adult ASD treatment, this book is designed to be a practical tool for counselors and other mental health professionals in how to best approach, assess and ultimately assist this population. In this guide we focus on a client population who exhibit mild to moderate ASD because they are the ones who can most likely benefit from collaborative talk therapy; as a result, this guide may not be as helpful for those who are diagnosed with severe language or cognitive impairments.

The majority of this book's content is dedicated to helping clinicians learn effective techniques designed to treat the primary symptoms of autism. The authors highlight evidence-based practices on how to effectively and comprehensively approach, assess, and treat adults with ASD. Since best practice in ASD treatment is based on a multidisciplinary approach, this guidebook features contributors with expertise in related fields such as clinical psychology, behavior analysis, exceptional student education as well as marriage and family therapy. Each chapter within will contain:

1. a description of that chapter's treatment focus,
2. clinical interventions and techniques that can aid practitioners in practice,
3. plus, an abbreviated case example of the presentation of ASD symptoms and interventions that highlight how they have actually been used with clients.

The introduction provides context through an exploration of this author's professional experience and journey and a brief historical review of her professional counseling experience with autism. The primary aim of creating this personal background is to demonstrate to the counseling community that working with this population is indeed within our scope of practice when we are provided with the appropriate tools and training. In my work, it's been essential to enter the worlds of other mental health professionals including exceptional student education, behavior analysis, and clinical psychology in which individuals with ASD have historically had a place either in the classroom or a treatment setting.

Yet, when introducing this work to my own mentors and colleagues in counseling, there has been a sense, an opinion, and even separation that sent the message that clinical and research interests in working with the ASD population didn't quite "fit" our profession, essentially trying to squeeze a square peg into a round hole. I challenge the notion that this work belongs only to other professionals and in this I and others have had to break ground within the field to insist and demonstrate, through awareness and education, that this indeed is a group that can benefit from working with professional counselors.

Square Peg, Round Hole

Square Peg: My Journey

When I sat down to write this book, I had a keen sense of imposter syndrome. How is it that I've arrived at a place where I, of all people, can confidently and competently teach others about counseling adults with autism? I found the answer to that question as I reflected on my career as a mental health counselor, educator, researcher, and supervisor, from its beginnings to the journey my career has taken me on over the last 14 years.

Two years after completing my bachelor's degree, I found myself in human services work that I liked but didn't love. This lackluster feeling about my career, led me to consider what I needed to do next to meet my ultimate goal of becoming a therapist. Therefore, my professional career truly began when I decided to apply for a master's degree in clinical mental health counseling. As I sat nervously in a group interview during the admission process, a question was posed to us: "What client population would you have the most difficulty working with?" I was frankly not prepared to answer this question, so I sat back, observed the others and tried to dig deep. Others responded in succession identifying groups of people such as sex offenders or violent criminals as those they would have a tough time helping. These logically made sense to me but didn't speak to my own personal feelings of discomfort and even seemed a bit obvious. Since I wanted to stand out among the group I continued to try to dig deeper. As the responses continued others discussed how issues that touched their personal lives would be difficult such as one woman who had lived through her brother's addiction issues. When the time came for me to respond, I was scared to share and open myself up to potential judgement from others. But, being a characteristically honest and direct person, I decided to take the plunge. My response was that working with people with disabilities would likely be my biggest challenge. I went on to explain that I hadn't had any meaningful exposure to "them" and went on to mention how I simply felt uncomfortable because how could I possibly know what to do. Writing about this now elicits feelings of condemnation and shame about my inexperienced, sheltered and naïve self. But in those days, when it came to people with disabilities and other groups with whom mental health professionals and counselors regularly work, I was clueless.

Although this response still makes me cringe, it did demonstrate that I was able to identify a significant bias and growth edge early on in training. To help admit my shame and to encourage others to explore their biases about this, or any other, population, I tell this story as often as I can. When I teach *Social and Cultural Foundations of Counseling*, it is a means to help graduate students expand their horizons about the kinds of clients they will work with. It is important to be vulnerable about my own journey through this profession and about how misplaced or uncomfortable I felt with what would later become my life's passion.

Given my lack of experience and self-proclaimed discomfort, how did I end up fulfilled and happy in a career of counseling people with autism? It was equal parts luck and persistence. Near the end of my master's degree, I was enrolled in a special needs counseling course where one of my peers said she was leaving her graduate assistantship and that the department she worked for was looking for her replacement. At the time, I was financially strapped due to the fact that I had to cut back my full-time job to make space for the master's degree practicum experience at a local substance use treatment center. A graduate assistantship was an excellent solution for me to get some part-time paid work and it could help with my tuition and fees. The department in question was the Center for Autism & Related Disabilities (CARD) and even though it was located in the same building, on the same floor where I'd taken dozens of classes for the last three years, I had never heard of it. With her help connecting me to the right people, I was interviewed and hired soon after to do administrative work, mostly covering phones and helping out wherever I could.

After starting I soon became fascinated by the work the clinical staff were doing to help families whose children or adult family members had recently been diagnosed with ASD. So, I began going outside my scope of administrative duties to help clinicians with other tasks, such as printing out therapeutic tools (i.e., PECS), lending a hand in a "Mommy & Me" group and shadowing intake sessions with their clients. I was inspired by how supportive counseling, treatment and clinical consultation resulted in demonstrable progress not just for clients with autism but also with their family members. The young children in the Mommy & Me groups learned new skills and improved their language in just eight weeks. Families who were once grieving and pessimistic after a new diagnosis were able to see the strengths in their child and move towards securing medical interventions and weekly therapies. In a short time, I learned an astonishing amount from my experience shadowing master's level clinicians and the families who allowed me to be a part of their process. Within three months of becoming involved in this work, I was hooked.

During my initiation into the field of autism, I began to notice how the master's level clinicians who worked at CARD identified themselves professionally. Most were exceptional student educators, speech language pathologists and behavior analysts (BCBAs). There was not a single counselor, licensed therapist or mental health professional in the group of professionals with whom I worked. I also began to notice that among my professional counseling colleagues, mentors and professors, very few had experience working with people with disabilities. Based on the kind of work I witnessed at CARD, especially through supportive counseling and consultation, both of which I had been trained in, I couldn't seem to understand why these two worlds were so separate. At the time, I was not familiar with the work my friends and colleagues in school and rehabilitation counseling were engaged in with the ASD population because even in my graduate program there was a separation between our counseling identities.

As I completed my practicum semester and first few months working at CARD, I had become so interested and invested in this work that I applied for a full-time clinical position. I was determined to fit my career path as a clinical mental health counselor into the world of ASD treatment. This was not an easy path as I confronted several barriers along the way, such as the need to find an appropriate supervisor and to convince faculty, mentors, and others that this work was the best fit based on my training and identity. My personal and professional journey and experiences are, as expected, not unique in that many professional counselors report feeling ill-prepared and incompetent when it comes to treating adults with autism.

Round Hole: Why Have Professional Counselors Not Been More Involved in Treating Autism?

Let's explore the context and parameters that have kept the worlds of counseling apart from clients with disabilities, and ASD specifically. Disability and multicultural competency are two areas of training that mental health professionals in varying fields continue to struggle with (Strike, Skovholt, & Hummel, 2004). These professionals include seasoned psychologists, speech language pathologists in masters' level training programs and social workers, who all report that their knowledge, skills, and awareness in working with clients with disabilities need improvement (Kemp & Mallinckrodt, 1996; Werner, 2011; Plumb & Plexico, 2013). One conclusion that can be drawn from this research, across mental health disciplines, is reassuring. It means that counselors are not alone in their sense of inadequacy, lack of training or discomfort in treating clients with autism or other disability diagnoses.

According to the literature, professional counselors began working with clients with ASD in the context of preschool children and their families only in the late 1980s (Hohenshil & Humes, 1988). In this capacity, counselors were able to positively affect not only children through early intervention but also their parents by helping them process the challenges faced during childhood and adolescence. This was capitalized on through counselors' training in strength-based therapy approaches with a focus on the therapeutic relationship. By providing services in schools, professional school counselors began to establish their roles in the ASD treatment context with the recommendation that counselors should receive special training in the needs of preschoolers and their families.

In addition to this important work within the schools for counselors, the ability to connect effectively with family members also provided counselors with an opportunity to use their unique abilities. With a focus on building a strong therapeutic relationship and shifting towards strengths, and away from a deficit-based model, counselors began to serve as important supports for families managing the impacts of a new ASD diagnosis. Supportive counseling for families is recognized as an integral component of treating children, teens, and adults impacted by ASD and can be provided by competently trained and experienced counselors (Bennett et al., 2012). The continued need for training programs to incorporate opportunities for expanding knowledge and practical experience of counselors is consistently recommended in research. Despite these consistent recommendations, the increase in the number of counselors within the field of autism has remained slow. From these early experiences working with young children and their families, other opportunities for counselors began to emerge in working with this population. Schools provided the best access for counselors to provide therapy to elementary, middle and high school ASD students.

Early on in our history, rehabilitation counselors, who are trained to work with individuals with disabilities, were given opportunities to work with the ASD population due to their specialization. With federal and state legislative funds allocated to improving human rights for individuals with disabilities, rehabilitation counselors have been in demand for the last three decades (Americans with Disabilities Act, 1990). Rehabilitation counselors helped to connect ASD clients with essential services such as job placement, coaching and case management.

The experiences of school and rehabilitation counselors in counseling clients with ASD have a more robust history; whereas the experiences of professional counselors with other specializations are more limited. It's unfortunate, that specialties within professional counseling programs are often siloed and don't allow for shared experiences when many trainees could benefit from such learning. Professional counselors can be equipped to work in a variety of settings with myriad populations, yet due to the fragmentation among specialties these opportunities are often unavailable (Rust, Raskin, & Hill, 2013). The clinical mental health and professional counseling specialty deserves a strong role in treating both the core symptoms of ASD as well as common comorbid diagnoses for which they typically have training and treatment experience.

Why Adults?

In my professional journey I was exposed to working with ASD clients of all ages, from those diagnosed via early intervention at 15 months of age to a 78-year-old who had, only two months prior, received his diagnosis after a life riddled with relationship issues. I've always loved children and babies so it would have been easy and enticing for me to specialize in early intervention and immerse myself in that age range. Yet, as luck and work demands dictated, it was the older population with whom I would end up finding my best fit.

My earliest memory of this work was when I shadowed a social work colleague who conducted a monthly social group for young ASD adults. The group had sporadic attendance and so the first night I attended there was, sadly, only one attendee. Let's call him Henry. Since he'd arranged transportation services and the time to come to the group, my colleague and I decided to conduct the social "group" with just the three of us. Henry had an exceptional memory and recounted the tales of some of his favorite Disney movies and family vacations in great detail. His attitude didn't seem to be negatively impacted by the fact that others didn't arrive, and he was perfectly content to have the interaction with just the three us. Aside from his obvious positive qualities, it quickly became clear to me why he would have challenges interacting with others. He had an apparent, robotic tone to his speech and atypical posture and gait that made it almost immediately clear he was different. I imagined what a childhood with these characteristics must have been like for him… certainly not easy. But I found Henry's brutal honesty charming, his dry sense of humor funny and his genuine, childlike interests, even naïveté, about the world fascinating. Generally, I just liked being around him, and as I continued to get to know him over the next eight years my fondness grew.

Henry is just one of the individuals I had the pleasure to get to know well during my working life. Even though I would ideally like to, it would be impractical for me to go through how each client like Henry impacted me. Given that my work involved facilitating hundreds of social and treatment groups as well as individual counseling, I believe that one of the reasons I've been so satisfied with my career is due to the ASD adults with whom I formed relationships. I truly wanted to witness them creating meaningful relationships, getting better jobs, and living fulfilled lives. There are many memories that pop-up for me as I think about seeing my clients and hearing about their recent relationship successes or a work promotion and I have a profound sense of joy for them; perhaps even more than I have for many other people in my personal and professional worlds.

Although I hope I have helped them over the years, it is also true that the adults with ASD that I have worked with helped *me* grow both personally and professionally. During my time in graduate school I struggled with my own relationships, job satisfaction and search for fulfillment. In researching and learning tools to help them build skills and create healthy relationships, I was able to make better decisions in ending some old and starting new personal relationships in my life. In fact, at the end of my doctoral research, during which time I taught ASD clients about romantic relationship skills for meeting a mate, I met my own husband. I also found the career that I consider my calling through my work as a counselor, but also an educator and clinical supervisor. The latter include credentials I would have not obtained without those adults with autism who volunteered to participate in the research we conducted. If it wasn't for them, I would not have a career in academia, or this work that I love so much. When all that is accounted for, I would say the community of ASD adults I've worked with have served me even more than I have served them.

Making it Work: Professional Collaborations

The opportunity to collaborate with other professionals is one the most valuable aspects of counseling individuals with ASD. In some circumstances, this includes connecting with other professional counselors who share in this work, but, honestly, this has been more rare than common for me. Most often I've collaborated with professional educators, clinical psychologists, and board-certified behavior analysts (BCBAs) who had a significant breadth of training and work experience treating clients with ASD.

My own training in how to work with clients with ASD began by learning the basics from a special educator about how to interact with families and train professionals on evidence-based practices. The first person I trained with, was a strong role model for how to effectively connect with parents of children with ASD and how best to relate to teachers in consultation. She confidently approached the subject due to years of experience in and out of the classroom in which she had had many successes teaching children how to communicate, overcome behavioral challenges, and learn core curricular lessons key to their education. Perhaps because of her years of experience and the confidence she exuded, she taught me how to effectively facilitate a room of teachers and other professionals who were typically mandated to attend professional development sessions and therefore quite often and understandably resistant. Her ability to engage both small and large audiences of parents, teachers and other professionals helped encourage me to develop my own way of counseling, consulting and training. She inspired me to be committed to this work and served as a model for how I would develop some of my professional skills. As professional counselors, we have a lot to learn from our colleagues in teaching and special education who excel at managing large groups of different ages (i.e., classroom management), individualizing instruction and understanding the complexities of consultation. Two of my colleagues and friends, Elisa Cruz-Torres and Alison Bourdeau have contributed their special education knowledge, experience, and specialties in their authored chapters in this guidebook.

Extensive training and expertise in testing and evaluation is an area of strength our psychology colleagues lend to treating clients with ASD. During my time in the field, I have been lucky to work with licensed clinical psychologists from across the nation who are clinical and research experts in the field of autism evaluation and treatment. I've been fortunate enough to be trained by Dr. Liz Laugeson from the UCLA PEERS® program where my group therapy clinical and research skills were honed. Currently, I get to work with Dr. Ryan Seidman, at the Children's Treatment Center, whose expertise in treating dual diagnosed ASD children, teens, adults, and their family members is vast. In this group practice, and its adult division – the Center for the Treatment of Anxiety and Mood Disorders – I work closely with licensed clinical psychologists and psychiatrists. The value of consulting with this team of professionals is priceless.

As mentioned before, the counseling profession's unique opportunity to treat adults with ASD from a strengths-based, relationship-focused approach is one that can fit well among these other disciplines. Finding our place within these professional circles is key to helping others understand our role. Our niche in providing feedback on the therapeutic relationship and focusing on strengths-based interventions to aid in both ameliorating symptoms and utilizing client's already existing resources is critical (Artman & Daniels, 2010). We can apply different ideas about case conceptualization and treatment modalities that may be different from traditional approaches. We're also able to serve as the conduits to successful professional consultation. Given that these are some of the hallmarks of professional counselors, it's important to honor and recognize many of the other professionals whose work with ASD has preceded our own and with whom we can and should collaborate. In my opinion it is our responsibility to work with these trusted parties in order to ensure the most well-rounded treatment outcomes for our clients.

Over my career, I've been honored to work with inspiring colleagues in related fields who have taught me the importance of interdisciplinary collaboration and consultation. The team approach should include not just the adult with ASD but also family members and professionals from assessment to treatment planning and should be designed to allow for the highest standards in ethical and effective treatment practices. Best practice treatment for ASD involves a multidisciplinary approach which often involves the integration of the fields of clinical psychology, psychiatry, behavior analysis, exceptional student education and other specialists. Both my clients and I have directly benefited from positive experiences with colleagues, peers and friends in each of these professions.

Clinical psychologists have taught me about best methods in assessing differential diagnoses and evaluating for co-occurring cognitive deficits. I have been exposed to some of the most impressive and complex diagnostic work through my colleagues and friends in this field whom I respect and from whom I've learned so much. I've witnessed my trusted colleagues in psychiatry provide medical interventions for clients that have helped stabilize their

ASD symptoms or comorbid conditions that would have otherwise made counseling and psychotherapy interventions nearly impossible. In many client's lives, these treatments have been life changing and/or lifesaving.

In my own work experience I've been lucky to have significant exposure to the wealth of research in applied behavior analysis and I've observed the value of behavior therapy in working with ASD clients through my dear friends and peers who are board certified behavior analysts (BCBAs). Their value will become increasingly important in treating adults with ASD as that population continues to grow, so will the need to collaborate with BCBAs who have an excellent grasp on ways to treat significant behavioral issues. I anticipate that the work they've been so effective in and famous for in ASD children's interventions will be replicated with adults. I've also learned an immense amount from exceptional student educators in schools from daycares all the way to college; people who excel in classroom management and the ability to differentiate instruction for a variety of students with ASD.

Counselors and counselor educators can learn an immense amount from these professionals in order to enhance their treatment of clients with ASD. In treating this population, it remains important to be immersed in the ASD community, which includes collaborating with professionals. The aforementioned professionals have certainly enabled me to grow both in openness to their discipline's approach to treatment and to understand how to fill gaps in treatment when they can benefit our clients.

Our Focus

In an effort to build a comprehensive network to enhance adult ASD treatment, this book is designed to be a practical tool for counselors and other mental health professionals in how best to approach, assess and ultimately counsel this population. The first section of this book, just like the first stage of treatment, will focus on how best to approach clients with ASD to cultivate a healthy therapeutic relationship within a culturally competent framework. Therefore, the first three chapters focus on how a counselor's attitudes about capability, the family system, and a client's thoughts and behaviors can inform the practitioner's approach. I've invited my colleague with a specialized master's degree in marriage and family therapy to author Chapter 2 because this training adds value to understanding how the family dynamic can impact treatment of an adult with ASD.

The assessment component of this book, which in treatment sequence co-occurs or follows soon after establishment of the therapeutic relationship, serves an important role and has its own dedicated chapter. Effective evaluation and assessment of ASD in adults along with differential and comorbid diagnoses is an essential step in planning for competent treatment. So much so that there are manuals and books solely dedicated to such topics. Historically, most of the literature in assessment and evaluation in ASD focuses on children, but over the last 10 years the number of assessment and evaluation resources for autistic adults has increased (Gerhardt & Lainer, 2011). Therefore, a variety of clinician observation, self and third-party reporting tools will be reviewed. An esteemed colleague of mine in clinical psychology will share expertise from her discipline to help break down these components in a way that is clear and comprehensive.

The majority of this book's content is dedicated to helping clinicians learn effective techniques designed to treat the primary symptoms of autism. The chapter titles and areas of treatment are based on those identified by the DSM-5 diagnostic categories and subscales of the gold standard ASD treatment assessment tool, the Social Responsiveness Scale-2 (APA, 2013; Constantino, 2012). There are five chapters dedicated to treatment, half of the book's content. In order to expertly address some of the most common behavioral challenges adult clients with ASD face, my colleague, a doctoral-level board certified behavior analyst, will take a stance in discussing how both traditional applied behavior analysis and contemporary behavioral approaches can be integrated to create positive treatment outcomes.

Lastly, the book will cover the array of extra therapeutic supports and services that are important for adults with ASD in order to promote independence. Since an ultimate goal of any adult's development is independent functioning in work, housing, education, transportation, and other aspects of daily life, the final chapter will review how independence may differ for autistic adults. Owing to the varying abilities and levels of potential, the concept of independence needs to be approached on a highly individualized basis. This chapter will provide an overview of how resources available in many communities can help improve the quality of life for adults with ASD when these pieces of the puzzle are integrated into treatment. As this is the last and final chapter of the book, its importance and value in the life of adults with ASD could arguably be the most impactful as it will determine how they access counseling and other vital services that will ultimately enable them to achieve the level of independence they desire.

Even though chapters are authored by clinical experts in subspecialties, who better to solicit information from on these topics than adults with ASD themselves who have the personal experiences? An important effort for me and my chapter authors in writing about how to effectively counsel adults with ASD was to provide a voice and personal agency for the clients we work with. One thing I'd like to note as part of my work within the ASD community is to acknowledge the language I'll be using throughout the book.

Due to the audience of practitioners and counselors who will be reading this book, I will be using person-first language. You've already read my multiple use of clients/individuals/adults with ASD in the beginning of this chapter. Person-first language began as an effort to move away from using a diagnosis to label or stigmatize people (Tobin, 2011). Parents and loved ones of people who were labeled as alcoholics, schizophrenics, or autistics wanted them to be respected as people not as diagnoses or conditions. It began as an effort to personalize clients with different diagnoses and became best-practice for clinicians in training. But there is a disconnect between how several autistic advocates view person-first language and their view of how people can support them.

Many argue that this language is not the way that autistic adults themselves would choose to be referred to. Much like different cultural groups who identify by their race, ethnicity, country of origin, or gender, some autistic adults would like to be acknowledged as such through identify-first language. This would be similar to the client who struggles with alcohol addiction and comes to embrace their identity as an alcoholic because it connects them to a community of support. There are prominent figures and organizations who consider person-first language clinical language dehumanizing, impersonal or even discriminatory (Brown, 2011).

In recent years, training in treating specific social and cultural groups has emphasized person-first language to humanize the client. But this assumption to adopt person-first language does not allow us to acknowledge how the client themselves would like to be referred to. Therefore, the adoption of the language that our client's identify with, whether it is person-first or identify-first, is important. As an attempt to speak to both perspectives, for those who prefer either person-first or identify-first language, the terminology *clients/individuals/adults with ASD* and *autistic adults* will both be used throughout this book.

The neurodiversity movement is one that has emerged over the last two decades as more people with autism have aged into adulthood and as more autistic adults began to receive new diagnoses later in life. This social justice movement is one that fights to recognize autism and other neurological and developmental conditions as a variance in the human genome (Jaarsma & Welin, 2012). Well-known variances in the human genome explain differences among us in height, hair color, and many visible or physical traits. It challenges all of us to consider neurological differences, much like any other and to hold them in respectful regard. Many have argued that these differences create an advantage in specific areas of life that can be viewed by institutions and society as preferential and privileged (Austin & Pisano, 2017). The autism advantage is nomenclature that is being used specifically in workforce policy and discussion for industries that value the strengths that autistic employees can bring to their organizations.

Family members and caregivers have also played a role in advocating that people with autism should be recognized, not by their deficits, but by how their neurodevelopmental differences can be valued and respected. This shifts the model of disability from a medical perspective, that tends to be pathology and symptom-based, to a strength-based perspective. The movement encourages the public, educators, clinicians, lawmakers and others to learn how to include people with autism in conversations about what structures can be put into place to benefit them. The neurodiversity movement and self-advocacy continue to be important parts of the autistic adult's experience.

It is therefore consistent and understandable that we have asked for permission from clients' to share their stories to help illustrate the primary concept or goal for each chapter. As each chapter concludes, a case example based on the clinical experiences of the authors will be used to illustrate treatment successes and challenges in the implementation of the recommended interventions. Case examples are based on actual clinician–client interactions but protect the identities of our valued clients; consent to share aspects of treatment in the scenarios presented was obtained for each chapter.

References

American Psychiatric Association. (2013). *Diagnostic and statistical manual of mental disorders* (5th ed.). Arlington, VA: Author.

Americans with Disabilities Act. (1990). Retrieved from: www.eeoc.gov.

Artman, L.K., & Daniels, J.A. (2010). Disability and psychotherapy practice: Cultural competence and practical tips. *Professional Psychology: Research and Practice, 41*(5), 442–448.

Austin, R.D., & Pisano, G.P. (2017). Neurodiversity as a competitive advantage. *Harvard Business Review, 5*, 96–103.

Bennett, E.D., Butler, M., Hunsaker, E., Cook, O., & Leland, B. (2012). Autism spectrum disorder: What counselors need to know. In *Ideas and research you can use: VISTAS* 2012. Retrieved from www.counseling.org/resources/library/vistas/2012.

Brown, L. (2011). *The significance of semantics: Person-first language: Why it matters.* Retrieved from www.autisticadvocacy.org/about/identity-first-language.

Constantino, J. (2012). *Social responsiveness scale 2*. Los Angeles, CA: Western Psychological Services.

Gerhardt, P.F., & Lainer, I. (2011). Addressing the needs of adolescents and adults with autism: A crisis on the horizon. *Journal of Contemporary Psychotherapy, 41*, 37–45. doi:10.1007/s10879-010-9160-2.

Hohenshil, T.H., & Humes, C.W. (1988). Roles of counselors in ensuring the rights of the handicapped. In D.R. Atkinson & G. Hackett (Eds.), *Counseling non-ethnic American minorities* (pp. 133–150). Springfield, IL: Charles C Thomas.

Jaarsma, P., & Welin, S. (2012). Autism as a natural human variation: Reflections on the claims of the neurodiversity movement. *Health Care Analysis, 20*, 20–30. doi:10.1007/s10728-011-0169-9.

Kemp, N.T., & Mallinckrodt, B. (1996). Impact of professional training on case conceptualization of clients with a disability. *Professional Psychology: Research and Practice, 27*(4), 378–385.

Plumb, A.M., & Plexico, L.W. (2013). Autism spectrum disorder: Experience, training, and confidence levels of school-based speech-language pathologists. *Language, Speech, and Hearing Services in Schools*, 44, 89–104.

Rust, J.P., Raskin, J.D., & Hill, M.S. (2013). Problems of professional competence among counselor trainees: Programmatic issues and guidelines. *Counselor Education & Supervision, 52*(1), 30–42.

Strike, D.L., Skovholt, T.M., & Hummel, T.J. (2004). Mental health professionals' disability competence: Measuring self-awareness, perceived knowledge, and perceived skills. *Rehabilitation Psychology, 49*(4), 321–327.

Tobin, M. (2011). *Put me first: The importance of person-first language. Innovations and perspectives: Virginia Department of Education's Training and Technical Assistance Center.*

Retrieved from www.ttacnews.vcu.edu/2011/05/put-me-first-the-importance-of-person-first-language.

Werner, S. (2011). Assessing female students' attitudes in various health and social professions toward working with people with autism: A preliminary study. *Journal of Interprofessional Care*, *25*, 131–137.

1 Presuming Competence and Capability

One of the first steps in effectively treating clients is to understand how our approach influences the therapeutic relationship. The approach we take with clients is informed by our personal preferences, chosen theoretical orientation, mentors, research in the field, a variety of professional experiences, and systemic factors (Erford, 2018). This chapter will specifically review the importance of presuming that our clients diagnosed with autism (ASD) are competent and capable. But doesn't this sound like a given? Absolutely, yes, it should be.

Yet, because of our historically entrenched ideas and inherent biases about ASD and other groups who have traditionally fallen into the "disability" category, it warrants an explicit review of why this is important (FitzGerald & Hurst, 2017). Unfortunately, like most people, mental health practitioners risk holding clients with autism to lower standards of achievement in many areas of their lives. Some may not think they can attain educational, work or relationship goals simply because of their ASD diagnosis (Artman & Daniels, 2012). Our inherent biases cannot be overlooked if we are to be at our best and fulfill our ethical obligations as practitioners to avoid doing harm or impose our own beliefs onto our clients (American Counseling Association, 2014). We have the potential to help significantly or harm depending on our own beliefs regarding autistic people. In one way this chapter serves as a reminder for us all that even though we may think we are presuming competence and capability in our clients, the work of monitoring our biases does not have a stopping point. We owe it to our clients, ourselves and our colleagues to refresh and reinvigorate our love for this work by learning ways to best acknowledge and address our biases.

But how do we move from simply taking on the mindset that our clients are competent and capable, to building this into our treatment approach? Guidelines and recommendations for taking action on how to build this mindset will be reviewed in this chapter. This starts with understanding the value of a strength-based approach and how to navigate the complicated clinical picture of splintered cognitive and behavioral skill sets. The chapter then reviews strategies that can help counselors best integrate these concepts into the treatment approach and provides a case example to highlight how this can be done in practice.

Starting with Strengths

In determining what actions to take in a competency and capability first approach to clients with ASD, this chapter will draw from best-practice, research-based recommendations for the general and ASD population. The first general recommendation is to assess and identify strengths from the start. How this can be approached specifically with ASD clients is discussed in how we can best identify both group and individual talents that will help guide treatment.

In order to implement this effectively we have to be intentional in the content and process of our initial contact with our clients. This can start simply and informally through initial screening and interviewing during which a counselor asks about their values, personal characteristics and aspects of themselves or their lives that they view as resources, and help to improve their mental health. Exploring both internal and external resources will be an essential first step to starting with strengths. It's amazing to witness the surprising encounter this affords clients who are used to starting and engaging in treatment that is typically problem-focused. It is in these clinical moments, that we're reminded about the importance of checking-in with ourselves and our colleagues so that we're delivering the best quality of care.

When considering how mental health professionals can deliver best-practices in care, it is critical to keep in mind that diversity among people diagnosed with autism is just as varied as with any other group of people. Because of this, each client should be treated based on individual experiences, strengths, and challenges. Acknowledging this at the outset of approaching all clients is helpful in order to avoid overgeneralizing or committing the common error of making assumptions about one person based on their association with a group (Sue & Sue, 2016). Therefore, acknowledging individual differences and unique abilities from the start of building the therapeutic relationship is key to success. But in understanding the tripartite development of personal identity on individual, group, and universal levels counselors go a step beyond that to understand commonalities across unique individuals (Sue et al., 2016). Therefore, an awareness of group similarities and characteristics that aid in our understanding of our clients is also important.

The neurodiversity movement is a cultural phenomenon that has shifted the neurological disability paradigm to a humanistic, strengths-based view on people diagnosed with a variety of conditions (Elder-Robison, 2017). As with many grassroots, cultural movements this one began and continues on because of the work of adults with neurodevelopmental and neurocognitive disorders themselves. Within this movement, treating ASD adults and children as a cultural group, much like those of minority race, ethnicity, or gender status, is an approach that honors and respects their experiences as a group that has been marginalized and discriminated against.

Yet the counseling profession has identified in research and clinical experience the importance of acknowledging the complexities of marginalized groups (Sue & Sue, 2016). This is because many within these groups also hold privilege in certain areas that are vital to surviving and thriving. For individuals with autism, their privileges and strengths lie in many areas. Some examples are an incredible capacity for memorization or an ability to spend long periods of time attending to detail on specialized topics and skills. The criteria that makes them eligible for the disorder can become an asset or advantage when cultivated successfully.

Another factor of ASD privilege is that, often, the skills they embody are ones that non-ASD adults find uncomfortable, difficult, or even impossible to acquire. This creates a unique opportunity for people with autism to create a niche for themselves in different domains, including educational settings, the workplace, and social groups. For example, people with autism can be particularly skilled in different technological domains. Areas of the world in which prevalence rates of autism are above the norm, such as Silicon Valley – the technology hub of California – could be a result of a cluster of people with autism or the broad autism phenotype (BAP) finding a niche and succeeding in this industry (Van Meter et al., 2010).

Even though each person's strengths should be assessed and identified individually, it's helpful to have an understanding of several identified group strengths (Sue & Sue, 2016). These can serve as a foundation in guiding initial steps in assessment, from written, intake form questions to interview, screening questions used in the beginning stages of treatment. These strengths include but are not limited to those given in Table 1.1.

Early identification of the unique strengths exemplified by clients diagnosed with ASD is part of our responsibility as counselors and mental health professionals. Missing the opportunity to identify and cultivate these will

Table 1.1 Group level strengths of individuals diagnosed with autism

Identified strengths	*Source*
Tendency to be investigative and conventional in approach to work tasks	Lorenz and Heinitz (2014)
Creative, resilient and able to find meaning in life	Wehmeyer (2015)
Detail-oriented, specialized skills in particular area(s), ability to learn or study deeply	National Autistic Society (2016)
Logical in decision-making, independent thinkers, strong visual memory and processing skills	National Autistic Society (2016)
Direct communication skills; loyal, honest and non-judgmental	National Autistic Society (2016)

Sources: this list comprises a collection of common strengths as identified in the autism research, disability literature, and by professional organizations.

likely lead to an ineffective approach, therapeutic relationship and even stagnation in treatment progress. The strengths-based perspective that counselors highlight as part of our professional identity aligns well with this recommendation. It is vital for us to integrate this part of our training into our clinical view and approach in working with ASD adults (Grothaus, McAuliffe, & Craigen, 2012).

From Self-Efficacy to Self-Determination

Amongst the most important reasons that a strength-based focus is successful in the area of adult outcomes are self-awareness, self-efficacy, self-advocacy, and self-determination. Self-awareness is the ability to observe and know one's internal states and characteristics (Goleman, 2005). This at the core of identifying strengths and tailoring treatment for achieving positive outcomes. It is essential to accurately assess and identify the ASD client's strengths and challenges to improve quality of life outcomes (Mason et al., 2018). In clients for whom self-awareness is impaired, they may not have a clear picture of their own attributes, this will be one of the first steps in counseling. This is helpful to introduce by first focusing on one's own strengths and continuing this work by exploring ways that clients can also become aware of their potential for growth. For those who demonstrate higher levels of self-awareness, repeating, emphasizing, and learning how to build on these strengths will be a goal in therapy.

Self-efficacy is the belief one has about one's ability to accomplish or execute a task successfully (Bandura, 1977). A person's measure of self-efficacy often reflects different levels of confidence and capability depending on the context. Among a small sample of college students with ASD, most reported confidence in a few features of self-efficacy, including getting information and other people to listen (Shattuck et al., 2014). But fewer than half of these same students reported being able to "handle most things that come their way", a higher-level self-efficacy skill. Finally, those who identified racially as white and those who had better communication skills reported the highest self-efficacy. Racial minorities in college settings have long faced challenges in getting their needs met in higher education, which seems to be reflected in these results on self-efficacy among autistic students (Sue & Sue, 2016). Self-efficacy is a cognitive determinant that leads to exerting oneself, attaining goals and making decisions and should be a focus of intervention for adults with ASD. It could have far reaching effects in getting basic needs met and is viewed as the first step towards self-advocacy.

Self-advocacy is a person's ability to speak up, stand-up for or represent oneself (Adreon & Durocher, 2007). Without the acknowledgment of one's strengths and capabilities, taking action to effectively represent one's views or interests is a challenge. When a person with ASD is able to self-advocate for accommodations and disclose their needs, this leads to better academic, employment and relationship outcomes (Shore, 2004). By focusing on strengths and taking action to build them, adults with autism can get their needs met in relationships, at work, and in the community. Without self-advocacy these possibilities are limited.

One of the best outcomes of counseling is when a client gains the self-advocacy skills of taking a stand, making a request and achieving their desired outcomes. Exploring the options from full to partial self-disclosure can open up the client's understanding of how to inform others of their needs. Full self-disclosure usually involves sharing a lot of details about one's diagnoses and medical history with accompanying paperwork in some circumstances (Shore, 2004). This kind of self-disclosure may occur in a workplace or formal setting in which accommodations are legally mandated. Partial self-disclosure is more limited in the amount of information shared and focuses on sharing characteristics about oneself that are important to know in order to get along well with others (Shore, 2004). This approach can be a good fit for clients who either reject their diagnosis or prefer to share more privately or generally about themselves. If a client can learn to disclose in a way that they are comfortable with, then their potential for sustaining a job, romantic partner or friends improves.

Self-determination is our natural ability to motivate oneself to behave in healthy and effective ways (Ryan & Deci, 2017). It allows people to be the cause of their own actions and freely make choices to meet their goals. Once a person experiences self-efficacy and successfully advocates for their needs, self-determination is the final step in building self-competence. Self-determination allows a person to be the change agent in the process of believing they are able to achieve and communicating those abilities (Wehmeyer, 2015). Therefore, the importance for building self-awareness, self-efficacy, self-advocacy, and self-determination will resonate throughout this guide.

In order to best understand our client's level of competence and capability in different domains, I will highlight the cognitive processes and behavioral components involved in a variety of ASD presentations. First let us review common schema presentations that lead an adult with ASD to demonstrate different levels of competence and capability. From there, we'll review the behavioral aspects of these clients that are commonly observed, which will help inform an effective way to approach and form a therapeutic alliance with them.

Cognitive Considerations

Adults with ASD have many years of childhood and adolescent experiences that help shape their cognitive processes. Depending on what occurred during their formative years, including family life, parenting dynamics, experiences in the educational system, and peer relationships, the manner in which they see themselves fitting into adulthood and how others will treat them have a significant influence. As it pertains to one's cognitive competence and capability, it will be helpful to explore the connection between schema dynamics and worldview.

Schema dynamics describe a triadic cognitive process including one's interpretation of self, others and the world. These schema dynamics are often connected to a person's worldview. Worldviews are comprised of one's reliance on internal or external loci of control and responsibility (Sue & Sue, 2016). This generally translates to how a person attributes responsibility and control in their lives, either to their own doing or factors outside themselves. Due to myriad factors, the results of schema dynamics and worldview of a client diagnosed with ASD present in a wide range.

On one end of this range are those who are self-assured, content, and have an exceedingly positive view of themselves and their fit in the world. Their experience during childhood likely involved supportive family members and effective parenting dynamics, academic success and relatively conflict-free experiences with peers. For individuals with these experiences they view themselves as in control and competent, others as helpful, supportive, and trustworthy and the world as a safe, trusting place. This resulting schema sounds like the best possible outcome. Yet, when amplified to an extreme this can lead to problems.

The results of this schema dynamic could lead an autistic adult to be overly trusting of others and be taken advantage of or have difficulty tolerating discomfort if they haven't had experiences that expose them to challenges with peers or in achievement-based settings such as school and work. It can also result in a scenario in which the adult views themselves as more independent than they are and, in some cases, entitled. They may often view others logically and with a purpose as resources who either help or hinder their ability to get what they want and meet certain goals. In my experience, those whose schema dynamics present at this end of the range have often been protected from adversity, which can lead to an inflated view of themselves, in which they are not realistic about their abilities (Lerner et al., 2012). They tend to be naïve about the impact of their interactions with others and the world.

At the other end of the schema dynamics range are adults with ASD who have more apparently negative outcomes. These are individuals who view themselves as helpless and hopeless, others as in control and power-wielding and the world as scary and unsafe. In this case, the adult clients have likely been treated as incompetent or incapable leading them to rely heavily on others for decision-making or guidance and can often minimize their own abilities. These negative views of the self, others, and the world can often lead to anxiety and depression, which can occur in up to 70 percent of adolescents and adults diagnosed with ASD (Lugnegard, Hallerback, & Gillberg, 2011; Hofvander et al., 2009). Many times, the core symptoms of ASD are contributors of these mental health concerns but some researchers posit that the way in which these adults were treated by primary caregivers as children and teens may play a more significant role (Durand, 2011). Both caregiver optimism and parenting or family dynamics will be explored further in Chapter 2.

In the first example of how an adult with ASD cognitively processes schema dynamics, the client may be unrealistic about what future goals can be accomplished and may expect others to be more flexible than they are willing to be. In the latter case, clients can be defeated, untrusting and require additional focus and support to trust themselves and others, which typically involves treatment co-occurring diagnoses. These commonly co-occurring conditions will be reviewed in Chapter 4. Where a client ends up in this range of potential schema dynamics can lead to more and less functional ways of navigating adulthood (Sue & Sue, 2016).

If adults with ASD have been treated or labeled as a person with a disability throughout their lives, they will have faced stereotypes and discrimination that will impact worldview and schema dynamics. Being a part of this minority group, many will have likely faced ableism and mistreatment (whether mild or severe) based on their disability status. Depending on the frequency and intensity of these experiences, adults with ASD can be accustomed to being treated as incompetent or incapable. This is true for the group of autistic adults who do not closely identify themselves as someone with autism or even rejects their diagnosis. In some research this is as much as 30 percent of the population (Shattuck et al., 2014). No matter what the self-identification, it is our task as clinicians to help accentuate the positive and ameliorate the negative to help influence how the autistic adult conceptualizes themselves (Olkin, 2001).

Presuming that individuals with ASD are competent and capable may provide a corrective experience for clients who have faced a range of issues from minor microaggressions to significant discrimination. When counselors and mental health professionals approach their clients by establishing an egalitarian relationship in which the client's personal voice is honored, this may be quite different to how they've been treated by many others in their lives (Sue & Sue, 2016). From those with both good and bad intentions, it could be likely that others have spoken for the person or on their behalf for most of their lifetime. This can be particularly true in the domain of getting psychological, social, and emotional needs met throughout their lives. Depending on the client's internal resources, such as motivation, level of insight and judgement, and external assets such as parents, siblings and others, a confluence of factors occurs that often ends up precluding the person with autism from having their voice heard in these matters. They need to be given this opportunity and being in counseling may be one of their first opportunities for this to happen.

Individuals with autism can be particularly confusing for others because of their clear strengths in some areas and significant deficits in others. This applies to both the behavioral mannerisms and social communication. The next section details how complex the differences in skills can be when examining the competencies and challenges of autistic adults.

Behavioral Peaks and Valleys: Understanding a Splintered Skill Set

One of the core symptoms of autism is the behavioral challenges individuals' exhibit, with restricted or limited interests and repetitive, stereotypic behaviors.

Yet, we all have specific interests which contribute to our quality of life, and behaviors we engage in that are routine and their repetition helps organize our lives. One way to conceptualize the behavioral symptomology of autism, from the stance of presuming competence and capability, is as an intensified presentation of the behaviors many of us naturally display. The extreme male brain theory of autism has found neuroscientific reasons to validate that people with ASD, both females and males, may have accelerated male features (Baron-Cohen, 2002).

In working with our clients we need to be able to understand how their behaviors might be impacting capability and competence in certain areas. One barometer for determining if behaviors are having this impact is when their interests are so limited and behaviors highly repetitive and intense that it interferes with their success in areas of their life where they would otherwise be capable and competent. This can be quite impairing in cases when inordinate hours are spent engaging in an eccentric activity that interrupts arriving at work on time or engaging in family events. But in other cases, these interests can be fairly mainstream and channeled productively in working environments and social contexts that naturally fit well together. Generally speaking, when interests and behavioral patterns are stereotypic and rigid, adults with ASD will likely experience fewer challenges (Garland, O'Rourke, & Robertson, 2013). Yet, within the behavioral presentation of ASD there are complexities due to a splintering of skills that lead to obstacles in life and treatment.

It is helpful to explore and understand the splintered behavioral skill sets that clients with ASD exhibit. Our clients are highly skilled in some areas and stunted in others. How can we best navigate ways to modify treatment to address both the high and low performing skills on splintered ends of the spectrum? The splintered skill set that people with ASD present with, can be naturally confusing for mental health professionals, parents, and others interacting with them (Seltzer et al., 2005). The advanced ability to perform in some areas while having significant challenges in others leads many to make assumptions based on low or high levels of performance that are observed. Most of us expect a more consistent match in performance. Therefore, when a person with ASD excels in academic writing skills and interacts effectively with teachers and older adults, but then struggles with oral presentations and cannot function well with peers, observing these differences in performance can be perplexing.

Declarative and procedural knowledge tends to be uneven for individuals with ASD, with better reported performance in declarative than procedural knowledge (Bellini, 2008). How this presents itself is that the adult with ASD is often well able to describe a skill but then when required to enact or perform the skill themselves problems arise. Therefore, it is important to keep in mind that even though the "right response" might be given when asked about a particular subject it is likely we haven't gone far enough in our inquiry. An additional step that would require the skill to be demonstrated or performed will give the most accurate representation of the comprehensive skill that person embodies.

We as counselors can also have declarative and procedural knowledge gaps when we know about the concepts but find it more challenging to act on these in therapy. With a firm grasp on the cognitive and behavioral patterns that autistic adults can present with, let's now move from a conceptual framework of presuming competence and capability to demonstrating it. The following are specific interventions to be integrated into our approach as practitioners to ensure we are clearly communicating that we believe our clients are capable and competent.

Clinical Interventions

There are historical and diagnostic contexts that help explain why adults with ASD have been perceived as less competent and capable than they have the potential to be. In creating a strong therapeutic relationship and corrective experiences with autistic clients there are specific ways to avoid the mishaps we've historically fallen into. At the core, this starts by shifting the clinical mindset to a strengths-based perspective. Yet, to expand beyond a mindset shift there are interventions that can be specifically applied to reflect this. These include the integration of empowerment models of counseling, making intentional language choices and using teaching methods that encourage personal agency and power.

Empowerment Counseling

Counseling and quality of life outcomes are enhanced for people with disabilities by improving self-confidence and empowering the client to actively engage in decision-making processes about their lives (Artman & Daniels, 2010). The concept of empowerment is more complex than it might seem. It both incorporates and goes beyond self-efficacy and self-determination through its incorporation of several steps, ideas, and goals for clients. One definition authored early on in the counseling literature describes empowerment as growth in skills, improvement in understanding one's role in power dynamics, identifying oneself with similar others and participating socially and in the community to empower others (McWhirter, 1991). The complexities identified in this definition involve several of the essential steps in helping adults with ASD increase skills, self-awareness, social belonging, and advocacy. This is one of the reasons that the empowerment model of counseling is a helpful tool in presuming competence and capability with ASD clients.

Building an egalitarian relationship with a client diagnosed with ASD should not differ significantly from the one you would build with clients from other groups who have faced marginalization and discrimination. Addressing the power dynamic between the privileged counselor and marginalized client is one of the first steps to ensuring a culturally competent approach (AMCD, 2015).

This can include at least one question during initial intake and assessment that helps review their experiences, in recent and long-term history depending on one's theoretical orientation, of being a person with ASD. For example, "How has your diagnosis impacted the way that other people in your life treat you?" Or "In what ways does your ASD diagnosis effect your relationships?"

Be mindful that some clients with ASD may strongly identify with the diagnosis in a positive way, in which is it is a point of pride in their identity, while others reject it. For those who reject the diagnosis, it will be important to approach these questions in a manner that gives the client space to have this reaction, and consider their reasons for seeking help as attributed to factors unrelated to symptoms of the diagnosis. Being able to respect the full range of reactions to a client's identity as a person with autism will be helpful in establishing an egalitarian dynamic in the therapeutic relationship. If the client rejects the diagnosis, taking on the position of attempting to convince them that it is important or relevant to treatment is likely to be ineffective. It may also have the counselor engaging in repetition of a theme from the client's lives that will impede productivity within the relationship and, ultimately, in treatment outcomes.

Allowing our clients to make their own decisions, from how they identify with their diagnosis to collaborating on treatment goals, is essential in empowering them in the counseling context. We can also help empower clients by assessing what needs they have that aren't fulfilled and by working through ways of fulfilling them. People with autism may have never been asked, "What's happening in your life that you'd like to improve or change for yourself?" This puts the client in the position of power in deciding what they'd like to improve in their lives and the practitioner can be the guide for how treatment can help them accomplish this.

Language Matters

As we encourage our clients to make decisions and find power, it is important that we model healthy and helpful language choices throughout the treatment process. The choices we make about the quality and quantity of language we utilize with clients can make an impact (Sue & Sue, 2016). In quality it is important as practitioners that we are intentional and deliberate about the kind of language, both verbal and nonverbal, we use with our clients. In quantity a helpful rule of thumb could be "the fewer words, the better". Making oneself clear, direct and concise in how we communicate with our clients will impact the quality and quantity of our language and likely be more successful in our interactions with autistic clients.

One matter of quality in our language pertains to a client's chosen identity. As discussed earlier, the use of person first language is a best-practice, clinical recommendation to decrease the stigmatization of those diagnosed with myriad mental health disorders. Yet, for some clients, their positive association as an autistic person can have mental health benefits and, if this is their chosen identification, our language should reflect that (Olkin, 2001). These clients will likely prefer identify-first language instead. Asking clients how they would like to be identified in this way, based on assessing their feelings related to their diagnosis is a good place to start. On the other hand, there are clients who experience rejection, anxiety, or depressive symptoms when they learn about their diagnosis (Academic Autistic Spectrum Partnership in Research & Education, 2018). For these clients, using person-first language may be a big leap towards encouraging self-acceptance without taking on the former label of "autistic". We should be able to challenge our own hesitancies about directly asking questions to clients with autism in order to honor their identity and demonstrate our own competence with this population (Olkin, 2001). Ultimately in this linguistic matter, the client's identity should be the determining factor and clinicians can adjust their language accordingly, just as we would for clients with other identities.

In the initial stages of treatment, when we are beginning to understand how clients identify in many ways, beyond their diagnosis, it is helpful to develop a set of interview questions that deliberately allow a client to discuss the areas in which they are competent and capable. These initial interview questions will naturally include, "Tell me more about why you're seeking counseling at this point in your life." Or, "What is the problems in your life that led you to counseling?" Whereupon clients are likely to be problem-focused in their response. The information gleaned from these kinds of questions is an invaluable and standard step in the therapeutic process. Therefore, the addition of strengths-based language in questions will be helpful. This could include "What is your favorite thing to do on the weekends?" Or "I'm wondering what characteristics you have that will make you successful in counseling?" These offer the opportunity for clients to discuss qualities about themselves and their lives they consider positive resources and it provides them with a different treatment experience.

Beyond the intentional focus on how we describe a client's identity and speak with intentionality, it is helpful to make deliberate choices about how our nonverbals impact the ability to demonstrate that our approach presumes competence and capability. The nitty, gritty details of "what we do not directly say" are included here and are often hard to identify in ourselves. These nonverbal communication tools start with wording or phrasing on a professional website or social media profile, initial paperwork and intake forms, and go on to include the body language and facial expressions we use that we are often not aware of.

In order to consistently take a strengths-based approach with our nonverbal language choices, intake forms should include questions such as "What are some good things happening in your life currently?" Or "Please list your top three strengths." Additionally, we should incorporate assessment tools aside from those used to measure ASD symptomology to identify areas of strength. Given the previously identified group strengths (Table 1.1), some potential choices could be the Brief Resilience Scale (Smith et al., 2008) or

The Meaning of Life Scale (Steger et al., 2006). Incorporating assessments that clinicians and clients can utilize to guide treatment that don't focus only on their symptoms or inadequacies, directly communicates to clients that we have a plan to help identify and monitor their positive attributes while ameliorating their presenting symptoms. These two things can and should be done simultaneously to demonstrate that we presume they embody both.

Teaching Methods

A basic counseling skill that most therapists are trained to use early on can be one of the most effective tools in communicating to our clients that we believe they are capable and competent. Socratic questioning, when executed well, communicates to our clients that they have the answers to important questions and the ability to contribute their ideas to the counseling process. But this technique often gets misused or applied superficially, which prevents it from being the powerful tool it has the potential to be.

One necessary assumption for effective Socratic questioning is that the client knows how to come up with a response. Even if the response isn't accurate or what the counselor is looking for, getting them to contribute through co-construction honors their abilities (Sue & Sue, 2016). We need to carefully construct the questions we pose, for a response they are likely to be able to provide and are validated by. The responses that the clinician then provides need to be affirming and encouraging, even if it's not the response we are looking for. This helps the counselor attend to the working alliance and connect the client's thoughts into the counseling process. It does not preclude us from working toward more accuracy when we provide psychoeducation or skill training, but this first step helps us eventually get to providing corrective feedback.

Effective Socratic questioning is based on the scaffolding of knowledge, so the questions we begin with should be based on what we know about our client's capabilities. Questions can be individualized to the client based on a variety of factors. Yet there are some question stems that you can use as tools to individualize through the client's response. If you use these question stems with repetition your clients will become accustomed to the method and can gain mastery in responding accordingly. My colleague Dr. Liz Laugeson teaches one of my favorite Socratic question stems, which is, "What could be the problem with ______________?" Depending on the therapeutic goal or activity, the blank at the end of the question could pertain to any problematic situation you elicit or the client reports. Other Socratic question stems that might be helpful include, "I'm curious about what you positively contributed to ______________?" "What did you do well?" Or "What would you do differently next time?"

Encouraging Personal Agency and Voice

The life experiences that an autistic adult is exposed to will lead them to different levels of dependence and communication. Whether it's out of force or by choice, family members often take on the voice of their adult loved one. In some cases, this can be incredibly helpful, while for others it has inhibited them from building and practicing the skill of communicating one's own needs. I've seen this manifest in adults with ASD in verbal and nonverbal communication. Examples of these are frequently responding with, "I don't knows" or just saying "yes" as an easy out of the conversation. Nonverbally this can show up for the client when, in response to a question, they physically look to a family member or support person to step in to share on their behalf.

Given that family members cannot always speak for or advocate on the behalf of adult with autism it's important to provide opportunities for the client to learn about their own decision-making abilities (agency) and how to effectively use their voice. Depending on the client's support system (Chapter 2) the method for approaching this will vary. One of my client's goals in therapy is to tell his parents "Hey, let me talk" so that he can demonstrate his competence and capability of communicating his needs within the family. Due to a history of him shutting down in social situations, his system has gotten comfortable with jumping in to explain things on his behalf, so this shift is significant for both the client and his family members.

As clinicians we need to be comfortable, reflecting our observations of the client and their support system regarding what patterns have developed that can help or hinder personal agency and voice. Several of the steps toward independence (Chapter 10) will directly promote these principles. For some adults it will start by making decisions in therapy, shifting from the counselor communicating with the family and getting the client to directly communicate therapeutic messages to them or setting limits on how much help they receive for different tasks.

Case Example

Paul is a 29-year-old, single, Caucasian, male who lives in a supported living apartment program with wrap-around services, including case management. During each session he presents as disgruntled reporting a lot of frustration with the amount of oversight and lack of independence he is afforded. He has been living in supported residences (with family or professional assistance) for the majority of his life. His interests are music, animals, and riding his scooter.

Some of the challenges that are immediately apparent when meeting Paul is that he has an atypical gait, poor hygiene and stereotypic hand ringing with repetitive arm movements. Unlike many of my clients whose autistic mannerisms present more mildly, Paul's symptoms of autism are moderate and, therefore, make him stand out. Because of traits that are attributed to autism, his competence and capability is automatically assessed at a lower level. Unfortunately, his challenge with hygiene has led him to losing jobs and volunteer opportunities that he truly enjoyed. He has experienced some behavioral challenges recently during which time he becomes verbally aggressive towards others (i.e., yells demeaning statements to other residents), isolates himself in his apartment and over-eats. This has resulted in the loss of his roommate and a 26-pound weight gain in the last three months. He is seeking counseling and his parents and supported living staff are seeking consultation for ways to best help him. Both family members and support staff at his residence have exhausted their best resources in helping Paul become independent and improve his health with limited success.

When meeting with Paul he reports that "no one is listening to me" and "they won't let me do what I want to do". He explains that the main reason for his recent decline in mental and physical health is due to his recent job loss caused by his hygiene issues. This has resulted in him having to complete, what he considers, menial and "boring" tasks at his residence which he also believes prevents him from getting experience outside of where he lives. He also reports having expressed an interest in attending college "multiple times" and doesn't understand why his parents or coach have not supported this. His goals for coming to counseling are to lose weight, get a job and make friends in college.

During consultation with his parent and coach, they are supportive of his goals but express concern about the realistic nature of them. His weight has fluctuated in the past and they don't trust his ability to self-regulate food intake. They inform me that Paul's mild intellectual disability resulted in the attainment of an alternate high school diploma, which precludes him from seeking a college degree. They're also unsure of how independent he can be in work because of his hygiene problems. The supported living coach echoes these concerns and is additionally worried about how Paul's anger is impacting him and his peers.

One of the first steps approaching Paul and his support system in presuming competence and capability will be to hone-in on identifying his internal strengths and external resources to build self-efficacy and work towards self-advocacy. In order to do so, individual time to assess and develop goals with Paul, without his support system present, is important. As we meet individually, Paul talks about how much he loved his position with the local animal shelter and how much he misses it. He also reports being motivated to lose weight because he thinks girls won't like him because of his weight. Lastly, he does seem to understand that college will be a different experience for him than it is for his sister (who is seeking a degree from a large university), but he'd still like to try it out. He is more insightful about his strengths and limitations and motivated to change than even the counselor has presumed.

The next step is to collaboratively develop some ideas and goals to later present to his support team. The first is that he can begin to earn money working in a nearby retirement community by dog walking and pet sitting.

He plans to go to apartment buildings to post flyers offering his service and charge a competitive fee that we research in session to determine. Regarding his weight, he's willing to enroll in a weight loss program that will help him track his food intake and incorporate mild to moderate exercise into his routine. He is also interested in participating in his residence's local garden to learn more about vegetables and to get physical exercise. Lastly, because he knows he is not eligible to pursue a college degree, we discuss the possibility of auditing one college level course in music, a special interest of his, at a local community college. Each of these goals was originated by him and modified in counseling through Socratic questioning so that his personal agency and voice is honored.

In the next phase of treatment, Paul and I join his support team including his parents and supported living coach to get their feedback. The reality is that in order to meet these goals he needs his parents and coach to buy-in so they can support him emotionally, financially, and energetically. During this session, Paul presents his ideas, in a way in which he behaviorally rehearsed in individual sessions leading up to this, yet during many moments he finds himself at a loss for words or the skills to express himself.

There are some helpful tools for helping to promote his self-efficacy (he's at a loss due to his belief that he can't communicate with them effectively) and self-advocacy during this joint session with the family. One way to apply Socratic questioning in this session will be to minimally help facilitate reminders of his upcoming points. This is to ensure that reliance on the counselor or other supports is avoided and his independence is encouraged. For example, the counselor asks, "Paul, I wonder how you think you'll try and meet that goal?" The experience of successfully communicating his plan as independently as possible can influence his belief that he can do this effectively.

Paul is accustomed to other adults in his life speaking on his behalf or even, at times, over him. This leads to frequent redirection during the family session because Paul and his family tend to focus their attention back to the counselor and supported living coach. For example, when Paul blanks in explaining his plan, he looks in our direction in the hope that we might take over this part of the discussion. This requires patience and more time in planning sessions to allow for this adjustment, which aims to promote Paul's self-advocacy. The clinician needs to be comfortable using nonverbal responses to redirect Paul to answer questions himself. This can be done through a hand gesture (i.e., pointing to him or patting the table in his direction) and preventing sustained eye contact or reinforcing attention to the dependence on others to respond for him. Verbally the clinician may encourage by saying "You got this" or "It's up to you".

Once his sense of personal agency and voice are more strongly developed and demonstrated, it'll be important to focus on improving behavioral challenges that are negatively impacting him. Since he has been fired from work due to hygiene issues this is an important treatment goal. Collaboratively, Paul and his support develop steps that he can follow in the shower to be sure he achieves cleanliness. The counselor assists in creating a visual aid and a plan for how much time he spends cleaning different areas of his body during a shower. Paul decides on favorite verses of Pink Floyd songs he can sing to, to make sure he spends about 30 seconds cleaning the most important parts of his body (i.e., armpits, genitals, hair). He also decides on songs he can play while he's in the shower that will help him with the total time he should spend thoroughly cleaning himself. The same is applied to toothbrushing. After a couple of weeks implementing this visual support and auditory plan for timing, Paul's hygiene improves. He still needs reminders to use dandruff shampoo, as his flakiness is an ongoing work in progress and potentially a next step in treatment once he masters current hygiene goals.

In the next steps in therapy, Paul exercises self-determination as he sets his own goal to lose weight. He decides to make changes to his diet and begin exercising in a serious attempt to become physically healthier and takes action quickly. A plan is co-developed with the treatment team but Paul leads the charge and demonstrates a high level of motivation for change on this particular goal. Through a scaffolded process of Paul believing in his abilities to succeed in different areas (self-efficacy) and self-advocating for what he needs in various settings he finally reaches the ultimate goal of being his own change agent. His family does not have to prompt him like they have in the past to motivate him to make changes and this shift in the dynamic is a positive treatment outcome when aiming to improve competence and capability. The reality is that when we treat our clients from a strengths-based perspective that honors their competence and capability, the potential for becoming more competent and capable in different areas of their life is possible.

References

Academic Autistic Spectrum Partnership in Research & Education (ASPIRE). (2018). Retrieved from: https://autismandhealth.org.

Adreon, D., & Durocher, J.S. (2007). Evaluating the college transition needs of individuals' high-functioning autism spectrum disorders. *Intervention in School and Clinic, 42*(5), 271–279. doi:10.1177/10534512070420050201.

American Counseling Association. (2014). *Code of Ethics*. Alexandria, VA: American Counseling Association.

Association for Multicultural Counseling and Development. (2015). *Multicultural and social justice counseling competencies*. Retrieved from www.counseling.org/resources/competencies/multicultural_competencies.pdf.

Artman, L.K., & Daniels, J.A. (2010). Disability and psychotherapy practice: Cultural competence and practical tips. *Professional Psychology: Research and Practice, 41*(5), 442–448. doi:10.1037/a0020864.

Bandura, A. (1977). Self-efficacy: Toward a unifying theory of behavioral change. *Psychological Review, 84*(2), 191–215.

Baron-Cohen, B. (2002). The extreme male brain theory of autism. *Trends in Cognitive Science, 6*, 248–254.

Bellini, S. (2008). *Building social relationships: A systematic approach to teaching social interaction skills to children and adolescents with autism spectrum disorders and others with social difficulties.* Shawnee Mission, KS: Autism Asperger Publishing.

Durand, M.V. (2011). *Optimistic parenting: Hope and help for you and your challenging child.* Baltimore, MD: Brookes Publishing.

Elder-Robison, J. (2017). The controversy around autism and neurodiversity. Retrieved from www.psychologytoday.com.

Erford, B. (2018). *Orientation to the counseling profession: Advocacy, ethics, and essential professional foundations* (3rd ed.). New York: Pearson Education.

FitzGerald, C., & Hurst, S. (2017). Implicit bias in healthcare professionals: A systematic review. *BioMedCentral Medical Ethics, 18*(19), 1–18. doi:10.1186/s1290-017-0179-8.

Garland, J., O'Rourke, L., & Robertson, D. (2013). Autism spectrum disorder in adults: Clinical features and the role of the psychiatrist. *Advanced Psychiatric Treatment, 19*, 378–391. doi:10.1192/apt.bp.112.010439.

Goleman, D. (2005). *Emotional intelligence. Why it can matter more than IQ.* New York: Bantam Books.

Grothaus, T., McAuliffe, G., & Craigen, L. (2012). Infusing cultural competence and advocacy into strength-based counseling. *Journal of Humanistic Counseling, 51*, 51–65.

Hofvander, B., Delorme, R., Chaste P., Nyden, A., Wentz, E., Stahlberg, O., ... Leboyer, M. (2009). Psychiatric and psychosocial problems in adults with normal-intelligence autism spectrum disorders. *BMC Psychiatry, 9*, 35.

Lerner, M.D., Calhoun, C.D., Mikami, A.Y., & De Los Reyes, A. (2012). Understanding parent-child social informant discrepancy in youth with high functioning autism spectrum disorders. *Journal of Autism and Developmental Disorders, 42*, 2680–2692.

Lorenz, T., & Heinitz, K. (2014). Aspergers – different not less: Occupational strengths and job interests of individuals with Asperger's syndrome. *PLoS One, 9*, e100358.

Lugnegard, T., Hallerback, M.U. & Gillberg, C. (2011). Psychiatric comorbidity in young adults with a clinical diagnosis of Asperger syndrome. *Research in Developmental Disabilities, 32*, 1910–1917.

Mason, D., McConachie, H., Garland, D., Petrou, A., Rodgers, J., & Parr, J.R. (2018). Predictors of quality of life for autistic adults. *Autism Research*, doi:10.1002/aur.1965

McWhirter, E.H. (1991). Empowerment in counseling. *Journal of Counseling & Development, 69*(3), 222–227. doi:10.1002/j.1556-6676.1991.tb01491.x.

National Autistic Society. (December 15, 2016). The strengths of autistic employees. Retrieved from www.autism.org.uk/get-involved/tmi/employment/blogs/blog-strengths-151216.aspx.

Olkin, R. (2001). *What psychotherapists should know about disabilities.* New York: Guilford Press.

Ryan, R.M., & Deci, E.L. (2017). *Self-determination theory: Basic psychological needs in motivation, development, and wellness.* New York: Guilford Publishing.

Seltzer, M.M., Shattuck, P., Abbeduto, L., & Greenberg, J.S. (2005). Trajectory of development in adolescents and adults with autism. *Mental Retardation & Developmental Disabilities Research Reviews, 10*, 4.

Shattuck, P., Steinberg, J., Yu, J., Wei, X., Cooper, B.P., Newman, L., & Roux, A.M. (2014). Disability identification and self-efficacy among college students on the autism spectrum. *Autism Research & Treatment*, 924182, doi:10.1155/2014/924182.

Shore, S. (2004). *Ask and tell: Self-advocacy and self-disclosure for people on the autism spectrum*. Shawnee Mission, KS: Autism Asperger Publishing.

Smith, B.W., Dalen, J., Wiggins, K., Tooley, E., Christopher, P., & Bernard, J. (2008). The Brief Resilience Scale: Assessing the ability to bounce back. *International Journal of Behavioral Medicine, 15*, 194–200.

Steger, M.F., Frazier, P., Oishi, S., & Kaler, M. (2006). The meaning in life questionnaire: Assessing the presence of and search for meaning in life. *Journal of Counseling Psychology, 53*, 80–93.

Sue, D.W., & Sue, D. (2016). *Counseling the culturally diverse* (7th ed.). Hoboken, NJ: Wiley.

Sue, D., Sue D.W., Sue, D.M., & Sue S. (2016). *Understanding abnormal behavior.* Stamford, CT: Cengage.

Van Meter, K.C., Christiansen, L.E., Delwiche, L.D., Azari, R., Carpenter, T.E., & Hertz-Picciotto, I. (2010). Geographic distribution of autism in California: A retrospective birth cohort. *Autism Research, 3*, 19–29. doi:10.1002/aur.110.

Wehmeyer, M.L. (2015). Framing the future: Self-determination. *Remedial and Special Education, 36*(1), 20–23. doi:10.1177/0741932514551281

2 Understanding Family Dynamics

Alison Bourdeau and Ali Cunningham Abbott

In order to begin understanding the complexities of family and support system dynamics, we'll start by introducing this chapter's case study. The purpose of this is so that as we move through the theoretical concepts and interventions, we will refer back to this family as the primary exemplar. The client in this case is learning how to navigate his family relationships and other support systems, which illustrates a common journey that adults with autism face when moving through life.

Case Example

Paul is a 22-year-old male who has just completed his associate degree at a local community college. While he has been able to complete the degree with some academic accommodations in place, his mother reports that she has put considerable time and energy into supporting his goal of completing this degree. Paul's mother, Frances, reports that she is feeling stressed because Paul is now reporting that he would like to transfer to the local state university and complete a bachelor's degree. While she supports his ultimate goal of independence, she thinks that she is the guiding force behind his academic successes. She's worried that if he moves away and attends this school he will likely not be as successful without her involvement. They are seeking counseling as a family to address this issue and their relationship dynamics, his desire for independence, and how she will function as the roles in their family may soon be shifting.

With further assessment, Frances discloses that she is a single mother who has done "everything" for Paul. Paul's father was not around much when he was young due to his job as a truck driver. When Paul was diagnosed with autism spectrum disorder (ASD) in middle school, Paul's father disagreed with the diagnosis. He responded by saying that Paul just needed to "be a man" and "toughen up" when it came to social challenges. This caused a significant amount of discord between him and Frances which ultimately led to divorce. After the divorce, Paul's father became more and more distant and rarely contacts Paul.

During one of the first sessions, Frances reports that she has been unable to work for years as her primary goal was supporting Paul. She has now gotten a new job and is fearful that his goal will put her new employment at risk because of "how much support he will need". She expresses significant concerns about the amount of effort the application process will take and the tight timeline in which it will all need to happen in order for Paul to make the deadline. She also expresses concerns regarding his ability to live independently and to keep up with a more rigorous schedule of a bachelor's degree at a larger university. As she expresses her concerns, Frances is quite tearful throughout. At this point in the session, Paul looks down and mumbles "she's always crying".

When meeting with Paul both individually and with his mom, he discloses his desire to get a bachelor's degree, live on campus, and be more independent. As he attempts to make statements about what he thinks will need to happen, Frances routinely brings up incidents in the past during which he had trouble or failed. Through her statements and body language, she communicates to Paul that because he has struggled with independence in the past, he is unlikely to be able to do so in the future. When Frances makes these statements, Paul appears to shut down by looking down and refusing to talk. A pattern has begun to emerge within the session. When Paul begins to show competency in an area that Frances expresses concern for, she moves to a different area of concern. No matter what successes Paul has demonstrated on his own, it is hard for her to validate anything that seems to move him towards autonomy from her. She seems to want to be in a position where she can be involved and even in control of his goals and successes.

The counselor sets a single, short-term goal for Paul to achieve in a week's time. He is tasked with going online and filling out the application for admission to the university by completing everything he can independently. This is a step towards assessing Paul's engagement in therapy and his motivation for meeting his goal of transferring to this university. Paul demonstrates the ability to follow through with this goal when it is broken down into steps and clarified over a two-week period. During sessions, the counselor offers check-in opportunities to see how well Paul can use social supports aside from Frances to get his goals met. The counselor reinforces his efforts consistently so as to continue the momentum of the motivation that Paul is demonstrating.

With this success in completing the application, Paul is exhibiting the initiative needed to branch out on his own. As he does so, what is interesting is that Frances appears to double down on the idea that Paul needs "more significant help". As he follows through on the goals set up by the counselor, she begins to bring up future concerns or tasks that he needs to accomplish and other areas of his life where he still needs support. While the need for these items to be addressed is important, they don't appear to be a current priority. She seems to be jumping several steps ahead of current treatment goals in an effort to remain involved. Acknowledging this role shift for Frances will be important in the work for this family. What should have been a moment to celebrate his independence and motivation, which are part of his treatment goals, she has turned into an opportunity for her to focus on his deficits, so she's not left behind.

This consistent attempt to return to the state in which Paul requires her support to function is important for the counselor to keep at the forefront of conceptualizing and treating Paul and working with Frances. The years of a dynamic in which she has been focused on him appear to feed her interest or desire to be problem-focused and she may even rely on some level of dysfunction to serve in her role as savior. If problems do not exist, she will likely find a way to create a scenario where she is needed and in which her involvement alone will help create a solution for Paul. Her frequent tears reflect her fear of not being needed by Paul and of losing the focus she's had on his progress over the last 10 years. This is a long-standing pattern that has developed between mother and son, and it will be hard to alter or shift. If this dynamic and pattern does not shift, it is likely that she will attempt to circumvent Paul's attempts to take more control by trying to communicate directly with the university and counselor. Even though she wants him to gain independence it will be hard for her to encourage and guide Paul in ways that will help him advocate for himself. Her words and actions communicated in counseling so far indicate that she does not have confidence in his ability to take control of his future. In many ways, the interactional style between Paul and Frances has the potential to be more disabling than the autism diagnosis.

Family Systems

In order to effectively conceptualize this case, and others, we'll be looking to understand and treat Paul through the lens of systems theory instead of an individual approach. This requires us to break out of our traditional view of how the diagnosis is impacting the individual and begin to look at the more complex relationship dynamics that have led to some of the outcomes the client is experiencing. The good news about taking a family and systems approach to treatment is that parents, caregivers, other family members and systems, such as schools or employers, can be some of the most valuable resources for clients with autism. Unfortunately, these systems also have the potential to cause the most harm when dysfunction is rampant.

Utilizing a framework that breaks down the individual roles, interactions, goals, and barriers within a family will be a useful tool in determining interventions. Furthermore, identifying how other systems in the person's life have oppressed or supported them can be a key to understanding the client's history and framing future recommendations. This chapter will take a deeper dive into how the strengths and challenges of individual members in a family work to contribute to the function and dysfunction of the system. It will also briefly introduce how other support systems, which will be more thoroughly covered in Chapter 10, can be integrated into treatment for long-lasting effects and positive outcomes.

Family Dynamics in Treatment

The family systems of people with autism are just as complex, diverse and multidimensional as any family we work with in counseling. Given that working with families in treatment can be hard because of these features, why is it important that we involve family members when we can just treat the individual with autism? When working with ASD children and adolescents, several of the evidence-based practices customarily used involve parent and peer (siblings) mediated interventions (Wong et al., 2013). In many practices, parent involvement is required, at least to some extent, because this aspect of treatment leads to better long-term outcomes for clients with autism (Mandelberg et al., 2013); this applies to adults with autism as well (Kirby, Baranek, & Fox, 2016; Laugeson et al., 2015; Gantman et al., 2012; Barnhill, 2007). This benefit is clearly one of the best rationales for taking an approach that incorporates families into the treatment process.

When changes happen in a system, it's considered disruptive. No matter what the change, good or bad, these shifts are usually uncomfortable and new. A system that is disrupted will typically, and unconsciously in many cases, do it's best to "right the wrong" that has been created through change. The sole purpose of this system is to return to whatever homeostatic status was in existence before it was disrupted. These states of homeostasis can be fairly healthy or quite damaging (Carlson, Sperry, & Lewis, 2005). Family systems theory allows clinicians to focus on the changes and shifts that occur within the group to understand its need to maintain whatever homeostasis it's been accustomed to.

McDaniel and Pisani (2012) support the use of family systems concepts and approaches when working with systems in which a member has a disability. They indicate that it has the potential to improve overall quality of life for all members in the system. Quality of life is a critical factor within the trajectory of all members of the system, as it impacts their ability to utilize optimism and process adverse experiences. Families naturally face several adverse experiences over the years, including children aging into adulthood. This leads us to consider what factors to attend to in order to best understand the dynamic between Frances and Paul.

Why would Frances act in opposition to her original goal? Her stated goal and her behaviors are communicating two different things. She indicated that she wants Paul to be more independent, yet every action she takes serves to make him less so. It appears that Paul is rising to the challenge and taking the necessary steps in order to achieve the goals that he had set for himself. On the surface it seems to defy logic that she would identify the areas in which he needed to grow, and then attempt to hinder his ability to develop these areas. As the counselor in this scenario, there would be two factors that would be essential to examine as you conceptualize this case.

Part of the process of conceptualizing this family is identifying both what the counselor and the family are bringing to the therapeutic work (Carlson,

Sperry, & Lewis, 2005). The first step in this would be for the counselor to identify a clear theoretical orientation from which each family and individual member is assessed and treated. This is helpful in determining if the family is a good fit for the clinician's approach to family work. The next step would be to identify which model of disability the individuals in the family and counselor are operating from. How we conceptualize disability can stem from family dynamics, so it is appropriate to utilize a family systems approach in order to identify areas of strength and areas of challenge within the system, as opposed to conceptualizing on purely an individual basis.

Theoretical Model

Murray Bowen was a founder of systemic family therapy and one of the early pioneers of family systems approaches to counseling (Bowen, 1976). His eight concepts are utilized in helping practitioners conceptualize treatment with families. Practitioners have developed tools that integrate these eight concepts to help treat families (Bowen, 1985). These concepts will be examined in the assessment section of this chapter and play an important role in initially understanding the case study. In order to comprehensively gather information on these concepts, the clinician can assess a few key areas, including the family projection process, patterns of differentiation or fusion, triangulation or cut-off, intergenerational transmission, and patterns as identified in genogram assessment (McGoldrick & Gerson, 2008).

The eight concepts developed by Bowen provide a framework in which to examine the dynamics of a family and to examine the dynamics of a family using the Bowen Intergenerational Family Therapy conceptualization model (Bowen, 1985). The concepts are outlined in Table 2.1 in order to clearly understand how these can later be connected to the dynamics occurring between Paul and Frances.

Let's look at how to sift through these concepts as they apply to the information we know about Paul and Frances' family system. One piece that the clinician is witnessing is the system fighting change in order to maintain homeostasis. Members of a family unit or system each have roles to play within the process. Within each system there is typically an identified patient or "IP", in this case Paul plays this role. This individual is directly or indirectly labeled the black sheep or scapegoat within the system, which is part of the family projection process. This would be the individual that the other members see as the reason for why there are issues in the family.

One important historical factor in this family is that Frances may still be wrestling with feelings related to the dissolution of her marriage as a result of Paul's diagnosis. It is not uncommon for parents of a child with autism to experience divorce, and they may be at more risk of divorce owing to additional stressors placed on a family who have one or more children diagnosed with ASD (Hartley et al., 2010). Frances may be unconsciously projecting feelings about her marriage ending onto Paul, which adds to her need to be

Table 2.1 Bowen's intergenerational family therapy concepts

Triangles (T)	A three-person relationship system. A building block of larger relationships as it represents the smallest stable unit of relationships. A two-person relationship is unstable as it is not a T.
Differentiation of Self (DOS)	Individuals vary in susceptibility to "groupthink". Groups vary the amount of pressure they exert for conformity. Differences between individuals and between groups reflect differences in levels of DOS.
Nuclear Family Emotional Process (NFEP)	Four basic relationship patterns that govern where problems develop in a family. • Marital conflict • Dysfunction in one spouse • Dysfunction in one or more children • Emotional distance
Family Projection Process (FPP)	Primary way parents transmit their emotional problems to a child. • Parents focus on child out of fear something is wrong • Parents interpret child's behavior as confirmatory • Parent treats the child as if something is wrong
Multigenerational Transmission Process (MTP)	Small differences in the levels of differentiation between parents and offspring lead to marked differences in differentiation amongst members of a multigenerational family
Emotional Cutoff (EC)	People managing their unresolved emotional issues with family members by totally cutting off contact.
Sibling Position (SP)	Position within family has impact on relational compatibility. Goal is to find partner with complementary positioning.
Societal Emotional Process (SEP)	How emotional system governs behavior on a societal level, promoting both progressive and regressive periods in society.

Note
All definitions derived from The Bowen Center for the Study of the Family (2018), https://thebowencenter.org.

desired as a support in his life. This end of the relationship between Paul and his father and Frances and her husband resulted in emotional cutoff. It is possible that he was struggling with his own dysfunction as identified in the nuclear family emotional process and therefore cut himself off from Paul and Frances. Because Paul required support as a result of his diagnosis, this dysfunction also seems like a key influence on the nuclear family's emotional process (Bowen, 1985).

Individuals within a system identify with their roles, and ultimately become comfortable with the expectations of the roles that they play (Carlson, Sperry, & Lewis, 2005). In the event that any member of the system attempts to shift their role, it causes a disturbance within the balance. In the event that the individual attempting to shift roles is the identified patient, the system is thrown even further into disarray. The system will attempt to fight the shift in roles in order to maintain homeostasis or balance. This will often explain why individuals seem to be fighting progress.

In the case of Frances and Paul, over the years Frances has become accustomed to her role as advocate and places a strong focus in her life on ensuring that Paul meets his goals. As Paul aged, he became comfortable with Frances handling everything for him. Since she has struggled to fade her involvement independently, Paul's self-advocacy skills were stunted and not allowed the opportunity to flourish. In this dynamic, Paul has not successfully differentiated himself from his mother, creating a fused relationship where she remains focused on him instead of shifting to herself (Bowen, 1985).

Meenakshi, Pareek, and Kaur (2018) looked at the population of parents of children with ASD. They found that the act of caregiving itself is a source of strain, and the required time, patience, and effort often can lead to symptoms of depression and anxiety. The burden of managing a child with a disability in the wake of a diagnosis, divorce and the subsequent absenteeism of the biological father have, understandably, been significant stressors for Frances.

Frances resents Paul's absentee father for the fact that she has to do so much for her son all by herself. These adversities have led her to focus on how she can be of help to Paul and given her life purpose in many ways.

Models of Disability

When conceptualizing the family impacted by a disability, it is necessary to consider the different models people tend to take on. These models are ultimately the lens in which an individual views disability, and understanding the differing perspectives provides guidance as to how it should be conceptualized. According to *Disability World*'s glossary, models of disability include medical, social, expert, charity, moral, legitimacy, empowering, social adapted, economic, market, and spectrum (*Disability World*, 2018).

Based on this history and the dynamics that have emerged, it seems Frances has adopted a model of disability that precludes him from involvement in major decisions in his life. She is reluctant to delegate responsibility to Paul for meeting his own needs, which has resulted in continued and worsened deficits. Unfortunately, this is not uncommon for parents with children with disabilities. They spend years of their lives advocating and meeting their children's needs. They are able to anticipate their child's needs without the child even having to indicate their desires or needs. There is a comfort and pride in the role of caretaker and advocate (McDaniel & Pisani, 2012). As the child gets older, this significant level of support becomes a burden for the parent and an intrusion for the adult, which creates strain on both sides.

Parents often feels overwhelmed by their responsibilities and begin to fear what will happen to their adult child when they are no longer around. The adult child begins to feel frustrated that they are sheltered or not permitted to take the same steps that their same age peers are. In some respects, this maintenance of the role of advocate and "doer" serves to enable the adult child with the potential to prevent them from meeting their potential. McDaniel and Pisani (2012) discussed how this asynchrony of parental support needed versus chronological age poses a challenge for caregivers, and even more so if there are typically developing children within the family. These factors all influence the model of disability the family and its members are likely to take on when conceptualizing how autism impacts their loved one.

The clinician's model of disability can take on a few perspectives. Traditionally, anyone providing treatment for those who have a disability would take a medical model approach. This model places a high value on treatment and legitimizes the role of doctors, therapists and other medical providers in the process of helping. It's easy to see why it is an appealing model to apply. Yet, other practitioners may take on other models in their treatment approach. Understanding what one's model of disability is (counselor) and that of the client will be helpful in navigating the therapeutic approach to the family being treated. This is where awareness and knowledge meet to help create a competent counseling relationship.

In order to build knowledge about the various models of disability, it's helpful to look into a comprehensive list of possibilities. Beyond the four primary models of disability, new ones have emerged that help depict more nuances of how one views disabilities. Examples of the different models and their descriptions are provided in Table 2.2.

In the case of Frances and Paul, the view of disability that is most likely to apply is the social adapted view. There is a potential for Paul's diagnosis to limit his abilities for success, but in many ways Frances' advocating for and enabling him has done more to limit him than his diagnosis. The environment that has been constructed around this family system serves to reinforce its existence and structure. In order for the system to change, all individuals participating within it would need to adjust their roles in order to adapt to a new and different stage of homeostasis.

Family Assessment and Interventions

The following will be a brief examination of this family system utilizing the concepts that apply based upon the information provided. Frances and Paul represent a two-person system, which is unstable. Stability within a system requires that there are at least three people, much like the visual representation of a triangle, it is supported on all sides (Carlson, Sperry, & Lewis, 2005). While we know a little bit about Paul's father, he seems to be mostly absent from the system and does not participate in meaningful ways. The divorce was an adverse event faced by this family (Hartley et al., 2010). This has created cohesion between Paul and Frances who have balanced out the missing link from the father who traditionally fills the role of a vital support to this triangle.

Table 2.2 Models of disability

Model	*Description*
Medical	Views disability as the result of a medical condition, with the focus being on treatment or a cure
Social	Views disability as a socially constructed problem
Expert	A combination of utilizing the medical model to identify the limitations of the disability, and then to take the necessary steps in order to improve the overall quality of life for the individual with a disability
Tragedy	Looks on the individual with pity, as if they are the victim of a tragedy
Moral	Looks at the individual as responsible for the advent of their own disability
Legitimacy	Looks at the explanations for the atypical conditions as a necessary part of membership to the disability community
Empowering	Looks to the individual with a disability to take an active role in making decisions regarding their treatment and services
Social adapted	Acknowledges that a disability has the potential to limit opportunities in the able-bodied world, but posits that the environment has the ability to be more limiting than the actual disability
Economic	Considers disability through the lens of one's ability to join the work force and be productive
Market	This model considers individuals with disabilities and their stakeholders as a category; as consumers, employees, and voters
Spectrum	Looks at disability as a range of visibility, audibility, and sensibility under which an individual functions. Acknowledges that a disability might not mean that functionality is reduced

Note
Definitions derived from *Disability World* (2018), www.disabled-world.com.

The level of differentiation between mother and son has been minimal over the years, and this has been reinforcing for Frances. As this shifts, Frances will struggle with Paul's attempts to think independently and will likely engage in behaviors that contradict the goal of Paul becoming more independent. While the marital conflict might initially look like it is where the conflict is within this family, because of his ASD diagnosis the *dysfunction* is identified within Paul and thus, in his mother's view, Paul is the IP. His disability represents a dysfunction within his presumed abilities and is a source of Frances' need to over-function. The emotional cutoff created by Paul's father is another significant issue within this system and has impacted both in different ways. The particular challenge is that this cutoff was initiated by the father, leaving unresolved issues for both Frances and Paul. Case conceptualization is a helpful tool for therapists in that it provides a framework from which to identify areas of deficit, protective factors, and the manner in which to most effectively intervene (Sperry & Sperry, 2012). As this is both an individual and family case, the utilization of the eight concepts and the Bowenian case conceptualization form is a more specific tool in which to identify the elements of a family system.

Another useful tool in the assessment of family dynamics is a genogram. This may be utilized in conjunction with the eight concepts as developed by Dr. Bowen. A genogram is a visual mapping system with symbols to indicate patterns, relationships, conflicts, and quality of relationships over generations. Genograms are related to the family diagram developed by Dr. Bowen, and it is believed that they first were developed by his student, Philip J. Guerin (Butler, 2008). Genograms were also utilized in the mid-1980s by Monica McGoldrick and Randy Gerson and continue to be a commonly used assessment in family therapy (McGoldrick & Gerson, 2008). Not to be confused with a genogram, the family diagram is also a visual tool that is utilized within the practice of family therapy, specifically systems theory.

Family diagrams originated in the 1950s, although the exact date of origin is unknown. Their purpose is to record the functioning of a family across three generations of the system. Included within this record are the physical, emotional, and educational factors associated with each individual. Genograms take the family diagram and add other variables to be examined, such as ethnicity, religion, race, migration, class, and sexual orientation (Carlson, Sperry, & Lewis, 2005). In essence, the genogram is a more in-depth view of the complexities of human dynamics, relationships, and interactions.

One benefit of using a genogram is that its visual presentation may be helpful in counseling adults with autism. Individuals with ASD benefit from the use of visual supports in combination with concepts that are presented verbally. So, in many ways, the use of genograms within the session can provide a visual reference point. Genograms also have symbols that have fixed meanings, which allows the individual with ASD to learn the meaning in a concrete manner. It can also help allay any anxiety or fear that dynamics in counseling will change from moment to moment, and that it is objective and explicit. This plays to the strengths of an individual on the spectrum in terms of concrete thinking and visual perception. Figure 2.1 is an example of Paul and Frances' genogram. The symbols in the legend provided are derived from a combination of family therapy resources, including Bowen's original work and newer updates to include diagnostic information.

What can be observed by the genogram of the family is similar to what is reflected within the Bowen case conceptualization tool. It provides general demographics, as well as information as to the dynamics of the relationships in this system. The clinician will not just be able to see a snapshot of these relationships, but a genogram serves as a "road map" to the dynamics over generations. While the initial key for the use of a genogram has the potential to be overwhelming for a clinician, its complexities are outweighed by its utility. There are also applications that can be downloaded so that it can be done electronically, as opposed to manually. Figure 2.1 is the genogram that was constructed based upon the information provided by Frances as to family dynamics.

After utilizing the assessment and intervention process provided by the multifaceted process of the genogram, other treatment interventions can be applied. It is clear that in order for treatment gains to be made, both parties will need to make adjustments individually and at the system or family level. If the family system dynamics aren't addressed therapeutically, Frances will likely continue to make efforts to regain homeostasis, at the cost of Paul's differentiation and individuation. It would be helpful for both parties to seek out individual sessions in order to gain insight into their particular patterns, and how to make the necessary cognitive and behavioral shifts.

Frances can benefit from individual therapy to deal with past issues related to the dissolution of her marriage, having a child with a disability, as well as managing her role as a single parent. It would also be important to deal with any anxiety she experiences related to her shift in role from parent of a young child to parent of an adult child. Thoughts such as "he will fail if I don't do [blank] for him", or "how will I support him when I get old?" are all intrusive thoughts that have an impact on how she interacts with Paul. These consistent fears govern her ability to phase out of her role, as well as sabotage any attempts Paul makes to become more independent. The use of cognitive-behavioral therapy could be effective to help her manage these thoughts as they come. Thought identification and shifting is a useful technique to interrupt the thought processes that occur that would be counterproductive to Paul's attempts at independence. This approach would provide skills for Frances to utilize, which will assist her in decreasing her over-functioning.

In the case of an individual counselor for Paul, the counselor would benefit from a direct, concrete approach as has been suggested by research

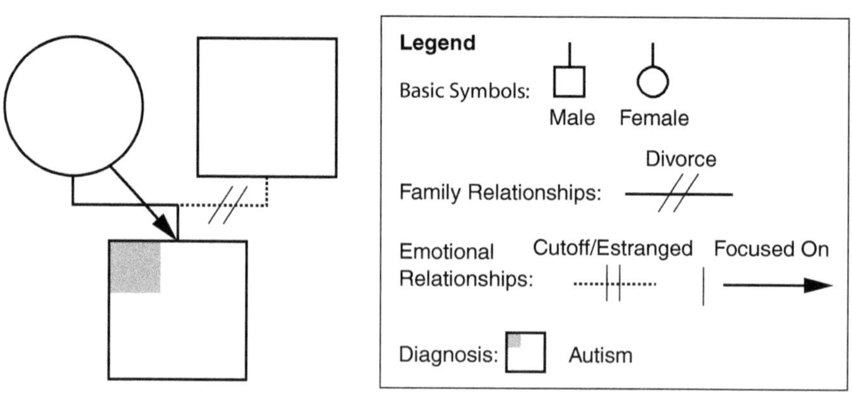

Figure 2.1 Paul and Frances family genogram and legend.

and best-practice in the field. Cognitive-behavioral therapy (CBT) has been shown to have success with individuals with ASD, understanding that there might be a need for adaptations such as being less Socratic and more explicit (Spain et al., 2015). The strategies utilized within this approach offer the individual with ASD concrete skills in order to manage the thoughts that have the potential to be intrusive and disruptive.

There would also need to be some psychoeducation about ASD, to empower Paul to understand circumstances in which he would need support to continue his path to independence (Graetz, 2010). Depending on expressed challenges, there can also be a component of social skills intervention and follow-up support. As will be reviewed in Chapter 10, connecting Paul and Frances with resources is an important part of the process. Services provided through Vocational Rehabilitation can help provide funding and support a move forward in his career. An agency such as this would provide the necessary supports in order for Paul to move ahead, and to gain education, training, and coaching to be successful in the long term. A plan should be developed both within this agency and in counseling sessions to create clear goals and track task completion. As individuals with ASD have strengths in visual processing, it would be beneficial to create a visual aid with Paul in order to give goals some traction outside of session.

The role of the therapist with this population has the potential to shift outside of the traditional talk therapy approach, with elements that integrate case management and coaching. Elements of the therapeutic plan should include a concrete plan of action to prepare the individual to function more independently, connect with applicable support agencies, as well as providing corrective feedback regarding social interactions and activities of daily living. This type of shifted dynamic supports the needs of the individual more so than traditional talk therapy. It provides a more supportive network around the individual and sets contingencies for change

When the ground work is laid with both parties, it will be necessary to engage Frances and Paul in family therapy to address the shifted dynamic and associated feelings that accompany this. In this process, helping Paul and Frances have the opportunity to apply and practice new skills learned in individual therapy will be helpful. Paul will apply communication skills towards assertiveness and self-advocacy. The practitioner can provide Frances with opportunities to reflect on how Paul's improvements are impacting her in both positive and challenging ways. It will be essential to process his improvements in a family context so Paul's understanding of his mother's position can lead to compassion while he responds, and the counselor can assist them in avoiding a return to their old, less functional patterns of communication.

The role of the counselor in treating this family is to utilize triangulation in a productive way (McGoldrick & Gerson, 2008). This will require the counselor to give opportunities to Frances and Paul to hash out their conflicts in session, while the practitioner deliberately inserts themselves when opportunities are present to do so in a healthy way. Finding these opportunities for getting involved when it'll be helpful to emphasize that a healthy skill was applied or backing out when they attempt to rely on the counselor too much is one way we can maintain healthy triangulation. This, in addition to frequently communicating healthy boundaries between the family and the counselor, will be important. There is often much attention given to the idea of managing expectations of the client, and this applies to the therapist as well. Managing the expectations of your role within this relationship is important to the process.

It will be critical to identify factors within the family that will promote resilience. Positive outlook, spirituality, family member accord, flexibility, family communication, financial management, family time, shared recreation, routines and rituals, and support networks are all examples of characteristics that promote resiliency (Meenakshi, Pareek, & Kaur, 2018). Therefore, utilizing optimism in treatment with families is a key component to building these features. The following chapter on increasing optimism will focus on how to integrate methods for promoting optimism for the ultimate goal of connectedness among clients with autism and their supportive families.

References

Barnhill, G.P. (2007). Outcomes in adults with Asperger syndrome. *Focus on Autism and Other Developmental Disabilities*, *15*, 146–153.

Bowen, M. (1976). Theory in the practice of psychotherapy. *Family Therapy: Theory and Practice*, *4*(1), 2–90.

Bowen, M. (1985). *Family therapy in clinical practice.* Lanham, MD: Rowman & Littlefield.

Butler, J.F. (2008). The family diagram and genogram: Comparisons and contrasts. *American Journal of Family Therapy*, *36*(3), 169–180.

Carlson, J., Sperry, L., & Lewis, J.A. (2005) *Family therapy techniques: Integrating & tailoring treatment.* New York: Taylor/Francis Routledge

Disability World. (2018). Retrieved from: www.disabilityworld.com.

Gantman, A., Kapp, S.K., Orenski, K., & Laugeson, E. A. (2012). Social skills training for young adults with autism spectrum disorders: A randomized controlled pilot study. *Journal for Autism and Developmental Disorder*, *42*(6), 1094–1103.

Graetz, J.E. (2010). Autism grows up: Opportunities for adults with autism. *Disability and Society*, *25*(1), 33–47.

Hartley, S.L., Barker, E.T., Seltzer, M.M., Floyd, F., Greenberg, J., Orsmond, G., & Bolt, D. (2010). The relative risk and timing of divorce in families of children with an autism spectrum disorder. *Journal of Family Psychology*, *24*(4), 449.

Kirby, A.V., Baranek, G.T., & Fox, L. (2016). Longitudinal predictors of outcomes for adults with autism spectrum disorder: Systematic review. *OTJR Occupation, Participation and Health*, *36*(2), 55–64. doi:10.1177/1539449216650182.

Laugeson, E.A., Gantman, A., Kapp, S.K., Orenski, K., & Ellingsen, R. (2015). A randomized controlled trial to improve social skills in young adults with autism spectrum disorder: The UCLA PEERS® program. *Journal of Autism and Developmental Disorders*, *45*, 3978–3989

Mandelberg, J., Frankel, F., Cunningham, T., Gorospe, C., & Laugeson, E.A. (2013). Long-term outcomes of parent-assisted social skills intervention for high-functioning children with autism spectrum disorders. *Autism, 1*, 1–9. doi:10/1177/1362361312472403

McDaniel, S.H., & Pisani, A.R. (2012). Family dynamics and caregiving for people with disabilities. In *Multiple Dimensions of Caregiving and Disability* (pp. 11–28). New York: Springer.

McGoldrick, M., & Gerson, R. (2008). *Genograms in family assessment.* New York: W.W. Norton & Company.

Meenakshi, Pareek, B., & Kaur, R. (2018). Perceived social support among care givers of children with autistic spectrum disorder. *Asian Journal of Nursing Education and Research, 8*(1), 51–56. doi:10.5958/2349-2996.2018.00012.5.

Spain, D., Sin, J., Chalder, T., Murphy, D., & Happe, F. (2015). Cognitive behaviour therapy for adults with autism spectrum disorders and psychiatric co-morbidity: A review. *Research in Autism Spectrum Disorders, 9*, 151–162.

Sperry, L., & Sperry, J. (2012). *Case conceptualization: Mastering this competency with ease and confidence.* New York: Routledge/Taylor & Francis.

The Bowen Center for the Study of the Family. (2018). Retrieved from https://thebowencenter.org.

Wong, C., Odom, S.L., Hume, K., Cox, A.W., Fettig, A., Kucharczyk, S., … Schultz, T.R. (2013). *Evidence-based practices for children, youth, and young adults with Autism Spectrum Disorder.* Chapel Hill: The University of North Carolina, Frank Porter Graham Child Development Institute, Autism Evidence-Based Practice Review Group.

3 Increasing Optimism

Optimism and positive psychology encourage fulfilling and life satisfying experiences, many of which may not be perfect or even immediately joyful events. During my career, I've encountered many clients, parents and professionals who interpret optimism and positivity as a naïve and unrealistic view of the world. This is understandable considering how often this view is perpetuated by popular culture trends and social media, which tend to imply that optimism equates "perfection", "rainbows and butterflies" or a "Pollyanna" approach to life. Christopher Peterson documented the challenges positive psychology has faced when being equated with "happiology" through misused smiley faces and positive images in the media (Peterson, 2006). Consider how when we're doing something engaging or interesting that we don't always smile or laugh happily, yet we can feel immensely fulfilled. Both challenging and successful experiences can be viewed through the lens of optimism.

When coming across these unrealistic or misleading messages about how "thinking positively can fix all of your problems", many people feel deflated. Consider how families who are encountering incredibly challenging situations and behaviors might feel when an "expert" or resource seems to convey that "positive thinking" is the key to solving their problems. This can be self-defeating when a person is simply looking for a concrete answer to "fix" the behavior. They usually do not want to see how a shift in their patterns of thinking and behaving can impact their loved one. Even though the former usually isn't effective, this is often what clients and families are looking for to help alleviate immediate distress. The latter is not as immediately satisfying and requires significant coaching and support over time to enact change. These are hard messages to receive when you're desperately trying to fix challenging behaviors.

In understanding the importance of optimism in approaching and treating clients with autism spectrum disorder, it's essential to acknowledge the roots of this work in positive psychology. The founder of positive psychology, Martin P. Seligman, is acknowledged for his effective approach in challenging the traditions of deficit or pathology-based treatment in the medical model-focused profession of psychology (Seligman et al., 1995). In many of his books, he describes the growing pains associated with helping to create this shift within himself and among colleagues (Seligman et al., 1995; Seligman, 2004; 2011). For problem-focused people and a problem focused discipline, this shift can be a hard pill to swallow for clients and practitioners alike. Therefore, this approach needed to make a strong scientific argument for why positive psychology should become evidence-based practice that is taught and practiced alongside traditional theories of and approaches to the treatment of mental health issues.

It is particularly challenging to embrace optimism for parents and caregivers who are using the powerful, yet flawed knowledge hub, the internet, to find answers to questions about their children. Much of the time they are confronted with messages of either doom or gloom, or unachievable, false hope when they are in the throes of grief, anger and frustration in managing their child's issues. One parent encounter helped remind of me of the importance of accurately explaining optimism in its real and practical sense.

I was at a local school presenting to a large audience on the topic of optimism in parenting children with autism. Halfway through the presentation, a parent of twins who had recently been diagnosed asked me a brutally honest question "How can anyone *really expect us* to have positive thoughts after a weekend spent with our boys who have meltdowns every two hours?" The helplessness and frustration coming from these parents who were hoping for an answer for how to help their children's behaviors were palpable and immediately gave me a moment of pause and reflection. Was the way I explained how optimism could be helpful for these parents just making them feel worse about themselves? It certainly seemed like it. Despite my attempts to communicate optimism accurately in the context of realistic expectations, the talk elicited this response. So, I had to try and understand how to do this better and grow from the experience.

I spent time with these parents after the talk and sought out feedback. They provided me with valuable reminders that can be applied to many families I've worked with. Namely, they told me the story of their autism journey with their twins; even though they were young children receiving early intervention, they'd gone through an arduous process of seeking diagnosis and treatment. What a humbling reminder that families impacted with autism face high levels of exhaustion and desperation when navigating care.

Family members and individuals with autism have typically been engaged in a long journey of finding their own solutions to problems and the best external resources, for quite some time before they seek help. Researchers and clinicians have discovered that children with autism, who on average are diagnosed between the ages of four and five years old, likely demonstrated signs and symptoms of autism for at least two years before receiving diagnosis (Howlin, 1997; Levy et al., 2003; Yeargin-Allsopp et al., 2003). A variety of factors contribute to an increase in age of diagnosis, including the severity of clinical presentation, socioeconomic status, parenting behaviors, being a racial minority, living in rural areas and the number of clinicians treating the child (Mandell, Novak & Zubritsky, 2015).

By the time they seek out a diagnosis or treatment, most have done their own research and come across a combination of good and bad clinicians who've provided either helpful or harmful feedback. Some of the harmful information that parents receive includes blaming them for not bonding effectively, and attributing their child's issues to a cold or "refrigerator" parenting style (Bettelheim, 1967). Even though this approach was more commonly taken decades ago, the fear and stigma surrounding this remains salient among parents who are already worried that something they've done (nor not done) has caused their child's autism.

Despite the consequences of bad practice that has resulted in decades of lasting stigma, most parents are able to push beyond this to help their children by seeking educational, medical, and therapeutic services. Therefore, after doing their own research and pushing themselves outside of their comfort zone, they finally reach out to a mental health professional to seek help. The first step of calling, emailing or texting to seek our services is significant and requires as much validation as we can provide. When they hear that a clinician's approach focuses on shifting their own thoughts and behaviors in order to create change for their child, by becoming more optimistic, this can be daunting and off-putting. Understandably, many families can become even more overwhelmed because this approach does not focus directly on the challenging behaviors they believe are causing them the most distress.

These historical contexts are imperative to practicing with compassion, care and sensitivity to this population. All of this should be considered as we think about the path that many of our clients and their families have walked in their efforts to seek help. We need to be careful that when we label a parent, caregiver or adult client's thoughts and behaviors as "pessimistic" this can be interpreted as unfair, unrealistic and even attacking. Therefore, navigating this territory must be done with realism, care and competence as to how we approach clients and their family members.

Realistic Optimism

When introducing this topic, it's helpful to start by realistically defining optimism and describing its influence and importance in treatment. Demystifying the idea that optimism is about "wearing rose-colored glasses" or "just smiling more often" is essential (Peterson, 2006). There are many lay and clinical definitions of optimism that can be useful to reference when explaining the influence of optimism to adults with autism and to their loved ones.

A realistic and relatable approach I often rely on with clients when explaining optimism is to use well-known historical figures or influencers to support a practical explanation of the concept. For my history buff clientele, I might refer to Winton Churchill's description of people with these traits as "a pessimist sees the difficulty in every opportunity; an optimist sees the opportunity in every difficulty". While for other clients I refer to the anonymous quote, "Pain is inevitable, suffering is optional" and ask them to process their understanding of this message.

The human condition is one that forces people to experience both immense pleasure and overwhelming pain. Life events that bring pain are by far and wide experienced by most people regardless of culture, age, geographical location or socioeconomic status. These events include death of a loved one, separation from friends and lovers, moving far away from home, and changing jobs. As counselors and mental health practitioners these are some of the most common life events that we regularly help people work through. Through this process we witness how different people, who encounter the same life stressor, manage the ensuing challenges in different ways. How they handle the stressor likely predicts their level of optimism in processing about said event. Those who embody more optimistic beliefs about these events ("This is rough, but I'll make it through") tend to suffer less; while those who are more pessimistic ("I'm totally incapable of getting through this") suffer more (Durand, 2011).

A common life stressor that many people around the world face is having a loved one with a diagnosed medical or mental health condition:

- About half of all Americans are diagnosed with at least one chronic medical condition, while one in four are diagnosed with at least two or more chronic medical conditions (Ward, Schiller, & Goodman, 2014)
- Half of the non-elderly population in America have one or more pre-existing health conditions (US Department of Health & Human Services, 2017)
- One in five (44.7 million) adults in the US are diagnosed with a mental health disorder (National Institute for Mental Health, 2018),

Given the above stated prevalence rates of chronic medical and mental health conditions, it is clear they impact a significant portion of the population. These people are our families, friends, neighbors and clients. We all face the inevitability that at least one person who we are close to will suffer because of these diagnoses. In many cases it can be difficult, if not impossible, to conceptualize how a person can think and act optimistically in the face of these circumstances.

This is when it becomes helpful to consider the clinical definitions of optimism because it provides for a more accurate depiction of how this can be achieved in a realistic and humanistic manner. According to Seligman's work in *The Optimistic Child*, "… optimism does not lie in positive phrases or images about victory, but the way you think about causes" (Seligman, Reivich, Jaycox, & Gilham, 1995, p. 54). The way we tend to think about causes of events in our lives involves three factors – permanence, pervasiveness and personalization.

People who view causes of a bad event as temporary or impermanent tend to be more optimistic (permanence). The optimistic person may also view the cause of a bad event as isolated or targeted and avoid generalizing to other areas of their lives (pervasiveness). Lastly, when a bad event happens to the more optimistic person they attribute its cause to a specific, behavioral issue within themselves instead of general self-blame for an unchangeable character flaw (personalization) (Seligman et al., 1995).

Let's explore an example of a typical bad event that most people have experienced: getting a bad grade. The optimistic person tends to think: "Oh no, this one grade will really bring down my final grade right now … I guess I still have the next few assignments to try my best and bring it back up." They also tend to compare this event with others in their past in which they did not fail in order to put the event in temporary context: "I'm really bummed that this happened, but it doesn't happen all of the time." And finally, the bad grade can be well understood or justified when looking back at what the person did that contributed to this performance: "I didn't spend enough time studying the concepts from Chapter 3, I really only skimmed over it." These three ways of thinking about the bad grade help the person avoid thinking it will last *forever*, will impact *everything* else and is due to a negative personal characteristic, such as *stupidity*.

It has been suggested in the literature that optimism and pessimism encapsulate two ends of one single concept (Rasmussen, Scheier, & Greenhouse, 2009). Viewing this on a continuum accurately describes the cognitive process humans experience when dealing with adverse events; low levels of optimism translate to higher levels of pessimism. People's optimism can be measured as a trait or state to determine how they generally view life's events, and how they deal with specific situations. Some research has identified that people have trait optimism, meaning there is a tendency towards optimistic thinking across situations, while others have argued that levels of optimism change for the same person under certain conditions or states (Kluemper, Little, & DeGroot, 2009). Regardless which camp you fall under as a practitioner, you can infuse optimism into the context of an issue the client is working through. You may decide to conceptualize the client as more optimistic or pessimistic by nature, but consider the outliers and look for opportunities to reinforce any trends toward optimism you may notice.

As one of its main goals, the science of positive psychology and optimism has researchers and clinicians demonstrating its effects across many of life's domains. Among those diagnosed with chronic and even terminal conditions, people who are optimistic about *how* they suffer in the face of the diagnosis have the following positive health outcomes.

- Optimism plays a positive role in objective assessments of one's physical health, including mortality and survival, cardiovascular and immune functioning, as well as cancer and pregnancy outcomes (Rasmussen et al., 2009).
- Lower levels of optimism result in less social support and more anxiety (Applebaum et al., 2014).

- Optimism is associated with improved health perceptions, vitality, mental health, and lower levels of bodily pain (Achat, Kawachi, Spiro, DeMolles, & Sparrow, 2000).
- Pessimistic styles and explanatory models predict negative immune system health effects in older adults (Karen-Siegel, Rodin, Seligman, & Dwyer, 1991).

As mental health professionals, we need to be cognizant of the research related to the clinical choices we make when we decide to focus on improving optimistic thinking and behaving. In addition to the physical health benefits mentioned above, optimism has also been linked to several psychological resources and strengths. These include having a wide array of coping skills, a sense that there are fewer barriers to meeting goals and the use of social support when facing stress (Groden, Kantor, Woodard, & Lipsitt, 2011). Therefore, having our own understanding of optimism's positive health impacts is imperative and, in some cases, can be used in counseling to psychoeducate clients. Since many adults with ASD are concrete, fact-based thinkers, many may be interested in the reasons why this should be a focus. And in these cases, diving into the clinical definitions and benefits of optimism can be helpful.

So how can we apply our understanding of optimism and its benefits to counseling autistic adults? One of the most useful ways for clinicians to explain the utility of optimism is to teach clients about scaling their levels on the range. Optimism and pessimism represent the opposing poles on this scale. We have a tendency towards one of these poles and can fluctuate between them depending on a variety of internal and external factors. It is an almost automatic part of the human experience to react to challenging life experiences with a flux of both more optimistic or pessimistic responses. For some these fluxes fall within a typical range and others have significant swings between the two which can lead to thoughts and behaviors that cause depression, anxiety, and resorting to the use of unhealthy coping strategies (Beck, 1987; Chang, D'Zurilla, & Maydeu-Olivares, 1994). Within the normal range, we shift in our reactions on this scale and the first step to understanding ourselves is noticing the situations we tend to process optimistic or pessimistically.

Once we can identify or notice trends in optimism about our clients, we also are likely to identify a tendency in ourselves that might tip us slightly or more significantly towards optimism or pessimism. Normalizing the natural fluctuation in our reactions and getting closer to identifying a pattern or tendency in ourselves can enhance self-awareness and move clients towards an openness to incorporating optimism into treatment. Therapeutic tools for increasing optimism with autistic clients will be explored in detail at the end of this chapter.

Optimism and Outcomes in Autism

Let's look at the roots of how a caregiver's reactions to their loved one with ASD throughout childhood can contribute to outcomes in adulthood. In most clinical research and practice, it's almost impossible to assert that one variable causes one or more outcomes; when examining human behavior, we understand and acknowledge that multiple factors are at play. As researchers and clinicians muddle through the myriad factors that contribute to successful outcomes for younger and older clients as they age, several common assumptions have been reported by caregivers and parents.

The assumptions are typically based on how parents and other caregivers process and respond to the news of a loved one's diagnosis. Many families and practitioners make assumptions about prognosis based on the specifiers of mild, moderate and severe; with the conclusion that those who are mild will go on to be more "successful" in adulthood. Although this contributes to managing expectations and the type of placement and services an adult will require, this isn't the most significant predictor of success in adulthood. Many with severe ASD symptoms can go on to live independently from their families, in residential care, and some hold part-time jobs or volunteer. Another common assumption that practitioners and family members make are that severity and frequency of problem behaviors is the strongest predictor of adult success. Although the extent to which challenging behavior problems are present during childhood and adulthood can impact one's level of success and independence in adulthood, it's not as strong an influence as one other key factor (Durand, 2011). Keep in mind that what success looks like or by what it is measured will need to be tailored to each person and their level of potential.

In fact, when evaluating thousands of families who have children with behavioral and emotional challenges, including ASD, the best predictor of success in adulthood is parental or caregiver pessimism (Durand & Hieneman, 2008). This means the way that primary caregivers view and respond to their child's behaviors has long-term impacts on that child's success as an adult. Caregivers who are classified as pessimistic tend to have automatic thought and behavioral patterns that can be paralyzing; whereas parents with more optimistic thought and behavioral patterns can more readily act. One example from the research demonstrated that a recurring thought of pessimistic caregivers is "I have no control over my child" while their more optimistic counterparts thought "Right now I cannot my child control, but I can do ______ to help" (Durand, 2011).

So how does the research and clinical treatment for children who are impacted by their caregivers' level of optimism translate to working with adults with ASD? Most ASD children will outlive their parents and develop their own personas, which are influenced by their experiences with family members, teachers, and other caregivers during their formative years. Therefore, the beliefs that an autistic adult has about themselves have been impacted by the way they were treated by these influencers. If the caregivers held beliefs that they, themselves were capable of handling challenging situations, this is communicated and interpreted by others as a covert message of efficacy and capability. As discussed in the previous chapter, it is important for counselors and mental health professionals to presume competence and capability, but when we confront a client who hasn't received this message from others before extra time, higher doses and more resources will be spent to shift the result of years of opposing experiences. Caregivers who demonstrate self-efficacy and self-determination raise children who become self-efficacious and self-determined adults (Durand & Hieneman, 2008). Therefore if this was lacking, the clinician will have to double down in efforts to expose them to these experiences through the therapeutic relationship.

These concepts are reflected in the literature and research on how applying the cognitive and behavioral tools from positive psychology, including optimism, have helped adults with ASD. One of the best tools for practitioners to apply positive psychology in counseling people with autism is the book, *How Everyone on the Autism Spectrum, Young and Old, Can ... Become Resilient, Be More Optimistic, Enjoy Humor, Be Kind, and Increase Self-Efficacy: A Positive Psychology Approach*. If you want to go above and beyond any of the concepts presented in this chapter, this book will be a resource you can enjoy. Research on how positive psychology interventions have assisted children with developmental disorders reflects how relaxation techniques can mitigate significant behavioral challenges (Groden et al., 2011). In addition to the tools of relaxation, the use of visual cue cards and video modeling through a positive psychology approach have also proven effective for those with ASD (Agran, Blanchard, Wehmeyer, & Hughes, 2002; Reeve, Reeve, Townsend, & Poulson, 2007). Based on the positive outcomes of promoting optimism and using positive psychology in treating the challenging behaviors people with autism exhibit, let's explore how interventions aimed at helping them reap these benefits can be applied in counseling.

Interventions

The interventions selected in the upcoming section are highlighted for clinicians to help clients increase optimism in order to improve physical and mental health outcomes. If you are reading this book, it is likely you have an established theoretical approach and treatment modality that you identify with and have mastered. Yet, if you've picked up this book, it's also likely you're looking for new tools to add to your therapeutic approach that can be easily integrated into your existing practice. The following recommendations were chosen with you and the client with ASD in mind for their ease of integration and concrete approach to understanding and shifting the cognitive processes associated with increasing optimism. On a final note, the interventions presented here can be used in this sequence (beginning, middle, end) so to provide the client with warm-up exercises that then lead to more rigorous therapeutic work and finishes with a treatment recommendation that can result in emotional catharsis.

Daily Gratitude Practice

To help clients create different, new, and healthy methods of increasing optimism, it is effective to develop habits and practices that support this. One of the best researched techniques derived from both positive psychology and mindfulness-based interventions is related to regular, intentionally scheduled and planned gratitude practices (Seligman, Steen, Park, & Peterson, 2005). The goal in initiating these daily practices is that eventually a person's automatic processes, both internal cognitions and externalized actions, are re-wired towards interpreting every day and, even, mundane aspects of their lives through a lens of appreciation.

In developing or improving an automatic tendency of this type, a few exercises for implementing these are outlined here. These are two that I regularly utilize for their clear and concrete nature and their ability to be tailored to clients at different levels of motivation and commitment to change. These are the three good things and the ten-finger gratitude exercises.

The three good things exercise promotes happiness and increases optimism through the mechanism of recording specific events throughout one's day that elicited a positive emotional state (Seligman et al., 2005). In the practice of writing down three good things that happened in one's day, the mechanisms in our brains that focus on negative events are replaced, even for a short time. This serves to interrupt depressive or anxious thoughts. This activity sounds simple and straightforward because it is. In fact, it has a high rate of completion in treatment compliance, and Seligman purports its simplicity and ease is likely one reason for this (Seligman et al., 2005).

An essential element of the three good things exercise is that the person not only lists the events that occurred, but it also asks them to immerse themselves in the event to consider its cause(s). The purpose of writing down and reflecting on the causes has the person identify the quality of the event and any role they may have played in causing it. When considering and reflecting on one's own role in the positive event, this exercise can help shift one's explanatory model towards optimism. Some prompts to consider recommending with clients who have trouble conceptualizing cause in a meaningful way would be to have them answer "Why did this good thing end up happening today? And how did I play a part?" This will require coaching and repetition of instruction for many clients who may not immediately adopt this successfully, but with visual aids in the form of a journal or smart phone app, this can be adjusted to smoothly.

The ten-finger gratitude exercise is a mindfulness-based practice as described by the science connected specifically to gratitude as the primary key to happiness and quality of life (Eammons, 2004). In this exercise, the counselor describes how one's anxious or depressed thought patterns have automatically developed neural pathways in the brain that become habitual and even "comfortable" for us. To shift these automatic patterns of thinking and pathways that have been developed in the brain, takes effort and work but not necessarily a lot of time in daily practice. The ten-finger gratitude exercise is a practice that asks one to reflect back on and identify ten specific, sensory and emotional experiences that they can identify as a positive or growing experience that occurred in one day.

One way I've found it helpful for clients to more manageably take on this task, is to break up the ten things they are grateful that happened in a day based on a meal schedule. What three things happened between waking up and breakfast that you are grateful for. The more detail that can be described about the sensory and emotional responses, the better. For example, if a client ate breakfast that morning, I might ask them to describe what they ate and what about it tasted or felt best. Was it the crunch of their Frosted Flakes or the delicious combination of the sugar with the milk that was most enjoyable? As for a growing experience that one might be grateful for, these can be trickier.

If a client had an experience that was challenging or initially frustrating, one practice that shifts a client towards optimism and gratitude is to help guide them toward identifying how this "negative" experience actually could have helped them. This isn't about forcing a bias or clinical opinion onto the client's experience in an effort to have them "realize this was a good thing" but instead to try to identify something they can learn from the unpleasant event. For example, a client may have not liked a work assignment they received earlier in the day. Perhaps this is because the assignment was unexpected, outside of their comfort zone, or they were not sure how to complete it successfully. They were annoyed and angry with their supervisor for this assignment, but the end result, to their surprise, and albeit continued frustration, was that they completed the task successfully and they are now eligible for a bonus. From our clinical perspective, we're likely to think "what a win!" so we need to skillfully, as gentle guides, help the more pessimistic client who will tend to focus on the challenging aspects of this event. We can do this by helping them see how this negative event may even be one that they're grateful for. Asking questions about how the negative experience was helpful may be the key to creating a shift towards gratitude and optimism. "How did their anger help propel them to conquer the task? Are they grateful for the potential bonus?" Practicing the ten-finger exercise in sessions with the client is an important starting point for having them generalize this skill into their gratitude practice outside of counseling. It's likely that continued practice with the practitioner will be the key to helping this become a habit for the client, so be prepared to integrate this into the beginning or end of a session as a regular check-in. This will help set the stage for changes in the client's pattern of thinking about challenging and successful events that occur in their lives.

Thought Logs and Disputation

The process of how to utilize thought logs and work through the process of disputation with clients is a two-step process and most effective in increasing optimism when used together (Durand, 2011). In the first step of the intervention, a client is asked to complete a log related to a challenging or successful incident that occurred between sessions. Traditionally, thought logs are tracked via hard copy, paper documents; but it is helpful to think about how thought logs can be used alternatively with technology as an aid.

As is essential to developing and maintaining cultural competence as mental health practitioners, it will be helpful to explore both traditional (paper forms) and modern (apps) formats for therapeutic interventions. To take the intervention of thought-logging to another modality, these can even be completed verbally using voice recording apps. Providing clients with various options that you are competent in facilitating to engage them in this process is a critical first step. In my practice, many clients chose to use a note taking app on their phone that they can then lock to prevent any private thought logs or related information from being shared with others. Technology is constantly evolving, and as cutting-edge, effective therapists we need to be open to incorporating these tools as readily as possible.

At the beginning stages of thought-logging one's challenging and successful incidents, I suggest starting in-session so you can guide the client through each part of the logging process. A thought log related to a recent situation is likely to include at least three sections or steps. The first is a description of the incident, that can include who, what, where, when, and how did this event occur. This provides the client with the opportunity to describe what occurred, so the counselor can then guide the next step of the process, which asks them to identify one to two thoughts that were occurring to them during the incident. It is a step that for some clients with ASD can be difficult and even impossible to access without prompting. This step takes significant efforts on both the part of the client who's being asked to complete a challenging cognitive task and for the therapist who tries their best to elicit this information from the ASD client. It is important to note that this task is one that can be hard for *any* client to identify so even though clients with ASD may struggle differently to identify thoughts related to an event, they are not alone in this being an unnatural part of the process for the majority of clients in counseling.

Since identifying thoughts can be difficult for most, there are some helpful tips to digging deeper for these cognitions. One is that I ask clients to visualize themselves being in the past event. The client can close their eyes to aid with this process, but primarily I need them to paint a visually clear and detailed picture of the incident during a session. Starting the thought logging with the description of the five Ws of the event can be a good place to start. After painting this clear picture, I'll provide a prompt for the client to describe any potential feelings they encountered in that moment. Feelings can include emotional and physical sensations since some are more readily accessible than others. Much of this guided visualization can then help the client with ASD move toward cognitive exploration about the experience in the present in a more direct, clear and concrete manner.

Once feelings are identified, thoughts are easier to access, but if they aren't, it is helpful to tentatively suggest possible thoughts that led to those feelings. This is our opportunity to apply our counseling expertise and use our own observations and insights about the client to help them determine what occurred internally. Being tentative and offering several options, not just one potential interpretation, is important here in order to avoid the power of suggestion or implanting our own thoughts into our client's experiences. Making a statement such as

> When I hear you describe the fight with your mother and that you felt frustrated, I wonder if you were thinking something like "She never listens to me" or "Why does she get to make all the decisions? Do either of those sound right to you?

Or "Is there another thought you can identify that is behind that anger or frustration?" One of the benefits in treating autistic adults is that they don't typically concede to a thought that they don't identify as being true; therefore, if you make an erroneous interpretation, they will probably let you know. Honesty can be one of their best assets or resources in therapy. The primary goal here will be to guide a client through the process of focusing on how their feelings and behaviors in the situation have been influenced by their less optimistic thoughts.

The final step in this process, after identifying a recent situation and the thoughts, feelings, and actions taken during the situation, is to process the opportunities to shift identified thoughts towards the optimistic. Unfortunately for autistic clients who are experiencing co-occurring symptoms of depression and anxiety, more pessimistic elements will be fairly easy to access. For other clients it may be more difficult because their level of self-awareness could be impaired, making it difficult to identify the internal processes, including thoughts and feelings. Nonetheless, once you've guided the client to identify at least one thought that conveys lack of control or a low sense of self-worth or efficacy you can move on to disputing it.

Disputation is the process of finding evidence that supports or contradicts the original or automatic thought presented by the client. Since clients diagnosed with ASD can be concrete and data-driven this can be a process by which you utilize these strengths to strengthen disputation. Asking questions to clients such as "What proof or evidence exists that confirms that this thought is true?" and "What proof or evidence exists that disproves that this thought is true?" Organizing the evidence for both categories in two columns through the use of a visual aid, executed by the clinician or the client is a helpful tool. Since the goal of this therapeutic exercise is to eventually shift a more pessimistic thought towards optimism, it'll be helpful to intentionally select a thought for which evidence exists to disprove it. In most situations, there is always evidence to disprove the permanence, pervasiveness or personalization of something they did so these three factors are a helpful place to revisit during the disputation process.

Gratitude Visit

For any readers who have been the recipient or deliverer of a gratitude visit, you've been fortunate to experience its poignancy. In a randomized control trail examining the effects of internet-based positive psychology interventions, this one had the strongest impact on participant's level of happiness for one month after the experience (Seligman et al., 2005). The way that this exercise is designed nicely supplements what clients have learned about and gained from their own individualized gratitude practice and the habits that they've worked to develop. Because the gratitude visit transitions gratitude practice from an intrapersonal to an interpersonal experience, the value in placing this at the end of this sequence of interventions can help this be more successful.

There are specific steps to executing a gratitude visit successfully, as outlined in the positive psychology literature (Seligman, 2004; Seligman et al., 2005). In brief, the first step is to choose a person who you can communicate with, ideally in person, about something they've done that you are grateful for. Visualizing a person who you feel was not adequately thanked for how they impacted you can be helpful. Next, you sit down and write a letter explaining to that person what you are grateful for and why. The letter should be no longer than one page. Finally, invite the person to get together with you casually, without informing them of your plan, and out of the blue you ask their permission to read them the gratitude letter aloud.

When describing these three steps, the gratitude visit may sound simple and even like something you or your client engage in on a regular basis. "I always say thank you to my parents for what they've done for me" or "My friend knows how much I appreciate them." We tend to believe that our day-to-day interactions include a lot more of this than they actually do. The act of planning a visit, sitting someone down and suddenly letting them know the details and depths of the gratitude in written and spoken form is a different and profound experience.

For individuals with autism who may not be used to engaging in such a task, the writing and delivery of the gratitude letter may benefit from support and supplements provided in counseling. One way to help support the efforts of a gratitude visit could be to help process the selection of the person who they have not adequately thanked. In this process, the counselor should utilize their knowledge of the family system and social supports in the client's life. It can be a symptomatic challenge for the ASD client to take the perspective of someone in their life who may have felt underappreciated by them. Providing clear prompts about this could help. For example, "Close your eyes. What people in your life have done things to help you? Does any one person or two people stand out the most?" or "Let's think deeply for a minute. Who have you relied on during a time of real need? How did you thank them?"

Getting the client to clearly identify how that person was thanked or appreciated during that time is a question that they may or may not have the answer to. Depending on many factors, the adult with ASD may have an expectation of support without ever having reflected on what that support means for others. This could be an incredibly powerful learning experience for the client to apply empathic thinking and behaving. Therefore, the preparation for the gratitude visit is likely to require some more specific planning in both how the client thinks about others in their lives and how to execute their authentic communication of appreciation.

You can imagine how unexpected, and even jarring, it could be for the caregiver or other loved one in the ASD adult's life to receive such a visit. The demonstration of a deep, shared, and emotional experience may be even more profound depending on the client's history and predisposition for showing gratitude. In planning for how the gratitude visit should be conducted, I suggest collaborating with the client on ideas for how this can occur authentically. There may be modifications or minor shifts in how it is executed based on the client's characteristics. I've worked with clients whose verbal communication can come off as flat, cold, or contrite, while their written communication is insightful, warm, and meaningful. Considering the strengths and resources of the client will be important to guiding them towards how to best execute the gratitude visit.

Case Example

Ben is an 18-year-old, high school senior who was diagnosed with ASD during elementary school when his parents and teachers noticed he was not regularly socializing with his peers. He was hesitant to initiate play and conversation with his peers, mostly avoiding interactions to engage in activities that he enjoyed, such as music and computers. From a young age, he describes feeling different, not understanding why but trying his best not to stand out among the crowd. Unfortunately, his fear of being different was exacerbated by an incident that occurred to him during late elementary school, wherein a teacher mistakenly posted private information about students on the board. Next to Ben's name was the word "autism", and even though it occurred for only few minutes before the teacher noticed and removed the posting, this event has been engrained as a traumatic memory.

As a result of his fear of negative evaluation by others for being different, as an adult Ben's symptoms of ASD and social anxiety are presenting issues to be addressed in treatment. After years of attempting to blend in among his peers at school, he maintains a close friendship with two popular friends but has a hard time developing friendship outside of these. Yet, because of the social status of his friend, Ben has partially achieved his goal of blending in. In treatment, he expresses strong feelings and reactions to his diagnosis. He "hates it" and has admitted to thinking "autism is a diagnosis worse than cancer". This is particularly hard for his parents to hear as they have a history of cancer diagnoses in their family and they are concerned with how his diagnoses have impacted his identity.

Ben's anxiety related to "being different" and how others perceive him cause him to have intrusive thoughts about how others view the clothes he wears, how he talks to others and how he walks down the hallways at school. His thoughts overwhelm him to the point that he is unwilling to engage in exposure tasks to help treat his anxiety. Ben has an interest in making more friends and potentially dating but believes that others will find out he is "different"; his negative self-view, coupled with his fear of being judged by his peers and others paralyzes him from taking action. He is interested in exploring how psychotropic medication and other recreational substances could positively impact his relationship goals.

Ben's parents are actively involved in his treatment and demonstrate concern for how intensely and negatively he interprets his diagnoses and issues. His views of himself have become exceedingly hateful and isolating to the point that he engages in computer games for hours without talking to others or eating. They aim to help convince him that ASD is not as "bad" as he thinks it is. Their hope is that he will shift his perspective to create a healthier self-identity.

One of the first steps in in Ben's treatment involves logging weekly events that occur and cause anxiety. He has been informed about his results on an anxiety scale (Subjective Units of Distress Scale, SUDS), that results in high rates of distress and avoidance. The logs he completes in therapy each week ask him to rate his levels of distress and also how likely he would be to avoid a similar situation in the future, on a scale from 1 to 100. He typically scores avoidance significantly higher than distress. As we process each weekly event that is logged, Ben is willing to explore alternatives to dispute some of his thoughts around how strange others must be interpreting him. From there we set a goal for exposing him to a somewhat distressing situation he would typically avoid. For example, texting friends to initiate a hang out. Although this generates about a 50 SUDS score, he rates his avoidance of this as a 95. Therefore, encouraging him to complete the task in session is essential.

Ben is also required to keep a daily log of the three good things that happen to him, and in therapy examples from his current day are practiced so generalization is easier. Despite the weekly sessions and goal setting, Ben does not report following through consistently with this exercise. In his case a weekly review of his gratitude is achievable in session, but recent discord among the family has emerged and Ben's parents feel taken advantage of by him. They feel he doesn't understand the value of money and is "spoiled". Given this feedback and the distress it causes Ben, we explore the concept of appreciate and expressing thanks to his parents; he admits it's not something he's ever truly done. So, to expand on the gratitude practice goal we set out to plan for Ben to conduct a gratitude visit within the next three months. This allows the counselor and Ben to prepare for this intervention with adequate practice and demonstration of optimistic growth in other areas of his practice.

After over one year of treatment, Ben's anxiety has measurably decreased in small increments and his automatic pessimistic thoughts have shifted slightly. Now when Ben attempts to initiate a hang out with his friends, he may ask for feedback on the text he'll send his friend, one out of every ten times. He also has moved away from hatred or shame about his clinical issues (although he's not been totally converted, which was not the treatment goal) and reports "I don't think I'm as bad as other people and I'm getting better". It is now easier for him to come up with reasons to dispute some automatic pessimistic thoughts and consider alternatives that may help him and which represent a healthier, less anxious perspective. He's easily able to call up his anxiety and avoidance scaling ratings before asked and uses this language to help communicate his distress in therapy and with his family, which has helped improve their tension. Finally, the gratitude visit experience made a tremendous impact on the relationship with his parents. They report, "We didn't know he could express himself like that. Hearing that he actually appreciates us in specific ways was an experience we'll *never* forget."

References

Achat, H., Kawachi, I., Spiro, A., DeMolles, D.A., & Sparrow, D. (2000). Optimism and depression as predictors of physical and mental health functioning: The normative aging study. *Annals of Behavioral Medicine*, *22*(2), 127–130. doi:10.1007/BF02895776.

Agran, M., Blanchard, C., Wehmeyer, M., & Hughes, C. (2002). Increasing the problem-solving skills of students with developmental disabilities participating in general education. *Remedial and Special Education*, *23*(5), 279–288.

Applebaum, A.J., Stein, E.M., Lord-Bessen, J., Pessin, H., Rosenfeld, B., & Breitbart, W. (2014). Optimism, social support, and mental health outcomes in patients with advanced cancer. *Psycho-Oncology*, *23*, 299–306. doi:10.1002/pon.3418.

Beck, A. (1987). Cognitive models of depression. *Journal of Cognitive Psychotherapy: An International Quarterly*, *1*, 5–37.

Bettelheim, B. (1967). *The empty fortress: Infantile autism and the birth of the self.* Oxford, UK: Free Press of Glencoe.

Chang, E.C., D'Zurilla, T.J., & Maydeu-Olivares, A. (1994). Assessing the dimensionality of optimism and pessimism using a multimeasure approach. *Cognitive Therapy & Research*, *18*, 143–160.

Durand, V.M. (2011). *Optimistic parenting: Help for you and your challenging child*. Baltimore, MD: Brookes Publishing.

Durand, V.M., & Hieneman, M. (2008). *Helping parents with challenging children, positive family intervention: Facilitator guide*. New York: Oxford University Press.

Emmons, R.A. (2004). The psychology of gratitude. In R.A. Emmons & M.E. McCullough (Eds.), *The psychology of gratitude* (pp. 3–16). New York: Oxford University Press.

Groden, J., Kantor, A., Woodard, C.R., & Lipsitt, L.P. (2011). *How everyone on the autism spectrum, young and old, can become resilient, more optimistic, enjoy humor, be kind and increase self-efficacy: A positive psychology approach*. London, UK: Jessica Kingsley Publishers.

Howlin, P. (1997). Prognosis in autism: Do specialist treatments affect long-term outcome? *European Child Adolescent Psychiatry, 6*, 55–72.

Karen-Siegel, L., Rodin, J., Seligman, M.E.P., & Dwyer, J. (1991). Explanatory style and cell-mediated immunity in elderly men and women. *Health Psychology, 10*, 229–235.

Kluemper, D.H., Little, L.M., & DeGroot, T. (2009). State or trait: Effects on state optimism on job-related outcomes. *Journal of Organizational Behavior, 30*, 209–23. doi:10.1002/job.591.

Levy, S.E., Mandell, D.S., Merhar, S., Ittenbach, R.F., & Pinto-Martin, J.A. (2003). Use of complementary and alternative medicine among children recently diagnosed with autistic spectrum disorder. *Journal of Developmental Behavioral Pediatrics, 24*, 418–423.

Mandell, D.S., Novak, M.M., & Zubritsky, C.D. (2005). Factors associated with age of diagnosis among children with autism spectrum disorders. *Pediatrics, 116*(6), 1480–1486. doi:10.1542/peds.2005-0185.

National Institute of Mental Health (NIMH). (2018, September 30). *Mental Illness.* Retrieved from: www.nimh.nih.gov/health/statistics/mental-illness.shtml.

Peterson, C. (2006). *A primer in positive psychology*. New York: Oxford University Press.

Rasmussen, H.N., Scheier, M.F., & Greenhouse, J.B. (2009). Optimism and physical health: A meta-analytic review. *Annals of Behavioral Medicine, 37*(3), 239–256. doi:10.1007/s12160–009–9111-x.

Reeve, S.A., Reeve, K.F., Townsend, D.B. & Poulson, C.L. (2007). Establishing a generalized repertoire of helping behaviour in children with autism. *Journal of Applied Behaviour Analysis, 40*, 123–136.

Seligman, M.E.P. (2004). *Authentic happiness: Using the new positive psychology to realize your potential for lasting fulfillment*. New York: Simon & Schuster.

Seligman, M.E.P. (2011). *Learned optimism: How to change your mind and your life*. New York: Random House: First Vintage Books.

Seligman, M.E.P., Reivich, K., Jaycox, L., & Gilham, J. (1995). *The optimistic child.* Boston, MA: Houghton Mifflin.

Seligman, M.E.P., Steen, T.A., Park, N., & Peterson, C. (2005). Positive psychology progress: Empirical validation of interventions. *American Psychologist, 60*, 410–421.

United States Department of Health & Human Services. (2017). ASPE Issue Brief: Health insurance coverage for Americans with pre-existing conditions: The impact of the Affordable Care Act. Retrieved from: https://aspe.hhs.gov/system/files/pdf/255396/Pre-ExistingConditions.pdf.

Ward, B.W., Schiller, J.S., & Goodman R.A. (2014). Multiple chronic conditions among US adults: A 2012 update. *Prevention of Chronic Diseases, 11*, E62.

Yeargin-Allsopp, M., Rice, C., Karapurkar, T., Doernberg, N., Boyle, C., & Murphy, C. (2003). Prevalence of autism in a US metropolitan area. *Journal of American Medical Association, 289*, 49–55.

4 Assessing Clients and Treatment Planning

Ali Cunningham Abbott and Ryan Seidman

The Diagnostic Journey

When a client with autism presents for counseling during young or older adulthood, it is likely that their journey of evaluation, diagnoses and treatment has been long and winding. Usually clients with autism have seen multiple service providers, from medical to mental health professionals, from whom they've been formally or informally evaluated for a myriad of conditions. Depending on the era the client grew up in, an adult client could have been diagnosed with attention deficit/hyperactivity disorder, obsessive compulsive disorder, oppositional defiant disorder, narcissistic personality disorder, and the list goes on (Punshon, Skirrow, & Murphy, 2009). Once a client is accurately diagnosed with autism spectrum disorder, especially if they receive the diagnosis after the age of 18, many have been through several rounds of evaluation, assessment and treatment attempts.

Over the last several decades, the provision of accurate diagnosis has improved in many ways and worsened in some. A wave of ASD awareness in the general public has led to widespread acknowledgement and acceptance about the condition and its various presentations. More knowledge about autism in the public has been supported by empirical efforts and research that have helped clinicians to better understand and identify children and adults who meet the criteria for this diagnosis (Mandell et al., 2012). Between the years 2015 and 2017, the prevalence of ASD diagnoses among children increased by 30 percent (Centers for Disease Control [CDC], 2018). Many researchers attribute the increase in prevalence to a combination of factors, including parental age, changing diagnostic criteria, and advancements in awareness and education among medical and mental health professionals (Weintraub, 2011). But there are also unknown contributing factors, such as environmental factors that continue to be investigated.

Improved awareness in the public and professional realms can also lead to the over-identification and diagnosis of conditions. Over-identification of autism spectrum disorders can occur in situations in which this diagnosis may be preferred over another or in an effort to gain specific support services. For example, if a young child is speech delayed and demonstrates behavioral issues that can be improved through early intensive interventions, a provider might diagnose with autism in order to help the client receive medical benefits. This might be an issue in the way in which ASD prevalence is gathered based on medical records that document one diagnosis for the purposes of helping improve similar symptoms even if the child doesn't fully meet criteria.

Adult clients may present to counseling after insistence from parents, friends or partners that they identify autism-like characteristics in them. Loved ones may infer that a person seems "Aspie", "awkward" or "somewhere on the spectrum". If they've known the person for many years, it's common to hear that the person has "always been this way" or "they just have a quirky personality". In some instances, adults who have autistic symptoms have only identified themselves after another family member, be it a child of their own, a cousin or even a grandchild, is diagnosed with autism. It is in these circumstances that after interacting with a younger member of the family who has autism that they may reach a point of realization that they too share similar traits.

The reality is that about 1 percent of the population is diagnosed with autism, which applies to both children and adults alike (Brugha et al., 2011; CDC 2018). Research into adult diagnosis has gained momentum in recent years, shedding light on how a diagnosis which should be identified in childhood is overlooked or mislabeled. Several barriers to diagnosis have been reported by adults with ASD and are important to helping improve our clinical practice in diagnostic assessment and treatment planning.

In qualitative research, many adults who were diagnosed with ASD reported positive impacts in their lives after receiving the diagnosis. These positive effects included improved self-acceptance, understanding of themselves, and strategies for improving their lives. Ultimately, it also helped to affirm, validate and normalize their life experiences (Lewis, 2016). The results of not being formally diagnosed with autism have demonstrated poor outcomes such as the deterioration of mental health, including depression and expressions of suicide, being misunderstood, not fitting in, bullied, isolated, having prolonged dependence on others, and underachievement (Wylie, 2014; Punshon et al., 2009; Portway & Johnson, 2005). Preventing these negative outcomes alone should help support the importance of early diagnosis.

Misdiagnosis and a history of negative experiences with mental health practitioners are two common barriers for an accurate and formal diagnosis (Lewis, 2017). Some adults report being forced to hide or camouflage their ASD symptoms if they had a history of being blamed or shamed for these traits by family members or medical professionals (Wiley, 2014). The diagnostic process is usually even harder for adults who are also female because they often get diagnosed at later ages compared with their male counterparts (Bargiela, Steward, & Mandy, 2016). Many autistic adults who seek a formal diagnosis have likely benefited from the process of self-diagnosis, which mental health practitioners traditionally dislike and make that known (Wiley,

2014). When they are dismissed by a professional from whom they are seeking support and assistance they not only lose trust in the system but also lose an opportunity to be accurately and formally diagnosed and treated.

In her research, Lewis (2017) quantitatively and qualitatively summarized data to inform practice guidelines to breaking down the barriers to adult ASD diagnosis. The resounding message, which confirmed strategies proposed by Wiley to support self-diagnosis, are to communicate trust in the client and to focus on establishing a trusting relationship. Specific suggestions from this research encourage clinicians to be curious and use open-ended questions about the client's journey to self-diagnosis, check our own biases about self-diagnosis that often get covertly communicated nonverbally, and actively educate and co-collaborate on learning more about autism (Lewis, 2017). It is our ethical and professional responsibility to be mindful of our views of the process of self-diagnosis in order to best assess, inform and treat our clients with ASD.

This chapter will explore the best-practice instruments and tools for screening and diagnosing adults with autism that involve self-reporting, caregiver-reporting and clinical observations. A discussion of common co-morbid conditions will also be included so mental health professionals can be prepared for ways to identify ASD when there are data that can support several differential diagnoses. From there, the Social-Responsiveness Scale, second edition, will be reviewed for its clinical utility in planning for and assessing treatment for improving autism symptomology. Lastly a case example will highlight how diagnostic screening and assessing treatment can be realistically incorporated into treating an adult client with ASD.

Best Practices for Diagnosing Autism in Adulthood

Diagnosis during early childhood is considered ideal when it comes to treating clients with autism spectrum disorder (ASD). With early identification, early intervention usually follows, which with an intensive therapeutic design has demonstrated the potential for improved prognosis for children who are diagnosed (Estes et al., 2015). Some of the adult clients that seek treatment will have benefited from this early intervention and have a long history of medical and therapeutic histories that will help inform current diagnosis. Yet, a portion of adults with ASD have not been identified in childhood and therefore seek a diagnosis of autism later in life.

This puts some clinicians in a dilemma if and when gathering data about childhood is difficult or impossible. Since the diagnostic criteria for an AD diagnosis requires that symptoms have been present since childhood, the process of verifying this can present challenges. If a parent or sibling is involved in the client's life, this can make gathering history on early development and childhood experiences easier. In some cases, family members may present with a history of medical records or psychological reports that have resulted in other diagnoses but help paint a clinical picture that is likely better accounted for by symptoms of autism. A range of data and information can be provided and help with a determination of childhood presence of ASD symptoms in order to meet this diagnostic criterion.

How do we go about providing a comprehensive diagnostic evaluation or assessment for adults with autism? Guidelines and best practices in the diagnostic process are still unclear and continue to be examined by organizations and researchers (Hayes, Ford, Rafeeque, & Russell, 2018). Among many different recommendations, there are a few common areas of agreement about including a multidisciplinary approach and seeking caregiver or relative report.

Since there are no generalizable biomarkers for diagnosing autism, the current scientific consensus requires agreement from a multidisciplinary team of assessors (Falkmer, Anderson, Falkmer, & Horlin, 2013; Woolfenden, Sarkozy, Ridley, & Williams, 2011). Depending on the diagnostic guidelines or recommendations being followed, the team would comprise at least two clinicians conducting a combination of formal and informal observations. In an ideal scenario, clinicians would be from different disciplinary backgrounds or training experiences with the involvement of at least one medical doctor (i.e., neurologist or psychiatrist). Medical examinations and testing can be complementary in helping explain the client's challenges, particularly if a genetic or neurological condition is identified that is contributing to the ASD symptom presentation. In a hospital or clinic-based model, seeking a multidisciplinary assessment is more realistic to accomplish; while those in solo private practice will need to consult with and refer out to colleagues to support this process. Being connected to the autism treatment community is essential for making informed clinical and diagnostic decisions across disciplines.

Another common practice in diagnosing adult clients with ASD is to interact with a caregiver or relative in order to obtain third-party information. Caregivers or relatives for adults extend beyond parents to include siblings, partners, friends, other family members, teachers, professional coaches, aids, or even employers. A few adult diagnostic and treatment assessment instruments include formalized, objective measures for data gathering from relatives or caregivers (for example ADI-R, SRS-2; these will be reviewed in detail in this chapter). In addition to collecting this objective data, subjective information collected from structured or semi-structured interviews will also be valuable to the diagnostic process. Family members, partners or friends are typically able to provide additional perspectives on diagnostic indicators that may or may not have been self-reported by the adult nor identified via clinical observation.

Putting these evidence-based practices into place can be a clinical hurdle to overcome but is essential to the diagnostic process. Once these practices are established it's important to seek information and training on the gold-standard diagnostic tools in the field. At present, the most effective methods for diagnosing autism combine the efforts of the clinician behavioral observation tool, the Autism Diagnostic Observation Schedule, second edition (ADOS-2), module 4 in combination with a parent or caretaker report, such as the Autism Diagnostic Interview-Revised (ADI-R) (Sappok, Heinrich, & Underwood, 2015).

Even though these are the two gold-standard approaches to formally diagnosing adults with autism, it is helpful to more extensively review all adult ASD screening and assessment tools available to clinicians. Screeners can be administered to determine whether more formal diagnostic evaluation is suggested and can help inform the selection of instruments utilized when diagnosing. Assessments can help inform diagnosis as well as provide direction for treatment planning and help monitor treatment outcomes. The following instruments for adults with ASD who have average to above-average intellectual functioning will be detailed.

Clinician-Administered Screeners and Assessments

Autism Diagnostic Observation Schedule

The ADOS-2 is a semi-structured, activity-based diagnostic assessment that engages the adult in a series of tasks to complete through clinician interaction and simultaneous observation. Based on how the client completes tasks in the assessment, observations are recorded in a corresponding module during the session, and afterwards the client's responses are quantitatively assigned values (Lord et al., 2012). During the assessment feedback session, results are typically coded after observation and presented to clients and caregivers. Coding requires assigning values to certain observations and summing these to determine if clients meet a cut-off score for autism (Wing, Gould, & Gillberg, 2011). These are then tabulated for a final score that will indicate if the person meets criteria for mild, moderate or severe levels of autism spectrum disorder. Multiple raters are involved in observations when clinicians are initially trained to administer the instrument to help develop assessor reliability in producing consistent results.

This assessment varies in administration time, but with clients who present with mild to moderate symptoms Module 4 takes an estimated 40–60 minutes to work through the tasks. Module 4 includes mostly conversation-based tasks that can be administered at a table or desk, such as telling a story from a book, reporting about school or work and describing a picture.

One advantage of this assessment is that Level C professionals from different disciplines can be trained to administer the ADOS-2. These professionals can include masters and bachelor-level psychologists, school counselors, occupational therapists, social workers, educators, or professionals in related fields. Since many, if not all, of these types of practitioners are typically involved in treating clients with ASD, this feature of the ADOS-2 makes assessment more readily available and possible. Other assessments and testing instruments require licensed psychologists to administer and interpret results, which limits options for those seeking diagnosis. This reflects the interdisciplinary nature of ASD treatment that creates a more well-rounded and robust clinical picture for assessment when professionals from multiple disciplines are involved in the assessment process.

The ADOS-2 has been examined for reliability and validity across adult age ranges, sensitivity, and specificity to severity scores (Hus, Gotham, & Lord, 2014). It demonstrated low specificity in adults with co-occurring intellectual disabilities (Sappok et al., 2015). Therefore, in its use with clients without cognitive impairment, this tool may be more accurate in assessing diagnostics and informing treatment.

Training for the ADOS-2 can be accessed via DVD training or via a live two-day seminar. This requires those who become certified to obtain between 24 and 30 contact hours in the observation and administration of the various modules included. For those attending the live two-day seminar, contact hours after training to become competent and a reliable assessor are fewer than those who are trained with the DVD package. The authors of the ADOS-2 advise any parties using this assessment for research purposes to receive the live training. This instrument is also available in 20 non-English languages. To learn more about the ADOS-2 and training options check out the following resources:

- Western Psychological Services: www.wpspublish.com (search ADOS-2)
- Cornell University's Center for Autism and the Developing Brain (CABD): www.psychiatry/weill.cornell.edu/education-training/autism

Autism Diagnostic Interview-Revised

The Autism Diagnostic Interview-Revised (ADI-R) should be administered by an experienced clinician who interviews parents or caregivers who are familiar with the adult who is being assessed. The instrument indicates that it can be used to assess any person with the "mental age" above two years old (Rutter et al., 2003). Translated into clinical terms, this means a person will need to demonstrate cognitive and verbal abilities equivalent to a typically developing two-year-old child or older.

The ADI-R is a 93-item interview that takes from 90 to 150 minutes to administer and score. It focuses on three categories of autism symptomology, as originally identified in earlier versions of the diagnostic criteria (DSM-IV-TR), including language, social interactions, and restricted and repetitive behaviors and/or interests (Rutter et al., 2003). Additionally, the instrument helps clinicians to gather important information about other content including biopsychosocial information and developmental and medical histories.

This instrument has been extensively used in the research community with strong scientific support as to its validity and reliability. It is also recognized as a helpful tool in differentiating ASD from other developmental issues and quantifying symptoms of autism to help inform diagnosis and treatment. One criticism of the administration of this instrument is that it is primarily based on parent or caregiver reports and does not include clinician observations. Because of this, the ADI-R is often used in conjunction with the ADOS-2 administration to gather more comprehensive data (Sappok et al., 2015); as is the recommended best practice for diagnosis discussed previously in this guide. Many institutional systems, including school districts and federally available healthcare coverage (i.e., Social Security Administration), require the administration of both clinical observation and caregiver report. An additional barrier when using the ADI-R is if a parent or caregiver is not available or has not given consent to be interviewed for the assessment. In this instance, the clinician must rely on self-reporting, clinician observation measures and attempts to discuss other people in the client's life who may be able to contribute valuable information as part of the diagnostic process. The ADI-R is available in 18 languages.

- Western Psychological Services: www.wpspublish.com (search ADI-R)

ASD in Adults Screening Questionnaire

This instrument was developed as a brief screener for autism spectrum disorder among adults in psychiatric care (Nylander & Gillberg, 2001). It includes nine yes or no response-style questions that target ASD symptoms and one question related to a history of psychiatric treatment. Yes and no responses are scored as 1s and 0s for a sum score that indicates symptom severity. A score of 5 or more is indicative of autism symptomology.

The ASD in Adults Screening Questionnaire (ASDASQ) is a free, brief, clinician-friendly screener that has demonstrated adequate psychometric properties in the research. It has been used in multiple contexts, including outpatient and inpatient hospitalization programs to help determine diagnostic and treatment next steps (Hare, Gould, Millis, & Wing, 1999). Yet a major issue in using this instrument was that it resulted in a high number of false positive in some research (Ferriter et al., 2001). Therefore, if this screening tool is being utilized it is essential to include it only in conjunction with clinical observations and follow-up assessment with one of the other instruments presented here to improve accuracy in the diagnostic process.

- Free: Gillberg Neuropsychiatry Centre Sahlgrenska Academy http://gillbergcentre.gu.se/English

Gilliam Asperger's Rating Scale

In an effort to distinguish mild forms of autism from more classic or severe autism, instruments to screen for Asperger's disorder emerged in the early 2000s. One that emerged during this time and has since been modified and reviewed for improvements is the Gilliam Asperger's Rating Scale, Third edition (GARS-3) (Gilliam, 2014). This instrument is only recommended for young adults 18 to 22 years old and therefore it is limited in work with older adults. A benefit of utilizing this assessment for treating young adults is that the instrument includes a resource for treatment goals to help connect results to interventions.

The instrument includes 58 items to rate which are optimally to be interpreted by an examiner who collects data from multiple sources and raters (Benjamin, 2017). Through this process, a trained examiner, who is typically a professional diagnostician, selects raters who are informed about how to complete the GARS-3. Raters are most often caregivers, parents, teachers and others who have at least two weeks of contact with the young adult. Depending on how the examiner choses to administer the instrument, it can be completed in a questionnaire or structured interview format.

The GARS-3 is psychometrically sound, after having undergone some significant revisions since its original publication in 2001. Yet, there are criticisms that the instrument demonstrates weaknesses in its results not being tested in non-ASD populations and being primarily based on white individuals between the ages of three and 19. Therefore, its applicability with people of color or in the 20–22 age range is cause for pause in considering this a best-practice tool among a more diverse group (Benjamin, 2017). This instrument is, however, available in a Spanish language form.

- Pro-Ed: www.proedinc.com (search GARS-3)

Self-Report and Caregiver Screeners and Assessments

Adult Asperger Assessment

The Adult Asperger Assessment (AAA), in its second version, is a tool that combines the efforts of three other tools with the aim of creating a comprehensive adult diagnostic assessment based on both adult and caregiver reporting (Baron-Cohen & Wheelwright, 2012). In combination, the instrument has 127 items with 50 items from the AQ, 40 items from the Empathy Quotient (Baron-Cohen & Wheelwright, 2004) and 37 items in the Relative Quotient, which is derived from a childhood measure, the Childhood Autism Spectrum Test (CAST) (Williams et al., 2004).

When using the AAA to assess adults who met criteria for an autism diagnosis, it has demonstrated accuracy in approximately 80 percent of cases (Baron-Cohen, Wheelwright, Robinson, & Woodbury-Smith, 2005). Administering the instrument is more complicated and time consuming than many other screening and assessment tools, creating a barrier for its clinical utility in practice. Yet, for those interested in collecting data from multiple sources on different constructs, including empathy it could inform treatment in a different way than other instruments presented in this chapter.

- Autism Research Centre Tests: www.autismresearchcentre.com/arc_tests

Autism Spectrum Quotient

The Autism Spectrum Quotient (AQ) (Baron-Cohen, Wheelwright, Skinner, Martin & Clubley, 2001) is a popular self-reporting instrument that has been applied in formal and informal assessment processes. The literature reflects that the AQ has been widely used in research, to inform formal diagnosis and in the self-diagnostic screening stage of adults with ASD (Vohra, Madhavan, & Sambamoorthi, 2017). The AQ has five subscales among the 50-item list (long-form) that helps measure social skills, communication skills, imagination, attention to detail and tolerance of change.

The scientific consensus on the use of the AQ is that is provides high sensitivity and specificity along with strong reliability and validity results (Ruzich et al., 2015). Yet, unfortunately in some research, scores can result in more than half of respondents receiving both false negatives (those with ASD not meeting the cutoff score) and false positives (those without ASD meeting the cutoff score) (Ashwood et al., 2016). The long-form version of the tool produces more predictive and accurate results than the ten-item short-form, which is important to know before selecting which to choose. One of the best features of this instrument is that it is available as an open-access tool that can be administered and scored easily. A visit to the Autism Research Centre's website allows anyone to respond to either the 10 or 50-item version of the test, which is available in at least 26 languages with regional variations based on country of origin.

- Autism Research Centre Tests: www.autismresearchcentre.com/arc_tests

Ritvo Autism Asperger Diagnostic Scale-Revised

The Ritvo Autism and Asperger Diagnostic Scale-Revised (RAADS-R) was designed as a screening tool to fill a gap for those with mild forms of autism spectrum disorder in adulthood (Ritvo et al., 2011). Clinicians across continents began to see a requirement to address self-referred clients who needed guidance in the diagnostic process and used this tool as the first step in determining more formal evaluation needs. This instrument is an 80-item self-report questionnaire that examines how frequently a respondent engaged in certain life experiences. Interestingly the frequency asks the adult to report on current and childhood experiences, therefore response options include "True now and when I was young", "True now only" or "True only when I was younger than 16" (Ritvo & Ritvo, 2007). This is distinct from the manner in which any other assessment instrument requires responses to be recorded. In summing the scores of each item, a score of 65 or more is consistent with a diagnosis of ASD. The RAADS-R also includes 23 pre-screening questions that gather demographic data, diagnostic and developmental history. This can present some challenges if the client does not have historical information about their early childhood development obtained from caregivers or documented records.

The instrument is intended to be administered in a clinical setting with guidance; it is not recommended for online use or completion. Within the 80 items, 4 factors have been identified as subscales that help determine one's social relatedness, circumscribed interests, sensory motor issues, and social anxiety (Ritvo et al., 2011; Andersen et al., 2011). It is a highly sensitive and specific instrument with strong reliability and validity scores when examined across three sites.

The RAADS-R is a long-form instrument that can help inform diagnosis and has been researched by the authors of the tool. More recently, another set of researchers created the RAADS-14, a 14-item, short-form of the original tool (Ericksson, Andersen, & Bejerot, 2013). This instrument has been assessed internationally and standardized as a helpful diagnostic aid in distinguishing those with, from those without, ASD. It is designed to be used in conjunction with other, third party or clinician obtained data, to formulate a more comprehensive diagnostic picture of the adult client (Ritvo et al., 2011).

- Springer Link article: https://doi.org/10.1007/s10803-010-1133-5 (RAADS-R)
- Queen's University: https://psychology-tools.com/raads-14 (RAADS-14)

Social Responsiveness Scale

The Social Responsiveness Scale (SRS-2) is a gold-standard in screening for diagnostic purposes and assessing treatment outcomes for children and adults with autism spectrum disorders (Constantino & Gruber, 2016). The instrument has been used in many of the most valuable empirical ASD treatment outcomes research published over the last ten years. It meets best-practice standards for many reasons. Aside from robust psychometric properties, it has utility in differentiating diagnostic issues, being gender sensitive and gleaning important clinical data to inform treatment. The instrument has two forms that can be useful in diagnostic screening and assessing treatment outcomes for adults, including an adult self-report and caregiver/relative form.

The SRS-2, adult and caregiver forms are used to assess social communication and restricted interests and repetitive behaviors (RRBI) in individuals with ASD ages 19 years and older. The design of the SRS-2 is aimed to be administered in a 15 to 20-minute time frame and consists of 65-items. Response options are on a four-point Likert scale that asks about the frequency of described behaviors or situations over the last month. The adult self-report form and the form for a caregiver (i.e., parent, partner, sibling, etc.) differs only in title, the items are the same for both. Caregivers who complete the instrument should have no less than a month's time of knowing the individual client; however, knowing the individual for a longer period of time is preferred.

According to clinical observations and comparisons between third-party reporting and diagnostic observation tools (ADI-R and ADOS-2 scores), the caregiver report yields a more closely matched response than self-report results do. Therefore, some consider the self-report form optional in the diagnostic process. This is a controversial position for clinicians and researchers to take since it discounts self-perceived ASD symptoms. In initial SRS-2 research to standardize the tool, adult and caregiver reports did not vary significantly (Constantino & Gruber, 2016). In order to maintain a strengths-based approach, and practice ethically by honoring our client's autonomy, it would be best practice to administer the adult self-report form in addition to caregiver and relative data collection.

Even if you decide to make adult self-report form optional in the diagnostic process, the use of both forms can provide a more accurate picture of self-perceived competence versus other-perceived competence. Additionally, some items ask about more abstract social or behavioral concepts, which may be hard for individuals with ASD to process and respond to. This may require time spent by the clinician to review the items in session with a client in order to assess their understanding of the meaning of some items that may seem more abstract.

The SRS-2 contains five subscales, with two of the subscales being compatible with the DSM-5. The five subscales are social awareness, social cognition, social communication, social motivation, and restricted interests and repetitive behaviors. The two subscales that are DSM-5 compatible are social communication and restricted interests and repetitive behaviors. Psychometric issues related to the SRS-2 are the length, the use of a four-point Likert scale, the optional nature of the caregiver/spouse report, and the need for further research of the adult report. While 65 items in neurotypical populations would be considered time efficient, in populations of individuals with inattention and disability, this has the potential to be problematic. The use of a four-point Likert scale also has the potential for challenge as there is not the option for a neutral response, as with the five-point scale. Additionally, having the spouse/caregiver report as optional does not provide as rich a picture as it would if it were a compulsory part of the assessment.

While the SRS-2 can benefit from continued research to establish reliability and validity, it is a tool that is utilized quite often in current autism research and has definite clinical applications. The five subscales break down the abstract construct that is "social competence" into five subscales that provide further delineation (Constantino & Gruber, 2016). For those outside of the field of autism and its related disabilities, being able to distinguish social awareness, social communication, social cognition, and social motivation can prove challenging. It also goes a bit further than simply being able to distinguish the four. In order for treatment planning to be effective, practitioners need to be able to distinguish and explain the four areas, as well as plan specific interventions that target areas of challenge. Therefore, each of these treatment constructs or clusters, as they're referred to by SRS-2 authors, is more thoroughly explored in Chapters 5–9.

Authors of the SRS-2 are clear in noting that subscales of the instrument were not intended to reflect the existence of independent factors in diagnosis. Instead, they are intended to be useful in describing and evaluating treatment goals (Constantino & Gruber, 2016). When used as a tool in the screening and diagnostic process it should be clearly communicated to clients and caregivers that social awareness, social cognition and social motivation are not standalone diagnostic indicators. For clinical and diagnostic purposes, the three subscales or treatment clusters above can fall under the broader autism symptomatology of social communication. The utility of each social communication subscale included in the SRS-2 can be applied to helping guide a treatment focus, aid in creating treatment goals and serve as the basis for assessing treatment effectiveness. Aside from its English version, the instrument is available in nine different languages.

- Social Responsiveness Scale, 2nd edition: www.wpspublish.com (search SRS-2)

In selecting a screening and diagnostic assessment tool kit to utilize in treatment, the aforementioned are all adequate to strong. See Table 4.1 for a summary of tools. Much of this process should be determined by the clinician's judgement and preferences based on their own individual experiences with clients. As long as the decisions have strong scientific support and clinical utility, one is likely on the best path towards assessing and informing treatment for adults with ASD. It is for these reasons that we have based this guide and recommendations on the use of the Social Responsiveness Scale-2 (SRS-2). One of the best reasons for choosing the SRS-2 as a gold standard for assessing and informing treatment is its utility in distinguishing autism from other commonly co-occurring conditions (Constantino & Gruber, 2016). Therefore, the remainder of this chapter will focus on the clinical utilization of this tool and its treatment clusters as a guide for the next steps in selecting clinical interventions.

Common Co-Occurring Conditions (CCCs)

There is a breadth of research that identifies comorbid conditions that often occur as secondary or tertiary diagnosis with autism. This is especially true when assessing children, who have been the most widely studied in autism research. But there are also many studies that explore co-occurring disorders in adults with ASD. In this section we will review the most common comorbid conditions that people with autism report across ages, populations and regions of the world.

It is now well-researched and known that children and adults with ASD experience high rates of multiple psychiatric conditions. Among the most common are other developmental disorders, depression, anxiety, bipolar condition, and schizophrenia (Croen et al., 2015; Vohra, Madhavan, &

Table 4.1 Adult ASD screening and assessment tools

Screening or assessment name	*Administration type and source*	*Number of items and time of administration/scoring*	*Availability*
Adult Asperger Assessment (AAA)	Self and caregiver report	177 total items (50:AQ, 40–60:EQ, 37:RQ); 20–30 minutes each, total of 60–90 minutes	Free: Autism Research Centre www.autismresearchcentre.com/arc_tests
Autism Diagnostic Interview-Revised (ADI-R)	Clinician interview; informed by caregiver	93 items; 90–150 minutes	Purchase: Western Psychological Services www.wpspublish.com
Autism Observation Diagnostic Schedule (ADOS-2)	Clinician structured observation; informed by adult	14 tasks; 40–60 minutes	Purchase: Western Psychological Services www.wpspublish.com
ASD in Adults Screening Questionnaire (ASDASQ)	Clinician interview; informed by adult	10 items; 2–5 minutes	Free: Gillberg Neuropsychiatry Centre Sahlgrenska Academy http://gillbergcentre.gu.se/English
Autism Spectrum Quotient (AQ)	Self and caregiver report	50 items (long-form), 10 items (short-form); 2–10 minutes	Free: Autism Research Centre www.autismresearchcentre.com/arc_tests
Gilliam Asperger's Rating Scale (GARS-3)	Clinician interview; informed by caregiver	58 items; 15-20 minutes	Purchase: Pro-Ed www.proedinc.com
Ritvo Autism and Asperger Diagnostic Scale-Revised (RAADS-R)	Clinician interview; informed by adult	80 items; 60 minutes	Free: Springer Link article: https://doi.org/10.1007/s10803-010-1133-5 (RAADS-R) Queen's University: https://psychology-tools.com/raads-14 (RAADS-14)
Social Responsiveness Scale, Second edition (SRS-2)	Self and caregiver report	65 items; 15–20 minutes	Purchase: Western Psychological Services www.wpspublish.com

Sambamoorthi, 2017; Hofvander et al., 2009; Lugnegard, Hallerback, & Gillberg, 2011; Lunsky, Gracey, & Bradley, 2009). Other developmental disorders include learning, attention deficit, communication, and intellectual disorders. In these large-scale prevalence studies some variance in overall results exists but the common overlaps identify these as the primary comorbid conditions that practitioners need to be informed about in order to provide effective care. Most medical professionals do not feel competent or knowledgeable in how to best treat adults with ASD as treatment guidelines do not exist, which makes it hard for these clients to receive quality care. This typically results in adults with ASD over-utilizing healthcare services, resulting in higher medical costs for them (Vohra, Madhavan, & Sambamoorthi, 2017).

Developmental Disorders

In some research, other developmental disorders (DDs) are described as the most commonly occurring in this population, with about 70 percent of those diagnosed with autism having a co-occurring DD (Vohra et al., 2017). People with attention deficit/hyperactivity disorder, learning disorders or intellectual disorders alone also report high rates of depression and anxiety (Simonoff et al., 2008). If a client is diagnosed with both ASD and another co-occurring developmental disorder the likelihood of experiencing either depression or anxiety are compounded.

Mood Disorders

Depression is consistently reported for individuals with autism, across children, adolescents, and adults. Unfortunately, there is a significant difference among what some research reports with regard to the prevalence of mood disorders among the ASD adult population. The prevalence of mood disorders among those also diagnosed with ASD is between 53 and 70 percent (Lugnegard et al., 2011; Hofvander et al., 2009). According to some research, between 70 and 80 percent of autistic adults have experienced at least one episode of major depression, with about half of the population reporting experiencing one or more episodes (Mazzone, Rutta, & Reale, 2012). Other research examining the medical records of adults in different hospital and insurance-based systems reports the rates of depression among adults with ASD as between 15 and 26 percent (Vohra et al., 2017; Croen et al., 2015). Social failures, loneliness, co-occurring anxiety and other behavioral challenges can lead to symptoms of depression for autistic people. These put them at a higher likelihood for self-harm and suicide (Kato et al., 2013). Life stressors that lead to low mood and feelings of hopelessness for those with autism understandably result in high risk factors in treatment that should be well-assessed and planned for. A screening tool that can help practitioners identify the presence of a co-occurring mood disorder is the Patient Health Questionnaire-9 (PHQ-9) (Kroenke, Spitzer, & Williams, 2001).

Anxiety Disorders

Anxiety disorders including generalized anxiety disorder, social anxiety disorder, panic disorder and agoraphobia have all been reported among people with autism diagnoses. On the high end of prevalence results, between 40 and 60 percent of children and young adults have reported experiencing symptoms of anxiety (Lugnegard et al., 2011; Hofvander et al., 2009). Yet, in other research, these numbers are reported in medical records as between 12 and 30 percent of adults with ASD (Vohra et al., 2017; Croen et al., 2015). Typically, these individuals tend to embody other characteristics that are highly correlated with an ASD person having co-occurring anxiety, including a higher intellectual quotient (IQ), more functional language, better social perception and understanding. As will be discussed in upcoming chapters, areas where social communication has fewer deficits make a person with autism more susceptible to anxiety.

Some of the most common anxiety disorders reported by adults with autism are social, generalized, and obsessive/compulsive. These co-occurring diagnoses can be identified when properly screened in treatment utilizing a variety of assessment tools. If scores are indicative of risk for experiencing generalized, social anxiety, obsessive compulsive, or phobias, integrating anxiety-based screening tools can assist in identifying how their symptoms of anxiety and autism intersect and impact one another. A gold-standard anxiety assessment tool that can be used during young adulthood is the Behavior Assessment System for Children (BASC-3), college age (Reynolds & Kamphaus, 2015). Other tools are available for the full range of adulthood, including the Beck Anxiety Inventory (BAI) that can help clients report anxieties they've been experiencing over the last month (Beck & Steer, 1993).

Psychotic Disorders

Schizophrenia and autism have a long-standing history of common occurrence and diagnostic overshadowing that can be confusing for families and clinicians alike. Before the diagnosis of autism existed, most people who in retrospect had symptoms of autism were diagnosed with schizophrenia in childhood, adolescence, and adulthood (Kanner, 1943). Clinicians have learned a lot about the relationship between psychosis and autism since then, with a clear understanding that ASD increases one's risk of experiencing a psychotic episode (Larson et al., 2017). Studies have reported from 5–28 percent of people with ASD experiencing psychotic symptoms in their lifetime (Selten, Lundberg, Rai, & Magnussion, 2015; Mouridsen, Rich, & Isager, 2008). Yet, recent work has linked specific subtypes of ASD to psychosis and indicates that most people with ASD will not experience psychosis in their lifetime (Larson et al., 2017). Nevertheless, it is important for us to be equipped with resources and referrals for assessment and psychiatric intervention for our clients who report, or we suspect are experiencing, psychosis.

Some assessments that may aid a clinician in determining the presence of psychosis in adults with autism are the Diagnostic Interview for Psychosis (DIP) or the Psychiatric Assessment Schedule for Adults with Developmental Disabilities (Mini PAS-ADD) (Castle et al., 2006; Prosser et al., 1998).

Substance Use Disorders

Adults with ASD have generally demonstrated less likelihood to engage in the use or abuse of alcohol and other drugs. Yet, some research indicates that adults with mild symptoms engage in frequent alcohol use as a social lubricant or facilitator (Santosh & Mijovic, 2006; Sizoo et al., 2009). Additional reports from autistic adults who have sought treatment for substance use disorders (SUD) support the assertion that substances can be facilitative socially as well as help medicate other co-occurring conditions (Clarke, Tickle, & Gillott, 2016). The two themes of self-medication and social facilitation are those that are most common in the limited research that exists. Owing to the reduced risk that autistic clients have to engage in substance use, it is important that clinicians do not ignore signs of abuse. With clients who have a history of using or at risk for other reasons, such as family history and co-occurring anxiety, depression or ADHD, it will be even more important to assess and treat. For clients with ASD and SUD seeking treatment, the research has demonstrated the need for instructional, supportive and directive approach. Therefore, our ability to honestly and directly assess for this is essential. Integrating the use of a substance use assessment tool such as the CAGE-AID brief questionnaire can be the first step to starting the conversation about a client's problematic use (Brown & Rounds, 1995).

Eating Disorders

Clients with eating disorders (ED) have been found to have overlapping cognitive processes and symptoms to people with autism (Huke et al., 2013). Research identifies that similar deficits in the theory of mind, identification of emotional states, and behavioral restrictions exist among those with ASD and ED. In particular there are overlaps between those with restrictive eating disorders, such as anorexia nervosa, and females diagnosed with ASD (Baron-Cohen et al., 2013). This has created interest into further investigating the prevalence of ASD in those diagnosed with ED and for those diagnosed with ASD who may be at risk for an ED.

People with autism can have food selectivity issues associated with sensory challenges. Selectivity and food intake restriction need to be carefully parsed out to determine if an eating disorder is present. One helpful screening tool to determine ED risk is the Stanford-Washington University Eating Disorder Screen (SWED; Wifley, Agras, & Taylor, 2013). When counseling clients with ASD it is important to understand that autistic women are at a higher risk of developing an ED and that it is important to attend to eating behaviors and nutritional intake. It will be helpful to develop relationships with ED mental health, nutritional and medical specialists who can help assess and intervene when necessary.

Treatment and Assessment Planning

After collecting the data from a comprehensive diagnostic evaluation, or screening for treatment utilizing a combination of reporters and diagnostic instruments, the next step is utilizing the information to plan for and monitor care. Treatment planning for an adult with autism should be collaborative and this can begin with a deliberate process of sharing assessment results with the client. From there goals and objectives can be co-constructed and time intervals for when progress should be monitored are determined.

In assessment, the results of the SRS-2 can be utilized to determine what ASD symptomology should likely be targeted in treatment as a priority based on primary presenting issues and sequencing of interventions. One place to start is by identifying which diagnostic category, autistic mannerisms (RRBIs) or social communication, is more impaired through objective results and subjective experience with the client. For example, if an adult's interests are so restricted behaviorally this may lead them to have significant difficulties in communicating with others. Therefore, before working on enhancing social communication deficits the client may need to work on behavioral flexibility and expanding their repertoire of experiences as a priority in treatment. The significance of the RRBI score on the SRS-2 being higher than the social communication score, coupled with clinical judgement, leads the mental health professional to prioritize behavioral goals and interventions.

As may already be obvious through this example, even though RRBIs take a priority in treatment because a restricted interest is considered a behavioral mannerism of autism, the aim or goal inevitably has a positive impact on the client's social communication. Even though they are separate in assessment and diagnosis, they overlap in presentation because a person's insistence in the same topic or subject area will typically translate to poor social interactions. The main distinction here is that there should be more of emphasis made early on in treatment related to behavior skills training (Chapter 9) over social communication skills training (Chapter 5).

In reviewing the complete results of assessment, it is important to identify areas where the client demonstrates strengths first. This will require not only the clinical interpretation of subscale results that were milder, or in some cases within normal limits, but behavioral observations of what the clinician has noticed that may help exemplify this in lay terms. Starting this process by telling the client (1) what you've noticed they're good at that is also (2) reflected in social communication, sub-domain and behavioral scores from formal assessment, may lead the client to be more receptive to the process of treatment planning.

From there the clinician can highlight areas of notable challenge from their formal and informal assessment results. In presenting these results it is imperative to focus on the provision of examples from the client's perspective that they can connect to. When a client has shared a story or situation that was challenging to them this is an opportunity to help conceptualize how the problem they faced is connected to an assessment result. Without a concrete example to refer to it may be more difficult for the adult to relate the psychological concept presented in an assessment to themselves. The goal is to help the client identify with the results or challenge them if they do not agree. When assessment results differ from subjective clinical judgement, the client may have a difficult time understanding and thus the practitioner will need to be flexible in their explanation and communication style.

Autistic clients, like any, are in different stages of change for therapy. And they also may be in different stages of change for different goals in therapy. A client could be motivated for action in therapy when creating a goal about social communication and dating yet in pre-contemplation when discussing how their restricted interests in video games might be a hindrance. The client will overtly or covertly inform the process of treatment planning through their interpretations of and reactions to assessment results.

Once assessment results are reviewed, the next step is to co-construct treatment goals and objectives that are relevant to the client. In comprehensive treatment of clients with ASD there will be social communication and behavioral goals in addition to addressing co-morbid symptom goals. Table 4.2 is a sample treatment table that highlights a few potential goals and objectives that align with SRS-2 subscale results.

Case Example

Seth is a 21-year-old college student who is currently in his first relationship. He's attending a four-year university course seeking a bachelor's degree and is in his first semester freshman year. The transition to college began years ago when his parents enrolled him in a small, private college preparatory school to help tailor his education to his needs and learning differences. Seth's parents report that he's always had trouble socially and behaviorally but they've been sure to make him as comfortable as possible by placing him in different programs throughout his life. They always feared him being stigmatized by his peers and helped to create an environment at school and in their home where his differences were honored and not pathologized. He presented to treatment to improve ruminating thoughts about girls, poor hygiene, awkward social skills and a desire to gain independence to prepare him for college.

It is important to note that because of his family's protective and accommodating nature, Seth has not been formally assessed or evaluated. The school environment where he was ultimately placed did not require it and provided supports regardless of any comprehensive evaluation. When presenting for

Table 4.2 Sample SRS-2 informed treatment plan with goals and objectives

SRS-2 subscale result	*Treatment goal*	*Treatment objective*
Social communication deficits	Learn how to initiate conversations with new people. Learn to share the conversation.	1a. Improve quality of relationships with colleagues in the workplace. 1b. Increase options for dating. 2a. Improve ability to work productively on teams at school and work. 2b. Allow others to feel understood and listened to.
Social motivation deficits	Find new social opportunities. Identify the frequency of social interactions needed to decrease loneliness.	1a. Find local activities where people engage in an interest. 1b. Make contact (phone call or in-person visit) with someone to discover details. 2a. Assess extraversion. 2b. Attend a social outing *X* times a month.
Social awareness deficits	Identify their character strengths and challenges. Utilize social coach to assess for accurate interpretations of social interactions.	1a. Create running list or journal characteristics that led to positive outcomes. 1b. Identify examples of situations in which social awareness negatively impacted them 2a. Collaborate with social coach to add to list of characteristics. 2b. Analyze thoughts and behaviors in situations that occurred to identify helpful methods for improving social awareness.
Social cognition deficits	Learn how to take perspective during a social interaction. Provide accurate interpretations of how others perceive you.	1a. Work with social coach weekly to identify a situation where lack of perspective-taking led to challenges. 1b. Practice social thinking questions with repetition to help create cognitive habit. 2a. Solicit feedback from social interactions and relationships to assess accuracy of perspective-taking. 2b. Process feedback received from others weekly with social coach and clinician to enhance accuracy in perspective-taking.
Restricted interests	Demonstrate flexibility by identifying other areas of interest. Join group activities to participate in, related to areas of interest.	1a. Demonstrate the ability to identify related areas of interest connected to current interests. 1b. Create ongoing list of related and newly developed interests. 2a. Engage in *X* number of activities related to the related interest and report on response. 2b. Plan an outing with someone who shares new or related interests.
Repetitive behaviors	Learn about and apply new behaviors to get needs met. Demonstrate a replacement behavior for current unwanted behavior.	1a. Identify what behaviors are undesired in own repertoire. 1b. Engage in instruction of new skills, consume materials and lessons from clinician and complete assigned homework. 2a. Practice *X* new behavior *X* times per week. 2b. Track the frequency of the application when replacement behaviors occur and its positive outcomes.

counseling, the clinician informs the parents and Seth about the value of better understanding how to help him by starting with assessing some of his characteristics. This is an opportunity to provide psychoeducation about how accurate diagnosis and assessment can best inform effective treatment and lead to an improved prognosis. Given their history of avoiding previous attempts at evaluation during Seth's childhood, it's helpful to guide the family and Seth to identify the current benefits and concerns they have about this process. After processing the topic of conducting an official evaluation for about four sessions, the family decides that now that Seth is an adult and preparing to move away for college, they consent to this being an important step in treatment.

Through the interactions with Seth and his family over the last month it is clear that his primary presenting issues are connected to symptoms of autism and anxiety. Therefore, the recommendation is made to conduct the Social Responsiveness Scale (SRS-2) as an ASD screening procedure and to help evaluate treatment. In addition to this, the Behavior Assessment System for Children (BASC-3) college age assessment is also utilized in order to determine the clinical significance of other issues that may be impacting him. To comprehensively evaluate ASD and anxiety symptoms both self and caregiver reports will be administered. Based on these assessment results, the clinician will determine if any other evaluations are necessary to include.

Results for the SRS-2 include total and subscale scores that are helpful to attend to and interpret for best informing treatment. There were not significant discrepancies between Seth's self-report and caregiver report in the total score results. Respectively, total scores were 61 and 65, which suggest mild autism symptomology. Subscale scores reflected important differences between autistic behaviors (64) and social communication (74), including social awareness (71) and cognition (68). Social communication, cognition and awareness scores were in the moderate range, suggesting more impairments in these domains. Repetitive behaviors and restricted interests yielded results in the mild range.

In order to evaluate co-occurring disorders that Seth may endorse clinical symptoms of, the BASC-3 with self and caregiver reports is administered. The results of the BASC-3 indicate scores of 70 (self), 73 (caregiver) for anxiety, 22 (self), 26 (caregiver) for interpersonal relations, and 15 (self), 10 (caregiver) for personal adjustment. All three of these domains are in the clinically significant range and help explain his current stressors in attending college, challenges with peers and anxious behaviors demonstrated in session.

Based on these results, a treatment plan is co-created and agreed upon among Seth, his parents and the clinician. In the process of interpreting the results and discussing them it becomes clear that Seth can identify several of his presenting issues and how they connect to the results. There are deficits within social communication, and the subsets of awareness and cognition, as well as repetitive behaviors, that will be the focus of treatment to address symptoms of autism and interpersonal relationships. Other treatment goals will be focused on helping Seth manage his anxiety and adjustment to the college setting.

Even though separate treatment goals and objectives are identified for social communication, awareness and cognition it is essential to be clear that these treatment clusters are integrally connected. Therefore, when aiming to improve an aspect of social cognition, both awareness and communication will also be addressed. There will be overlaps in treatment interventions that reflect this. There is also overlap in the SRS-2 goals related to social communication and the BASC-3 interpersonal relations goals since his issues with peer relationships can likely be attributed to autism. The following is a suggested sequence and structure for scaffolding these treatment goals in order to help predict or determine the best possible treatment outcomes.

Within the domain of social communication, he identifies having trouble in knowing how to start a conversation with new people and how to ask someone out on a date successfully. Both of these are connected to knowledge and skills deficits that can be approached in treatment through best-practice interventions in social skills instruction. The social communication goals are inherently motivating to Seth and this is intentionally planned to help increase treatment compliance and buy-in to therapy.

To work on building social awareness Seth has decided to improve his understanding of his position in social situations, specifically related to being embarrassed by others and understanding how others perceive his strengths and challenges. It is clear within the first session with Seth, that he has hygiene issues that cause him to have noticeable body odor. He reports that others have "picked on him" by calling him "smelly" or "gross", but he assumes this is a form of bullying that doesn't reflect how he truly presents. There is a difference between feeling embarrassed by this feedback and bullying so it will be important to assess his interpretations of this. As this is connected to how he fits into the social landscape, he is not self-aware of the potential social repercussions of poor hygiene and self-care practices on dating. This is precarious for clinicians because it can often be the case that we are the first to bring this to a client's attention; most are uncomfortable broaching this subject. To improve his ability to understand how body odor impacts his social relationships, we need to be comfortable providing coaching and feedback on personal care and cleaning. Working through personal hygiene as a first step to resolve this objective issue will then lead to improved awareness of his social strengths and challenges.

After addressing social communication and awareness symptom goals, it will be important to get Seth working towards improving his social cognition skills. The rationale for choosing this order is first because social thinking is inherently built into the former goals and second because a better skills foundation has been built that will set him up for more success. Without remedying the social awareness issues (i.e., personal hygiene) and improving social communication skills, working towards more action-based interventions connected to social cognition could be counterproductive.

It's important for Seth to learn how to assess if someone else is interested in his friendship or a romantic relationship. Given his previous experiences in approaching and asking out any woman he found attractive, in an attempt to increase his chances for dating, it's helpful for him to learn a different approach. The likelihood of being rejected with the old approach is high. He will benefit from learning how to "test the temperature" of an interaction by paying attention to signs from another person that improve his ability to take their perspective. A secondary objective for this treatment goal aims to help Seth use the information from assessing the other person's interest by applying a more successful approach to the actual asking for a date.

In Seth's autism mannerisms results, repetitive behaviors resulted in a mild symptom presentation and he, reticently, confirms that he engages in hypersexual behaviors related to masturbation. These repetitive behaviors have caused him issues in class when he becomes sexually aroused and embarrassed by, what he considers to be, an obvious erection. Therefore, he compulsively masturbates before going to campus and in the bathrooms on campus, in an attempt to manage this. He's also been "caught" trying to hide masturbatory behaviors during live video chats with friends and in the public restrooms. The goal for this would be to help Seth practice safe masturbation practices that he can manage less impulsively and compulsively.

The results from assessing Seth's co-occurring issues indicate a need to help him manage his anxiety and adjustment to college. In sequencing treatment this should be primarily to prevent any barriers anxiety creates from allowing him to make improvements on ASD goals. Most clients who experience adjustment and anxiety symptoms need to have these resolved so they don't interfere with attempts to generalize social communication skills through homework and real-world application. If a client's anxiety is primary or secondary diagnostically and goes untreated, the likelihood that goals to manage ASD symptoms are met is diminished.

For Seth to make gains in college, he can benefit from learning and applying relaxation techniques to manage his anxiety. Examples of this can be through explicit breathing lessons and practice and progressive muscle relaxation. It is essential to model and rehearse this in session because many times clients do not use diaphragmatic breathing, which is the key to reap the benefits of relaxing breathing. Guided progressive muscle relaxation is another concrete method to implement in session and to encourage to be practiced outside of session (at least once a day) upon treatment inception. From there, the clinician can encourage Seth to connect with group support for those who experience autism or anxiety to assist with any feelings of isolation due to his diagnoses that are adding to his adjustment issues. To continue to connect him socially, he can also identify a few potential student organizations on campus so that he becomes more connected to the university community and works toward goals of adjusting to this new environment.

It is important to note that to help Seth with all his treatment goals, ongoing social support will be practiced within sessions (see Table 4.3 for

Table 4.3 Assessment results and treatment plan

Treatment domains and assessment results	*Treatment goal*	*Treatment objective and interventions*
Social communication (74)	Improve conversation skills to meet new people.	Learn how to start a face-to-face conversation. (Socratic questioning, didactic instruction, role-play, behavior rehearsal, homework.) Allow others to feel understood in conversation. (Behavior rehearsal, coaching and feedback about conversational experience, homework with feedback from social coach and/or conversation partner.)
Social awareness (71)	Improve current hygiene practices. Reduce embarrassing feedback and social rejection based on body odor. Identify own social strengths and challenges.	Create and apply a personal cleaning routine to improve methods (i.e. use of soap, deodorant, etc.) and time spent. (Visual aid app and timer, coaching and feedback from social coach.) Record of steps applied, and challenges met to track data daily. (Journaling, coaching and feedback.) Improve accuracy in identifying social successes and errors with immediacy. (Socratic questioning with social thinking focus, coaching and feedback by social coach and others.)
Social cognition (68) and interpersonal relations	Increase options for dating.	Assess someone's potential for romantic interest via flirting and asking a mutual friend. (Instruction through in vivo and video modeling, behavior rehearsal through choice between social coaches of different genders.) Ask someone out on a date. (Homework assessment and feedback, behavior rehearsal for coaching.)
Repetitive behaviors (64)	Improve self-regulation of impulsive sexual behaviors.	Identify places and times best suited for masturbation. (Socratic questioning, decisional-balancing.) Ensure safe masturbation practices (video instruction and modeling).
Anxiety and personal adjustment	Learn and apply behavioral and cognitive anxiety management skills. Identify local resources for recreation and support.	Create a routine for relaxation through diaphragmatic breathing and progressive muscle relaxation. Apply relevant coping skills when placed in anxiety or distress provoking situations. Engage with local support group. Join social club on campus directly related to interests.

treatment goals). As for many of the social communication related goals, this is vital to be continuous and intentionally sequenced throughout treatment. For continuity of care, it is essential that the counselor also involves people in Seth's life that can help him maintain and generalize social support outside of the treatment context. Since his family is an integral part of treatment, they should be coached on ways to help him maintain these goals. Exploring other social supports in his life that can be useful in continuity will also be important, including professionals in his university. Sharing treatment successes and goals with Seth's support system of family members and other informed parties will help him maintain treatment gains over time.

References

American Psychiatric Association. (2013). *Diagnostic & statistics manual of mental disorders* (5th ed.). Arlington, VA: American Psychiatric Association.

Andersen, L.M. Naswell, K., Manouilenko, I, Nylander, L., Edgar, J., Ritvo, R., Ritvo, E. & Bejerot, S. (2011). The Swedish Version of the Ritvo Autism Asperger Diagnostic Scale: Revised (RAADS-R): A validation study of a rating scale for adults. *Journal of Autism & Developmental Disorders, 41*, 1635–2645.

Ashwood, K.L., Gillan, N., Horder, J., Hayward, H., Woodhouse, E., McEwen, F.S., … Murphy, D.G. (2016). Predicting the diagnosis of autism in adults using the Autism Spectrum Quotient (AQ) questionnaire. *Psychological Medicine, 46*, 2595–2604. doi:10.1017/S0033291716001082 www.ncbi.nlm.nih.gov/pmc/articles/PMC4988267/.

Bargiela, S., Steward, R., & Mandy, W. (2016). The experience of late-diagnosed women with autism spectrum conditions: An investigation of the female autism phenotype. *Journal of Autism & Developmental Disorders, 46*, 3281–3294. doi:10.1007/s10803-016-2872-8.

Baron-Cohen, S., Jaffa, T., Davies, S., Auyeung, B., Allison, C., & Wheelwright, S. (2013). Do girls with anorexia nervosa have elevated autistic traits? *Molecular Autism*, 4–24.

Baron-Cohen, S., & Wheelwright, S. (2004). The empathy quotient: An investigation of adults with Asperger's disorder or high functioning autism, and normal sex differences. *Journal of Autism and Developmental Disorders, 34*, 163–175.

Baron-Cohen, S., Wheelwright, S., Robinson, J., & Woodbury-Smith, M. (2005). The Adult Asperger Assessment (AAA): A diagnostic method. *Journal of Autism and Developmental Disorders, 35*, 807–819. doi:10.1007/10803-005-0026-5.

Baron-Cohen, S., Wheelwright, W., Skinner, R., Martin, J. & Clubley, E. (2001). *The autism spectrum quotient (AQ)*. Cambridge Autism Research Centre. Retrieved from: www.autismresearchcentre.com/arc_tests.

Beck, A., & Steer, R. (1993). *Beck anxiety inventory manual*. San Antonio, TX: Harcourt Brace and Company.

Benjamin, K.C. (2017). A test review: Gilliam autism rating scale (3rd ed.) [GARS-3]. *Journal of Psychoeducational Assessment, 35*, 342–346.

Brown, R.L., & Rounds, L.A. (1995). Conjoint screening questionnaires for alcohol and other drug abuse: Criterion validity in a primary care practice. *Wisconsin Medical Journal, 94*, 135–140.

Brugha, T.S., McManus, S., Bankart, J., Scott, F., Purdon, S., Smith, J., ... Meltzer, H. (2011). Epidemiology of autism spectrum disorder in adults in the community in England. *Archives of General Psychiatry, 68*, 459. doi:10.1001/archgenpsychiatry.2011.38.

Castle, D.J., Jablensky, A., McGrath, J.H. Carr, V., Morgan, V., Waterreus, A., ... Farmer, A. (2006). The diagnostic interview for psychosis (DIP): Development, reliability and applications. *Psychological Medicine, 36*, 69–80.

Centers for Disease Control [CDC]. (2018). Prevalence of autism spectrum disorder among children aged 8 years – autism and developmental disabilities monitoring network, 11 Sites, United States, 2014. *Morbidity and Mortality Weekly Report (MMWR), 61*, 1–23.

Clarke T., Tickle, A., & Gillott, A. (2016). Substance use disorder in Asperger syndrome: An investigation into the development and maintenance of substance use disorder by individuals with a diagnosis of Asperger syndrome. *International Journal of Drug Policy, 27*, 154–163.

Constantino, J.N., & Gruber, C.P. (2016). *Social responsiveness, scale – second edition (SRS-2) [Manual]*. Torrance, CA: Western Psychological Services.

Croen, L.A., Zerbo, O., Qian, Y., Massolo, M.L., Rich, S., Sidney, S., & Kripke, C. (2015). The health status of adults on the autism spectrum. *Autism: The International Journal of Research and Practice, 19*, 814–823.

Ericksson, J.M., Andersen, L.M.J., & Bejerot, S. (2013). RADS-14 Screen: Validity of a screening tool for autism spectrum disorder in an adult psychiatric population. *Molecular Autism, 4*(49). doi:10.1186/2040-2392-4-49.

Estes, A., Munson, J., Rogers, S.J., Greenson, J., Winter, J., & Dawson, G. (2015). Long-term outcomes of early intervention in 6-year-old children with autism spectrum disorder. *Journal of the American Academy of Child & Adolescent Psychiatry, 54*, 580–587. doi:10.1016/j.jaac.2015.04.005.

Falkmer, T., Anderson, K., Falkmer, M., & Horlin, C. (2013). Diagnostic procedures in autism spectrum disorders: A systematic literature review. *European Child Adolescent Psychiatry, 22*, 329–40. doi:10.1007/s00787-013-0375-0.

Ferriter, M., Hare, D., Bendall, P., Cordess, C., Elliot, K., Hudson, I., Humpston, R., Jones, J., Souflas, P., & Taylor, M. (2001). Brief report: Assessment of a screening tool for autistic spectrum disorders in adult population. *Journal of Autism and Developmental Disorders, 31*, 351–353.

Gilliam, J.E. (2014). *Gilliam Asperger's rating scale* (3rd ed.) [GARS-3]. Autism, TX: Pro-Ed.

Hare D.J., Gould J., Mills R., & Wing L. (1999). *A preliminary study of individuals with autistic spectrum disorders in three special hospitals in England*. London: National Autistic Society.

Hayes, J., Ford, T., Rafeeque, H., & Russell, G. (2018). Clinical practice guidelines for autism spectrum disorder in adults and children in the UK: A narrative review. *BMC Psychiatry, 18*, 222. doi:10.1186/s12888-018-1800-1.

Hofvander, B., Delorme, R., Chaste P., Nyden, A., Wentz, E., Stahlberg, O., & Herbrecht, E. (2009). Psychiatric and psychosocial problems in adults with normal-intelligence autism spectrum disorders. *BMC Psychiatry, 9*, 35.

Huke, V., Turk, J., Saeidi, S., Kent, A., & Morgan, J.F. (2013) Autism spectrum disorders in eating disorder populations: A systematic review. *European Eating Disorders Review, 21*(5), 345–351. doi:10.1002/erv.2244.

Hus, V., Gotham, K., & Kord, C. (2014). Standardizing ADOS domain scores: Separating severity of social affect and restricted and repetitive behaviors. *Journal of Autism and Developmental Disorders, 44*(10), 2400–2412. doi:10.1007/s10803-012-1719-1.

Hus, V., & Lord, C. (2014). The autism diagnostic observation schedule, module 4: Revised algorithm and standardized severity scores. *Journal of Autism & Developmental Disorders, 44*, 1996–2012. doi:10.1007/s10803-014-2080-3.

Kanner, L. (1943). Autistic disturbances of affective contact. *Nervous Child, 2,* 217–250.

Kato, K., Mikami, K., Akama, F., Yamada, K., Maehara, M., Kimoto, K., … Matsumoto, H. (2013). Clinical features of suicide attempts in adults with autism spectrum disorders. *General Hospital Psychiatry, 35*, 50–53. doi:10.1016/j.genhosppsych.2012.09.2006

Kroenke, K., Spitzer, R.L., & Williams, J.B. (2001). The PHQ-9: Validity of a brief depression severity measure. *Journal of General Internal Medicine, 16*, 606–613.

Larson, F.V., Wagner, A.P., Jones, P.B., Tantam, D., Lai, M.-C., Baron-Cohen, S., & Holland, A.J. (2017). Psychosis in autism: Comparison of the features of both conditions in a dually affected cohort. *The British Journal of Psychiatry, 210*(4), 269-275. doi:10.1192/bjp.bp.116.187682.

Lewis, L.F. (2016). Realizing a diagnosis of autism spectrum disorder as an adult. *International Journal of Mental Health Nursing, 25*, 346–354. doi:10.1111/inm.12200.

Lewis, L.F. (2017). A mixed methods study of barriers to formal diagnosis of autism spectrum disorder in adults. *Journal of Autism & Developmental Disorders, 47*, 2410–2424. doi:10.1007/s10803-017-3168-3.

Lord, C., Rutter, M., DiLavore, P.C., Risi, S., Gotham, K., Bishop, S.L., Luyster, R.J., & Guthrie, W. (2012). *Autism Diagnostic Observation Schedule™, second edition (ADOS-2).* Torrance, CA: Western Psychological Services.

Lugnegard, T., Hallerback, M.U., & Gillberg, C. (2011). Psychiatric comorbidity in young adults with a clinical diagnosis of Asperger syndrome. *Research in Developmental Disabilities, 32*, 1910–1917.

Lunsky, Y., Gracey, C., & Bradley, E. (2009). Adults with autism spectrum disorders using psychiatric hospitals in Ontario: Clinical profile and service needs. *Research in Autism Spectrum Disorders, 3*, 1006–1013.

Mandell, D.S., Lawer, L.J., Branch, K., Brodkin, E.S., Healey, K., Witalec, R., Johnson, D.N., & Gur, R.E. (2012). Prevalence and correlates of autism in a state psychiatric hospital. *Autism, 16*, 557–567. doi:10.1177/1362361311412058.

Mazzone, L., Rutta, L., & Reale, L. (2012). Psychiatric comorbidities in Asperger syndrome and high functioning autism: Diagnostic challenges. *Annals of General Psychiatry, 11*, 16.

Mouridsen, S.E., Rich, B., & Isager, T. (2008) Psychiatric disorders in adults diagnosed as children with atypical autism. A case control study. *Journal of Neural Transmission, 115*, 135–138.

Nylander, L., & Gillberg, C. (2001). Screening for autism spectrum disorders in adult psychiatric out-patients: A preliminary report. *Acta Psychiatrica Scandinavica, 103*, 428–434.

Portway, S.M., & Johnson, B. (2005). Do you know I have Asperger's syndrome? Risks of a non-obvious disability. *Health, Risk & Society*, 7, 73–83. doi:10.1080/0950083050004286.

Prosser, H., Moss, S., Costello, H., Simpson, N., Paterl, P., & Rowe, S. (1998). Reliability and validity of the Mini PAS-ADD for assessing psychiatric disorders in adults with intellectual disabilities. *Journal of Intellectual Disability Research, 42*, 264–272.

Punshon, C., Skirrow, P., & Murphy, G. (2009). The "not guilty verdict": Psychological reactions to a diagnosis of Asperger syndrome in adulthood. *Autism, 13*, 265–283. doi:10.1177/1362361309103795.

Reynolds, C.R., & Kamphaus, R.W. (2015). *Behavior Assessment System for Children, third edition (BASC-3)*. Pearson Clinical.

Ritvo, R.A., & Ritvo E.R. (2007). *Ritvo autism Asperger diagnostic scale – revised*. Retrieved from: https://link.springer.com/article/10.1007%2Fs10803-010-1133-5.

Ritvo, R.A., Ritvo, E.R., Guthrie, D., Ritvo, M.J., Hufnagel, D.H., McMahon, W., & Tonge, B. (2011). The Ritvo Autism Asperger Diagnostic Scale-Revised (RAADS-R): A scale to assist the diagnosis of autism spectrum disorder in adults: An international validation study. *Journal of Autism & Developmental Disorders, 41*, 1076–1089. https://doi.org/10.1007/s10803-010-1133-5.

Rutter, M., LeCouteur, A., & Lord, C. (2003). *Autism Diagnostic Interview™, revised (ADI™-R)*. Torrance, CA: Western Psychological Services.

Ruzich, E., Allison, C., Smith, P., Watson, P., Auyeung, B., Ring, H., & Baron-Cohen, S. (2015). Measuring autistic traits in the general population: A systematic review of the Autism-Spectrum Quotient (AQ) in a non-clinical population sample of 6,900 typical adult males and females. *Molecular Autism, 12*, 45. doi:10.1186/2040-2392-6-2 www.ncbi.nlm.nih.gov/pmc/articles/PMC4396128/.

Santosh, P.J., & Mijovic, A. (2006). Does pervasive developmental disorder protect children and adolescents against drug and alcohol use? *European Child & Adolescent Psychiatry, 15*, 183–188.

Sappok, T., Heinrich, M., & Underwood, L. (2015). Screening tools for autism spectrum disorders. *Advances in Autism, 1*, 12–29. doi:10.1108/AIA-03-2015-0001.

Selten, J-P., Lundberg, M., Rai, D., & Magnusson, C. (2015) Risks for non-affective psychotic disorder and bipolar disorder in young people with autism spectrum disorder: A population-based study. *Journal of American Medical Association of Psychiatry, 72*, 483–489.

Simonoff, E., Pickles, A., Charman, T., Chandler, S., Loucas, T., & Baird, G. (2008). Psychiatric disorders in children with autism spectrum disorders: Prevalence, comorbidity, and associated factors in a population-derived sample. *Journal of the American Academy of Child & Adolescent Psychiatry, 47*(8), 921–929. doi:10.1097/CHI.0b013e31879964f.

Sizoo, B., van den Brink, W., Gorissen van Eenige, M., & van der Gaag, R.J. (2009). Personality characteristics of adults with autism spectrum disorders or attention deficit hyperactivity disorder with and without substance use disorders. *The Journal of Nervous and Mental Disease, 197*, 450–454.

Vohra, R., Madhavan, S., & Sambamoorthi, U. (2017) Comorbidity prevalence, healthcare utilization, and expenditures of Medicaid enrolled adults with autism spectrum disorders. *Autism, 21*, 995–1009. doi:10.1177/1362361316665222.

Weintraub, K. (2011). Autism counts: Shifting diagnoses and heightened awareness explain only part of the apparent rise in autism. Scientists are struggling to explain the rest. *Nature, 479*, 22–24.

Wilfley, D.E., Agras, W.S., & Taylor, C.B. (2013). Reducing the burden of eating disorders: A model for population-based prevention and treatment for university and college campuses. *International Journal of Eating Disorders, 46*, 529–532.

Williams, J., Scott, F., Stott, C., Allison, C., Bolton, P., Baron-Cohen, S., & Brayne, C. (2004). The CAST (Childhood Asperger Syndrome Test): Test accuracy. *Autism, 9*, 45–68.

Wing, L., Gould, J., & Gillberg, C. (2011). Autism spectrum disorders in the DSM-5: Better or worse than the DSM-IV. *Research in Developmental Disabilities, 32*(2), 768-773. doi:10.1016/j.ridd.2010.11.003.

Woolfenden, S., Sarkozy, V., Ridley, G., & Williams, K. (2011). A systematic review of the diagnostic stability of Autism Spectrum disorder. *Research in Autism Spectrum Disorders, 6*, 345–354.

Wylie, P. (2014). *Very late diagnosis of Asperger syndrome (autism spectrum disorder): How seeking a diagnosis in adulthood can change your life*. Philadelphia: Jessica Kingsley Publishing.

5 Treating Social Communication Impairments

The ability for human beings to communicate with one another is fundamental to our survival. Communicating with one another allows us to meet basic needs and more complex desires via human interaction and belonging. Depending upon your theoretical orientation and approach, terminology and definitions to describe this basic human need may differ. However, one agreement remains regardless of approach or orientation, humans are social beings for whom communication is a critical skill for cooperation and collaboration

Since social communication is a skill primarily involving language and pragmatics it helps to rely on the definition of this construct from the American Speech-Language-Hearing Association (ASHA). Social communication is the use of language in a social context (ASHA, 2018). In working with ASD clients, speech-language pathologists (SLP) are another essential group of professionals I have collaborated with to successful ends. Their expertise in promoting effective expressive and receptive communication strategies for clients is therapeutically relevant as in some cases SLPs have been vital in moving clients into more verbal states wherein they can benefit from counseling and psychotherapy.

Communication takes on two main forms, verbal and nonverbal. For most people, verbal skills are learned based on exposure to the use of language by others in their natural environments (ASHA, 2018). At home a family speaks Spanish and their child learns to communicate in this language. When they go to school and English is spoken, they can often learn that language too. The same learning principle is universally applied to learning nonverbal communication. Yet, for children who learn differently or have neurological, developmental disorders this is often not the case.

Young children with autism often have atypical language development with different presentations. The classic autism diagnosis is marked by a lack of language when developmentally expected, between 18 and 24 months old (American Psychiatric Association, 2013). This is usually the most immediately apparent and concerning symptom of autism for parents and pediatricians alike. If language is completely lacking during early childhood, important gains can be made through intensive therapeutic interventions during which time some children gain language skills. Some children diagnosed with ASD early on improve to the point that they no longer meet criteria for the diagnosis (Fein et al., 2013; Orinstein et al., 2014). This is one of the most promising parts about early detection and treatment of social communication skills; even when there are significant deficits, improvements can be made. But every person has their own level of potential and most children's ASD diagnosis remains stable throughout older childhood and through adulthood (Ozonoff et al., 2015).

The delayed language characteristic of autism is one that most in the general public are familiar with if they've been exposed to the news, social media or fictional stories portrayed in entertainment. It is a helpful piece of information for the public to be equipped with because it may help increase awareness, screening efforts and treatment for young children. But another kind of communication difference is detected among young children with autism that is less subtle or obvious as a sign of ASD. This is understandably less concerning because in these cases the child is able to use language, a sign of healthy development, but does so in atypical and stereotypical ways.

Atypical ways that children with early language skills can demonstrate symptoms of ASD are by using more advanced language or vocabulary than would be expected for their age. Parents often report these children engage in reading books well-beyond their years including dictionaries or encyclopedias. Of course, this is impressive and often a point of pride for parents whose young children seem to be demonstrating high levels of intelligence. It's directly opposed to the other children who are clearly at a deficit; in these cases, the children seem savant or genius-like in their skills (Treffert, 2009). One of the challenges with the use of advanced language and vocabulary is that often it is not being applied in a functional or meaningful way. Because of this, these children are much more likely to get along with or gravitate towards adults or older children in social situations. Relationships with same-aged peers are typically much harder for these children who seem advanced in one realm of communication and struggle in others. The realm they tend to struggle in most is reciprocal interactions during social communication.

Social Communication is Complicated

The struggle exists primarily because using language in social contexts is complex for several reasons. One thing required during social communication interactions is the knowledge and use of a vast number of skills. These include verbal tasks such as making requests, comments and questions while using tone and prosody that will lead others to understand us well. Social communication also involves the use of nonverbal tasks such as making gestures and creating congruent facial expressions. And these examples only scratch the surface of all the skills listed in verbal and nonverbal communication task categories.

Another reason for this complexity is that language is bidirectional, meaning you have to be able to express it to (output) and receive it from (input) others in a way that helps you, at the very least, "get-by". For clients with ASD, many times expressive and receptive language skills are splintered and uneven (ASHA, 2018). This means that a client might present in therapy with an incredibly impressive vocabulary and seemingly great insight, but when asked questions to expand on ideas they've presented they may have difficulty processing the question or be confused about how to respond to an unfamiliar topic. The mismatch between a client's ability to express themselves (high level) and understand the social interaction (low level) in the therapeutic context can create its own issues that are a parallel process to their interactions in the world.

A third reason that complicates communicating within a social context is that, as with the requisite skills required above, their array of social contexts is almost limitless in definition. There are social contexts that are helpful to focus on due to the person's frequency in exposure to them, such as interactions with primary groups (i.e., family, friends, close/loved ones) and secondary groups (i.e., teachers, boss, co-workers, etc.) (Gladding, 2019). Learning how to navigate the nuances and rules in these main social contexts is tricky enough, but with the addition of other social contexts, such as casual social interactions at the grocery store, coffee shop, bar or online, the rules change again. And even when we think we've conquered some social rules of communicating in these contexts, things evolve and change over time, which require us to be flexible to new social demands when they arise. Thankfully, there are helpful resources and guides available that review verbal and nonverbal communication rules in specific public spaces, such as elevators and restrooms (Gerhardt & Lainer, 2011). Therefore, when working with ASD clients, it is helpful to be able to specifically identify the groups or environments in which they have the most difficulty navigating to prioritize contexts that are most important.

One final factor that adds to the complex nature of this domain, is that the social context is constantly changing and evolving. Consider the different social contexts that have emerged with technology. The communication rules for social networking and media platforms is ever-changing and depends on a variety of demographic factors its users contribute to its interface. This also applies to face-to-face interactions, as is illuminated when someone from an older generation is fascinated by how a younger generation approaches social relationships. What worked for the grandparents in our families, may not be successful for the teens or young adults who are trying to initiate or maintain relationships. Across decades and generations, the types of verbal and nonverbal tasks that apply to different contexts need to be considered. As clinicians who treat ASD clients, it is vital to understand the most up-to-date rules, and this can often be done by following the latest trends in news and research. And, it just so happens, our clients can be the best resources about the current trends in communication. Therefore, we can allow *them* to teach *us* about the latest expectations for electronic and face-to-face communication.

Challenges for ASD Adults

For adults with autism, social communication is impacted by a few main factors. One of these is difficulty starting and taking turns in conversation, which leads to a perceived lack of interest from others. Another factor to consider is a limited range in verbal and nonverbal repertoire, which leads to a lack of using and understanding their own and other's attempts at communicating social subtleties. Lastly, and likely due to the aforementioned factors, many people with autism struggle to connect with peers within two or so years of their own age (APA, 2013). As far as socializing with ease or success, these core diagnostic criteria set up an adult with autism to be at a disadvantage when attempting to connect smoothly with others.

Social communication is a broad concept that can be confusing and overwhelming to tackle clinically. This is why the use of an assessment tool that breaks down this broad skill into sub-categories, including motivation, awareness, and cognition, can be incredibly helpful. Because these each fall under the broader category of social communication, this chapter will focus specifically on forms of self-expression and interpretation of verbal and nonverbal communicating, while the next three chapters will dive into the sub-categories of social motivation, awareness and cognition.

When assessing a client's different levels of social communication, the results of the SRS-2 will help inform and guide treatment planning (Constantino & Gruber, 2016). The first step to informing treatment will help a counselor determine the level of diagnostic category of social communication for the client. It will also provide a gage or comparison to that of the second diagnostic criteria regarding behavioral tendencies so treatment can be tailored and focused accordingly. If social communication results indicate more of a need than behavioral issues, treatment planning should reflect this. In this first step of determining how social communication and behavior issues compare, a foundation for treatment can be set.

Be mindful that even though social communication deficits can be more severe or marked than autistic mannerisms or behaviors, the intersection of behavioral challenges and communication issues typically cause the clinician to address both simultaneously. The utility of understanding the results of the SRS-2 is that this can help inform how you can tackle collaborating on treatment on these issues. If the client endorses more problems with social communication, it's possible they'll be more open to starting with improving aspects of how they express themselves socially. If they endorse more problems behaviorally, this could reflect their own ideas that this is a priority for them in treatment. Collaborating with the client on the results of social communication from assessment is helpful in determining treatment prioritization and the client's openness to tackling specific areas. The next step in presenting SRS-2 results involves the parsing out the sub-categories within social communication to determine whether expression, motivation, awareness or cognition should take priority.

For adults with autism, all of these are connected and work in conjunction with one another. We suggest starting with assessing the social communication picture because it is typically the clearest and most concrete to identify early on. Since verbal and nonverbal expressions are required for interacting with the clinician, these can become apparent almost immediately. From there, social motivation can be assessed to help determine the quantity and quality of social relationships and interactions. Next, the client and counselor can work to assess how socially aware a client is and move on lastly to social cognition or thinking abilities. This sequence is suggested because it can make practical sense in approaching the social communication domain but should be individualized based on client and the prioritization of needs.

An example of how a practitioner can apply this sequence to treating social communication issues will be reviewed in Matt's case study at the end of this chapter. This case helps illustrate issues in social communication for one client and does not cover the breadth of errors made in social communication by people with ASD. Let's look at some of the most common social communication deficits that are likely to arise when treating clients with autism, so as a practitioner you can be prepared.

Social Communication Skills

Autistic clients share a diagnosis that can help practitioners identify criteria and symptoms that are similar in presentation. In the area of social communication, a variety of challenges can arise that have group similarities and individual differences. Individual differences will be determined on a case-by-case basis, but shared group challenges are helpful to understand as you prepare to provide counseling for this population.

One of the interesting things about people is that we can identify some shared common social interests and errors based on different characteristics we share. Adults with autism tend to commit common social errors that are inherent in the description of the condition with which they are diagnosed. We can improve our competence by understanding what some of the most common social communication challenges are for autistic clients.

Table 5.1 shows commonly identified social errors that people with autism demonstrate in three domains of communication. These lists are not all-inclusive but highlight some of those that are most reported in research and practice.

It can be helpful to put these common social errors into the communication categories listed above in order to understand context in each. Rules for how to improve skills in each domain can be broken down into concrete steps, which is a useful approach for clients with autism. Understanding what the ecologically valid, concrete steps to managing these errors are is what can present a challenge for the counselor in providing instruction and feedback. We have to be well equipped with the proven methods that make others socially savvy in order to execute this well. Without that we will typically make our own errors in assuming what these concrete steps are.

Table 5.1 Examples of common social communication errors

Verbal communication	*Nonverbal communication*	*Electronic communication*
Difficulty starting conversations	Misinterpreting another person's experience during a conversation	Contacting someone repetitively without receiving a response
Taking up too much time during a conversation	Giving too much eye contact (staring) to express interest	Contacting someone too early or too late in the day
Asking too many questions in a row during a conversation	Standing too close or too far away from a conversation partner	Randomly friending, following or direct messaging someone on social media
Making an abrupt change in topic or going on a tangent in conversation	Thinking another person is laughing at a joke when they're actually laughing at them	Asking for explicit or sexual materials from people who don't expect it or reciprocate interest
Using too little or too much vocal volume in conversation	Getting visibly upset when teased, embarrassed or bullied	Reacting defensively to trolls who tease or bully online by making more comments online
Providing feedback in a brutally honest manner that others are not expecting	Having poor hygiene	Engaging in texts or online communication with someone while hanging out with another person
Having a disagreement that results in ending relationships	Difficulty choosing a physical look or style that blends in with the crowd	Engaging in repetitive attempts to contact that result in harassment, stalking or cyberbullying claims
Difficulty joining a group conversation, often times interrupting	Abruptly walking away from a conversation without any warning	Difficulty creating an appealing online persona

Source: Laugeson (2017).

Verbal communication skills tend to be more concrete and, therefore, can be easier to address in therapy. Learning how to share a conversation may be easier to gage for an autistic client who is trying to limit or increase how much time they take up in conversation. Following steps for starting a conversation by asking a question, making a comment or giving a compliment may seem simple and straightforward. Electronic communication may also be considered a more concrete form of social interaction that requires written expression that can be accurately interpreted in a literal sense. The abstract concepts related to both verbal and electronic communication that can go unnoticed or misinterpreted by a client with ASD are nuanced tones, sarcasm and exaggeration that are socially idiosyncratic.

Distinguishing the idiosyncrasies and nuances of social communication usually requires strength in interpreting the abstract or non-linear meaning behind the literal words used during a social exchange. In face-to-face interactions where verbal communication occurs, this requires an ability to accurately interpret nonverbal communication. In electronic interactions, this requires an understanding of the person with whom an interaction occurs in order to best interpret meaning behind the messages being sent. Most times this means electronic communication partners turn into those with whom you need to interact with face-to-face (even via video) in order to better learn about their nonverbal communication tendencies.

Even the most socially savvy people can experience challenges in interpreting nonverbal communication messages being sent by someone they're interacting with. Nonverbal messages can be so subtle and indirect that we are trained to automatically pay attention to these and interpret them by making assumptions based on little effort. The lack of social communication deficits enables most of us to be so good at interpreting nonverbal communication that we assume others pick up and use the information well. Yet, when interacting with an autistic person, automatically assuming that they're picking up on or accurately interpreting our nonverbal communication is almost as far reaching as assuming the person you're speaking to is bilingual. It's often a dual task for the ASD adult to pay attention to both verbals and nonverbals simultaneously. Imagine speaking with your French–English bilingual friend and suddenly they seamlessly go back and forth between both languages. What happens is that we'll miss all of the important messages being sent in French because of a lack of understanding the language. This is analogous to what some people with autism experience during social communication when they can best attend to the concrete, verbal messages being sent and miss out on all of the nonverbals that are often equally or more important. Since an estimated 50–75 percent of social communication is nonverbal (ASHA, 2018), it's possible that our clients with ASD are missing out on much of that.

Much of the work we do with clients to help improve social communication skills will be to help fill the misinterpreted language gap highlighted above. Therefore, understanding many of the common issues that arise for them and the methods for how to help them improve in these areas are both essential. Applying the treatment steps above to clients who are engaging in verbal, nonverbal and electronic interactions provide an evidence-based approach to improving social communication deficits for clients with ASD.

Social Communication Interventions

The best practice treatment recommendations for improving social communication are derived from social skills treatment for people with ASD across the lifespan. Since social communication is an essential social skill, it is the best place to begin understanding the literature and creating treatment goals. Even though social skills treatment primarily focuses on social communication, in ASD-specific social skills treatment, how to manage repetitive behaviors and restricted interests is also addressed. In Chapter 9, information will be reviewed for behavior skills training that involves many of the same approaches and interventions with a focus on working with challenging behaviors. For the purposes of this chapter, the focus will be on how social skills treatment can benefit the social communication repertoire for adults with ASD.

At each stage of the lifespan, different social communication skills are required in order to be successful. During the early years of childhood, social communication is mostly done through play with peers (Frankel & Myatt, 2002). As we age into adolescence and adulthood, social communication is carried out through conversation (Laugeson & Frankel, 2010). Therefore, early on in the treatment of autistic clients they may have experienced play-based social skills treatment prior to treatment they receive later in life. A history with and foundation in social communication skills treatment has the potential to help or hinder adult clients in counseling.

If the autistic adult has built successful skills for social communication in previous treatment this may have been the catalyst and change agent that allows them to have improved function in social interactions and relationships. Early intervention in speech and behavior therapy may have created the foundation for a teen or adult to have the ability to express themselves verbally and know about nonverbal tools for communication. The importance of effective early intervention cannot be over-stated in its importance in determining good prognoses for outcomes in adulthood (Wong et al., 2015).

Yet, for those who have received social communication skills treatment before entering your care, there is potential for a history of experiences in treatment that resulted in learning invalid skills, in ineffective skills. Unfortunately, there are both effective and ineffective treatments available to this vulnerable population. Most ineffective work is carried out by clinicians who are well-intended but are not well-equipped or trained on evidence-based, social skills treatment strategies. Treatment as usual for social skills has most therapists finding themselves pulling together materials from various sources to integrate into one approach (Laugeson, 2013).

One issue is that there here are so many available resources to sort through. At the time of writing, an Amazon books search of "social skills treatment autism", produces over 1000 potential products. And that's only in the books department, thus excluding therapeutic games and activities. Identifying which of these products will lead to effective treatment requires effort and time that many clinicians find themselves short of. The good news is that when searching for "*evidence-based* social skills treatment autism" on Amazon books the list of results is much more limited; the results list 15 products.

As clinicians it is our ethical and professional imperative to find and use treatment that is evidence-based in order to provide the best-quality treatment to our clients (American Counseling Association, 2014). Evidence-based social skills treatment has improved in research rigor, through randomized control trials, and practice is improving as a result of more widespread training. Over the last decade, some of the best resources for social skills training for adults, teens and children alike have been identified and share essential elements (see Table 5.2). Let's explore these elements in detail for the best understanding for how to treat social communication skill deficits.

Table 5.2 Elements of evidence-based social communication skills treatment

Treatment element	*Method*
Didactic instruction	Identification of and instruction on *ecologically-valid social communication skills*. Integration of Socratic questioning and role-play for the co-creation of social rules.
Modeling	Utilize clinician-led *role-plays* that allow clients to identify wrong and right ways to execute skills being taught.
Behavior rehearsal	Providing structured *opportunities to practice* what was identified and instructed didactically. Allows for the assessment of strengths and barriers.
Coaching and feedback	Utilize assessed strengths and barriers to *encourage growth and plan for ways to improve.*
Homework	Providing *planned opportunities,* outside of therapy, for the skill to be generalized and practiced.
Caregiver assisted	Identification of a social coach in the person's natural circle. The caregiver needs to be provided with specifics on social skills rules and involved in planning homework to support practice and generalization.
Group format	Allows for varied opportunities with peers to learn through didactic instruction and behavior rehearsal. A *small group format*, 7–12 people, is ideal for positive treatment outcomes.

Sources: Laugeson (2013); Laugeson and Frankel (2010).

Didactic Instruction

The foundation for integrating these elements for successful treatment outcomes is to ensure ecologically valid social communication skills are being instructed (Laugeson, 2017). This should be considered the compass that guides treatment because without it we may be, unknowingly, equipping clients with skills that are invalid and lead to more challenges than they began with. When this happens, it is primarily done with good intention and the assumption that a socially savvy clinician knows how to teach what they already practice socially. Unfortunately, we aren't often good at teaching other people skills that we have inherently, instead of deliberately, learned. This can often result in a tendency to teach skills that are too formal or what people "should do" in social situations but that often do not occur in natural social interactions.

After speaking on this subject to many audiences over the years, I've asked them to reflect on the phenomenon that what we teach is often not what we actually do. In talks, I pose two questions. "How would you teach someone to start a casual conversation?" and "How do you start a conversation with someone in line at a coffee shop?". The first question's responses tend to include the "shoulds" such as "They should introduce themselves" or "Walk up, say hello and offer a handshake." But the second question's responses look quite different. Typical responses to this include "Ask if they've been waiting for a while" or "Comment on the new seasonal drink or item". The good news is that there seems to be momentum toward a shift to teach socially and ecologically valid skills in the ASD treatment community.

What we think others should do socially tends to be distinct from what we would deem appropriate or savvy ourselves. As mentioned above, it may be that we just find it particularly difficult to teach skills that we naturally apply. Therefore, it is imperative that we take from the latest research and information from people in the age group that we are treating to gather the best resources for social communication skills instruction.

A final reason that it is important to pull from the most current literature on ecologically valid social skills is that they are frequently evolving. The fast-moving trends, fads and patterns in social communication require us to learn about the language and tools clients utilize to interact with one another. It would be nearly impossible to conduct all of the research on this topic as clinicians because the research itself has a hard time keeping up with these trends. Thus, the best resource for this will be our clients and like-aged people with whom we interact in our personal lives. Direct questions that get clients and others to teach us about what's most popularly done in social media and what younger and older adults do when they get together are important to growing our knowledge-base about current trends.

Modeling

The demonstration of social errors and successes is an essential factor for instructing the autistic client about how to apply social communication skills (Laugeson, 2017). It is helpful to explore various options for how modeling can occur and many times this is based on resources available to the clinician. For in vivo demonstrations, more than one person is required to engage in an interaction so that the social example can be executed. As mental health professionals, most realize resources can be sparse and that this is not always possible. Therefore, using the next best thing, video demonstrations, can be a good and recommended alternative.

An important point about modeling, otherwise called role-playing, is that you do not want the client to engage in this when providing social communication skill instruction. Instead, this needs to be carried out by others, so they can learn from watching how others interact and identify both what to (1) avoid and (2) achieve. In the effective modeling of errors, this is used to point out the clear problems that can occur during social interactions. This helps encourage independent learning and assesses their understanding of the declarative knowledge they have about social communication. The modeling of social successes then gives clients the opportunity to have a visual representation of what instructions taught look like procedurally. Ideally, modeling secures the final stage of learning the social communication rules taught during instruction.

Behavior Rehearsal, Coaching, and Feedback

Once the two phases of didactic instruction and modeling are complete, the next step in sequencing social communication skills training is to have the client rehearse the skills they've learned. This provides an opportunity for the counselor to assess the strengths and challenges of these newly learned communication tools. As is essential in most treatment, this is an opportunity to emphasize what the client has done well in practice and areas they can improve on (Laugeson, 2017). Encouragement for demonstrated strengths must proceed any corrective feedback a clinician will provide so that the rehearsal and coaching process is well-received.

When delivering corrective feedback after observing the behavior rehearsal, it can be helpful to refer to visual aids or gestures that serve as reminders for the rules or steps that the client can improve on. For example, if the client forgets Step 3 of 6, the clinician can provide a physical prompt to re-read a rule or guide them with a gesture as a reminder of what to do next. A gestural prompt, such as extending your arm out and parallel with the ground, can work well when reminding a client about body boundaries (Laugeson, 2017). Coaching and feedback in social skill treatment delivery provide opportunities for the client to engage in the repetition of instruction and refine their skills before generalizing them in the real-world.

Homework and Caregiver Assistance

The assignment of homework or take-home tasks is the primary method for clients to have planned opportunities to generalize skills learned in session (Laugeson, 2017). This step of treatment is essential to the trouble-shooting process of social communication skill development. Realistically, when a client learns a new or improved skill, they are not likely to master it immediately. It is only in these real-life experiences that more significant trouble-shooting, beyond what occurs during behavior rehearsal, can occur.

Homework compliance improves when a client's task is planned out in detail. This includes pre-planning the who, when, where and what aspects of the homework task. For example, if the client is planning on practicing flirting with someone, the preparation piece can be essential to making it happen. A client can identify the person they're interested in (*who*), that they're going to a mutual friend's house this weekend for a get together (*when* and *where*) and that it'll be a Halloween party with games (*what*). From there the client and counselor can work together to review the steps for "the *how*" they can engage in successful flirting (through the aforementioned steps). Following up on homework assignments require the client to report back during the next session how the attempt at flirting went.

Processing homework attempts, whether successfully executed or not, is the final part of homework. Being able to have the client identify the steps they took in the process that helped them make their attempt and the barriers to achieving their goal will both be important. Any attempts should be encouraged while assessing for complacency or resistance if homework compliance is low (Laugeson, 2017). One way to increase the chances of homework completion is by involving the client's social coach or caregiver in the process. In this role they can serve as homework reminders and help the client generalize the skills to different environments and people when natural opportunities arise.

Group Treatment Format

Ideally, social skills treatment is provided in a small-group treatment format. Essential to effective group therapy is a screening and interview process where selection of group members is strategically executed (Laugeson, 2017). Not everyone is a good candidate for group treatment and therefore conducting initial interviews to assess for fit is a vital first step in planning this format of therapy. When social skills treatment is the focus, major behavioral problems and other co-occurring issues that should take precedence in treatment may be exclusion criteria for group treatment. The focus of the clinician in delivering group therapy is to ensure the group can function effectively, which makes screening a priority.

The reality of group treatment is that recruitment can be difficult, and attrition can directly impact the effectiveness of the group. Recruiting a group of approximately seven to 12 adults is ideal in order to provide group members with options for practice with different people. It also helps prevent the problem of ending up with too few members in a group after accounting for those who will inevitably drop out. Due to the challenge of providing group therapy in out-patient settings, individual therapy can still be utilized to provide social communication skill instruction, but it may require additional support for it to be effective. To make similar gains to those that are possible in group therapy, individual treatment may require more treatment (higher dosage) and a serious commitment from caregivers to help generalize and practice skills outside of treatment.

The evidence-based interventions for effective social skills instruction will be an important foundation to establish in one's skills set when preparing to counsel adults with autism. I was lucky enough to be trained by the autism field's most respected social skills training professional, Dr. Liz Laugeson. She founded the UCLA PEERS® program and she taught me everything I learned about how to best execute the interventions above. I cannot recommend the UCLA PEERS® training enough to practitioners who want to obtain the highest quality social communication skills training. Although this training is not the only one that exists, the gold-standard research supporting its efficacy far outweighs its value for practitioners.

Having said that, myriad training options are available to enhance these skills and if these are areas you can improve in your repertoire this will help you grow professionally and will positively impact your client's treatment outcomes. If you find this guide useful, you've likely engaged in a lot of professional development on this topic to date. Now, let's elaborate on how these methods of treating social communication skill deficits may be applied to an autistic client receiving individual therapy services.

Case Example

Matt is a 27-year-old, straight white male who presents to counseling with the social goals of learning how to get a girlfriend and lose his virginity. These two goals are common among the clients I see, particularly for those who have little to no experience in dating or sexual relationships. For Matt, these two goals don't necessarily converge, and his priority is to have sex for the first time. His logic is that he needs to first get sexual experience and then this will lead to him being able to get a girlfriend. In further understanding Matt's history and background, it appears that his motivation for getting a girlfriend could be to fill a caregiving role that he will need to replace with the eventuality of his parent's mortality, which they often bring to his attention in an effort to motivate him.

In assessing the core symptoms of ASD and how they impact Matt, it is apparent that he is limited in his verbal expression. He has the ability to communicate verbally, yet he infrequently initiates topics of conversation and his responses to questions are brief and blunted. He often responds with two to three word phrases and rarely expands on situations that could use more details to better understand his perspective. In addition to these verbal language deficits, Matt has a hard time using and interpreting nonverbal communication. He does not demonstrate a range of emotions through varied facial expressions when communicating and awkwardly uses gestures, and his body language portrays a person who is closed off and guarded.

His social communication barriers have impacted his family, social and work relationships in a variety of ways. Among his family he is encouraged to express himself, yet with two dominant and differing parenting styles he has developed a pattern of "yesing" both parents and only responds with more substance and meaning when prompted and probed. This has led to a lot of frustration for his parents who want him to "stand up for himself" and more readily express his appreciation for their support.

Socially, Matt has one to two friends who he connects with on a sporadic basis. At most he hangs out with friends every other month. Overall, Matt is lower in social motivation requiring less interaction than many of his same-age peers. He reports overall satisfaction with his friendships but significant challenges in romantic endeavors. To better understand his objective social communication picture, the SRS-2 pre-treatment self and caregiver assessment results will be important to review. In the self-assessment, Matt reports mild ASD deficits in social communication. In the caregiver assessment, his parents collectively report more severe ASD deficits in social communication. After understanding Matt and his caregivers, the counselor's clinical judgement leads to the conclusion that Matt is likely under-reporting symptoms while his parents are probably over-reporting them. This is a common phenomenon in self and caregiver reporting, which the practitioner has been trained to identify. All of the data indicate that Matt is likely in the moderate range of impaired social communication, with more significant challenges in the subdomains of social motivation and social cognition.

In order to remain focused on social communication as one of Matt's treatment goals, social motivation and cognition will be addressed as connected goals with distinct foci. For social communication skills, Matt's verbal and nonverbal expression requires improvement if he is to meet his goals for improved relationships with women. The first addresses his aforementioned challenge with initiating a conversation and fully expressing himself when responding to a question. The second goal will address how his facial expressions and body language can communicate flat, uninterested and awkward to others. Within the goal of nonverbal social communication, Matt will need to learn how to accurately interpret more complicated, social messages others are trying to send him. Mostly, he needs to be more aware when his advancements are unwelcome. These will be targeted and approached in the context of improving his interactions with women to include his stated goals for counseling.

To address the issues Matt has with verbal communication skills it is helpful to begin by assessing his understanding, or perspective, on how a conversation partner experiences interacting with him. He has relied on prompting from others in his life for so long that if not asked a direct question, he's unsure of what to say or do in a conversation. Years of therapy and specialized services have helped Matt considerably but have also created a pattern of dependence in socializing that he is now accustomed to. This is likely what has led him to seeming blunted or uninterested in conversation; he's always waiting for someone else to start and maintain it. The question is, does he realize the effect this has on others? In order to effectively assess and improve his social cognition, three social thinking questions are utilized (see Chapter 8). In responding to these questions, Matt is accurately able to identify that these interactions are likely awkward, weird or confusing for others and it leads them to be less likely to want to interact with him again. This introduction to enhancing Matt's social cognition aims to become a habitual thought process that will optimize his ability to socially communicate with others.

It's clear that Matt "gets" how others feel when interacting with him and is now building the thinking skills to help him self-correct in social situations outside of therapy. Now, Matt is eager to learn skills for how to make his social interactions more successful. Since initiating skills are difficult for him, a review of conversation starting skills is important. He has to identify places or scenarios where he can start conversations with others who share similar interests. Then he is taught specific steps for a successful conversation including ecologically valid physical and verbal and nonverbal skills. For example, when he sees someone at the comic book store who he'd like to talk to, he can (1) slowly approach them by picking up a book or item in the same aisle; (2) move close to the person (but not too close); and, lastly, (3) ask them a question, make a comment or give them a compliment related to comics (Laugeson, 2017).

Teaching these steps for starting a conversation is ideally done through Socratic questioning and visual aids. Asking questions that elicit the client's collaboration in creating the steps allows them to buy-in to the process and is best practice for working with adults and adolescents. Even though the steps are co-created with the client, the clinician is responsible for knowing about the ecologically valid skills in order to frame Socratic questions in a way that elicits the best responses. Once the steps are identified, with the clinician's guiding expertise, it is important to integrate them into a visual, through written instruction or video modeling. Repeating the steps with some frequency helps solidify instruction and the visual representation is a best-practice in teaching individuals with ASD (Laugeson, 2017).

After the initial instruction of the conversation starting skill is complete, it'll be important for Matt to be able to rehearse the steps with the therapist in session and outside of the session with his social coach. This should all take place before Matt attempts this in the real-world so the next step of coaching and feedback to help him improve his skills can be integrated. The clinician and Matt rehearse his approach and the conversation starting question, comment or compliment he might use in a comic book store. Matt does not like the rehearsal aspect of treatment and is resistant because, ironically, he finds it awkward. The counselor reminds him of its value in exposing him to these opportunities so he's more likely to do it in the real-world when approaching women; he agrees to partake but does so reticently. In rehearsing Matt is effectively able to come up with an effective question, "Hey … I'm thinking about getting this new Green Lantern. Have you read this one?" This is a real success and his specific ability to ask a question that is on-topic is well-done. But in his physical approach, Matt comes too close which is likely to be uncomfortable for a stranger. With this nonverbal element of starting a conversation, Matt needs some correction through coaching and feedback.

Because Matt doesn't like rehearsing skills in therapy, even though his homework is to engage in practice with his social coach, he's noncompliant with the recommendation. This makes it harder for him to generalize and improve on his nonverbal communication skills as much as he could. Instead, Matt is eager to move forward toward his goal of getting a girlfriend, so he rehearses this skill at work and in the comic book store with mixed reviews. At work he struggles because he's been too persistent and, as a result, been written up for inappropriate co-worker interactions. In processing these experiences, Matt is slightly annoyed in describing his failed attempts, but he is not dissuaded from continuing to try. This resilience in Matt is an important trait for protecting him from the development of anxious or depressive symptoms, but it may eventually lead him to become increasingly frustrated with future failed attempts.

In continued work with Matt, he settles into an improved skill set of social communication skills, specifically with how effectively he is able to verbalize in conversation. His family reports hearing more from him and that in conversation with friends he is more successful. His flow is more natural, less forced or pressured by prompts from his conversation partner. In treatment, the focus has moved beyond conversation starters to how to maintain a conversation and there has been a marked improved in this domain. Nonverbally, Matt is able to make improvements in some areas, including more natural eye contact and respecting other's personal boundaries and space. These behaviors have caused him some trouble in the past and in the last six months there have been no reported incidents of these nonverbal behaviors interfering with his personal or professional goals.

Matt continues to have troubled interactions with women and struggles to meet his initial goal of getting a girlfriend. Matt's level of social motivation to find new opportunities to meet women or other male friends is low. Therefore, suggestions about increasing in-person or online opportunities to do so have not been embraced. Even though he is still aspiring toward that goal, Matt reports better social interactions at work, with family and the friends he does have. He seems satisfied with the progress he's made but is still holding out for the hope that one day his interests, work or online interactions, will lead him to finding a mate.

References

American Counseling Association. (2014). *Code of ethics*. Arlington, VA: American Counseling Association.

American Psychiatric Association. (2013). *Diagnostic and statistical manual of mental disorders* (5th ed.). Arlington, VA: Author.

American Speech-Language-Hearing Association. (2018). Social communication disorders. Retrieved from: www.asha.org/practice-portal.

Constantino, J.N., & Gruber, C.P. (2016). *Social Responsiveness, Scale – second edition (SRS-2) [manual]*. Torrance, CA: Western Psychological Services.

Fein, D., Barton, M., Eigsti, I.M., Kelley, E., Naigles, L., Schultz, R.T., … Tyson, K. (2013). Optimal outcome in individuals with a history of autism. *Journal of Child Psychology and Psychiatry, 54*, 195–205.

Frankel, F., & Myatt, R. (2002). *Children's friendship training*. New York: Brunner-Routledge.

Gladding, S. (2019). *Groups: A counseling specialty*. New York: Pearson Education.

Gerhardt, P.F., & Lainer, I. (2011). Addressing the needs of adolescents and adults with autism: A crisis on the horizon. *Journal of Contemporary Psychotherapy, 41*, 37–45.

Laugeson, E.A. (2013). *The science of making and keeping friends: Helping socially challenged teens and young adults*. San Francisco, CA: Jossey-Bass.

Laugeson, E.A. (2017). *PEERS® for young adults: Social skills training for adults with autism spectrum disorder and other social challenges*. New York: Routledge, Taylor & Francis Group.

Laugeson, E.A., & Frankel, F. (2010). *Social skills for teenagers with developmental and autism spectrum disorders*. New York: Routledge, Taylor & Francis Group.

Orinstein, A.J., Helt, M., Troyb, E., Tyson, K.E., Barton, M.L., Eigsti, I.M., … Fein, D.A. (2014). Intervention for optimal outcome in children and adolescents with a history of autism. *Journal of Developmental & Behavioral Pediatrics, 35*, 247–256.

Ozonoff, S., Young, G.S., Landa, R.J., Brian, J., Brysaon, S., Charman, T., Chawarska, K., … Iosif, A.M. (2015). Diagnostic stability in young children at risk for autism spectrum disorder: A baby siblings research consortium study. *Journal of Child Psychology and Psychiatry, 56*, doi:10.1111/jcpp.12421.

Treffert, D.A. (2009). The savant syndrome: An extraordinary condition. A synopsis: Past, present future. *Philosophical Transactions, Royal Society London B Biological Science, 364*, 1351–1357. doi:10.1098/rstb.2008.0329.

Wong, C., Odom, S.L., Hume, K.A., Cox, A.W., Fettig, A., Kucharczyk, S., Brock, M.E., … Schultz, T.R. (2015). Evidence-based practices for children, youth and young adults with autism spectrum disorder: A comprehensive review. *Journal of Autism Developmental Disorders 45*, 1951–1966. doi:10.1007/s10803-014-2351-z.

6 Understanding Social Motivation

One of the most common myths about people with autism is that they have little to no interest in socializing with others. Many assume that autistic children and adults alike will mostly prefer solitary activities to those where interacting is required. For those who don't have exposure to or experience with many people with autism, these assumptions can lead them to being confused and even taken-aback by social attempts made by a person with autism. Looking at each autistic person differently to assess their individual social preferences is one way that clinicians can actively avoid making stereotyped assumptions about a lack of social interest among their ASD clients. By doing so they can begin to help their clients understand and manage their level of social motivation, so the clients can be as successful as possible in different areas of their lives.

It is important to understand the theory of social motivation as it applies to adults with autism and the psychological underpinnings that help us understand people in general. An assumption about this theory is that challenges in social thinking (cognition) are the result of social motivation deficits (Chevallier, Kohls, Troiani, Brodkin, & Schultz, 2012). When we can help teach, guide or coach a client towards understanding their level of genuine interest in others across a variety of social contexts, we can then begin to work towards how to improve perspective taking and empathic responding in these situations. In essence, many of the autistic social communication skills deficits can be addressed through social motivation. Hence the choice to begin the next series of treatment chapters with the overview on how this cluster of autistic symptoms can be effectively addressed at the outset of counseling.

If we continue to pay attention to ASD-only research and assumptions, we may be missing the bigger picture of understanding human behavior on a broader spectrum than autism alone. As clinicians who practice from a culturally competent framework, we are responsible for taking a neurodiversity approach to our clients by seeing how general psychological explanations of the human condition can apply to our work with autistic adults. Let's explore the primary and ASD focused theories about social motivation before diving into assessing and treating different social motivation needs.

Theories of Social Motivation

The most robust model of personality theory in the social and behavioral science research is the Big-Five factor structure (Goldberg, 1992). According to the research, this theory identifies five areas of the most common personality traits humans use to interact with the world and one another. These factors that Goldberg identified are openness, conscientiousness, agreeableness, neuroticism, and extraversion. Most people don't necessarily engage in a formal assessment of these personality features, but many do commonly self-identify with some of them, in particular, about extraversion.

Extraversion is a personality factor that describes a range of differences in people's interest in being around or socializing with others. The range from high to low extraversion represents polar ends of this one personality factor. Low trait extraversion describes those who prefer solitude, feel tired after too much social interaction and dislike attracting the attention of others (Goldberg, 1992). Those who rate extraversion as low are likely referred to as introverted in lay or colloquial terms. High trait extraversion describes those who seek out social attention and become energized from their social interactions.

In new interactions with others, we are often attempting to identify early on if they exhibit introverted or extraverted personality traits. It is part of the lexicon of how we describe the process of understanding ourselves and others. Knowing one's degree of extraversion may be one of the first steps in conceptualizing the level of social motivation. People who are low in extraversion are likely to value social interactions but in a limited or specific manner and be less socially motivated than others who are high in extraversion.

In the context of providing services for adults with autism, social motivation refers to the level of interest in engaging in social interactions and relationships (Constantino & Gruber, 2016). When considering this in treatment, we're looking for the answer to the question "How interested is this client in the social landscape?" When the clinician finds it valuable, this can be assessed through a personality trait lens, through the Big-Five, and recommended ASD-specific assessment tools – such as the Social-Responsiveness Scale 2. In tandem, results from these assessments may be the key to clinically conceptualizing and collaborating with our clients about solutions for social motivation if it's an area that is negatively impacting them.

The social motivation theory of autism is one that puts into context a client's inherent interest in engaging in the social world. In an effort to better understand this theory of how interested people with autism are in social interactions, researchers have broken down social motivation into several constructs, including attention, seeking, and liking and maintaining (Chevallier, Kohls, Troiani, Brodkin, & Schultz, 2012). From a young age, most children with autism demonstrate difficulty orienting and attending to social sounds and faces, which speaks to differences in social attention (Elsabbagh et al., 2012). In addition to this, children and adolescents with ASD tend not to bid for others' attention in the same way as those without ASD do, and can be less responsive to verbal praise, which reflects differences in how they seek feedback from others socially (Demurie et al., 2011). Lastly, when compared with non-ASD individuals, they tend not to succumb to pressures related to impression management as easily. This may manifest in refusing to engage in social "niceties" such as greetings or adjusting their behaviors in order to maintain a positive reputation among others (Hobson & Lee, 1998; Chevallier, Molesworth, & Happe, 2012). Without these social maintenance skills, this aspect of social motivation can be interpreted as aloof or uninterested in others.

Given these observed and reported social motivation challenges, it is easy to see how autistic adults have been lumped into labels or stereotypes of "loner", "hermit", or "recluse". And even though these challenges are demonstrated in the research, it is important to be mindful and critical of the way they are interpreted. The reality is that even though adults with autism may demonstrate some of these traits, it does not mean they don't value or benefit from social interactions. Unfortunately, the myth that people with autism aren't social has been perpetuated by negative stereotypes in the media or news. Please be cognizant that this overgeneralization of a select few to the whole population is, in many cases, wrong.

Yet there are some proven characteristics that adults with ASD embody that lead them to be less motivated socially. In assessing social motivation and interest of autistic adults, researchers have found that adults with ASD are more likely to be asocial and asexual than their non-ASD counterparts (Silvia & Kwapil, 2011; George & Stokes, 2018). Those who are asocial, or high in social anhedonia, are different than those who are introverted or shy. Individuals who are asocial don't have a genuine interest in social interactions and relationships (Silvia & Kwapil, 2011). Most adults with autism self-report being interested in social interactions and relationships and would not identify as asocial.

Even though fewer autistic adults are asocial than they are low in social motivation, there is a range of different levels of motivation that helps depict a more complex picture. Some have low levels of social motivation but do value interactions with others with less frequency or intensity. For example, if the average person plans social outings with friends two to four times a month, a person with low social motivation may only seek out a get-together once a month or every other month. Even though low levels of social motivation should be acknowledged and respected, it's helpful to identify when this leads to isolation, loneliness and depression. Others have extra-high levels of social motivation, which can lead to other problems including anxiety or hyperactivity related to a need to interact more frequently than usual.

In some research these sub-groups of people with autism have been identified in different ways. One of those is the "active-but-odd" group (Chevallier, Kohls, Troiani, Brodkin, & Schultz, 2012). These are individuals who display authentic interest in others, are highly socially motivated, and are perceived as hyper socially motivated. This type will be explored later in our case study. Another sub-group is described as the "aloof" group, which describes those who are hypo socially motivated and don't seem interested in others (Chevallier, Kohls, Troiani, Brodkin, & Schultz, 2012). Because an autism diagnosis describes a heterogeneous group of people, it is incumbent upon us to determine the level of social motivation for each client to determine best treatment steps. A place to start the conversation about social motivation can be about the quantity and quality of social interactions and relationships that a client currently maintains and aspires to have in the future.

Quality or Quality?

Our expectations about the quantity and quality of our social interactions and relationships can often be unrealistic and unattainable for others. This is demonstrated in research about romantic relationships in which many partners or spouses describe expectations of one another that are nearly impossible to meet, especially when they are assumed instead of intentionally communicated. A common conflict between coupled partners arises when one or another engages in the expectation of mind-reading. Mind-reading is an assumption that one partner makes that leads them to believe the other knows their desires or needs without them being explicitly explained. Sounds like magic, right? It does not *feel* like magic when you're in an intimate relationship with the person who *should* know you the best but who does not automatically respond to these needs or wishes. When we assume a high level of intimacy in longer-term relationships it can lead to poor quality interactions in which we assume the other person can understand us without having to communicate it. This is just one way in which many people place qualitative expectations on the relationships we engage in.

In working with ASD adult clients, it is essential to understand how family and social dynamics may influence expectations about the quantity of social interactions. One family dynamic that can impact social motivation depends on the expectation of how much socialization the family member engages in themselves. For example, parents of an adult with autism may expect them to socialize a few times a week because of their own experiences or preferences. If they *had*, in comparison with their own childhood or young adulthood experiences, or *have*, based on current social activity, a high level of social motivation there's a tendency to assume that a matched or markedly similar level of social engagement is the best fit for their autistic adult. They want their loved one to feel connected socially and the frequency of social get-togethers is often an indicator of this. It is understandable that family members become concerned when these expectations for how often they socialize with others don't match.

If a higher frequency of social interactions is insisted upon or forced by family members or other loved ones, this dynamic can lead to a strain and potential rupture in the relationship. One thing that family members seek through counseling is the hope that we can influence a client's frequency of social interactions. This is tricky for the clinician who may understand that a person's level of social interest is, at least partly, inherently dictated and can only be influenced to a certain degree (Chevallier, Kohls, Troiani, Brodkin, & Schultz, 2012). This means that treatment can realistically focus on assessing the level of social motivation and in which areas the client would like to focus on their motivation to socialize. But it is essential to identify what they believe is their desired set-point for quantity of social interaction. If, or when, a parent or family member tries to force an increase in social motivation that is achievable or realistic for an adult with autism this may result in feelings of pressure and carries the risk of further demotivating their attempts at socialization. This can result in the opposite outcome the family members were hoping for. Therefore, approaching the construct of how much social motivation a client needs should be carefully considered and attempts to increase it must be well-planned.

It may be that clients with low levels of social motivation may be satisfying their own needs by engaging in fewer social interactions and relationships. These individuals may have one or two close friends with whom they spend time once every two or three months but mostly correspond electronically. Those with high levels of social motivation may get more enjoyment from frequent, in-person or electronic communications with friends and acquaintances alike. Time spent engaging in these social interactions and relationships will differ significantly and can be one of the first quantitative measures of how often and with whom social interactions occur (Laugeson, 2013). Yet, inherent in the above depiction of the highly and poorly socially motivated clients are qualitative factors that should not be ignored.

The quality of one's social interactions and relationships is hard to pinpoint for most people since these involve our subjective experience and reports of them. Qualitative features of most relationships are hard to verify, unless there is reciprocal feedback provided by people or a third party involved who can report on experiences in or about the relationship. Helping our clients identify some concrete ways in which the people in their lives provide them with shared experiences is helpful in assessing the quality of these relationships (Laugeson, 2013). We can also encourage our clients to elicit feedback from their friends or family members on the quality of their relationship. But this is often awkward, uncomfortable and difficult for most.

How many of us are in the regular practice of giving and receiving feedback to one another about the quality of our relationships? It's can be an uncomfortable process for most since it requires transparency and directness in a dynamic in which we hope others can read between the lines. For some, accurately interpreting the quality of a relationship can be difficult and this applies to adults with autism.

The literature on friendship quality has identified some categories and common characteristics for types of friendships – based on the level of intimacy or closeness – that shed light on to the quality of a relationship. The six core friendship characteristics as identified by researchers include self-disclosure, validation, companionship, instrumental supports, conflict, and conflict resolution (Yau & Reich, 2018). It is important to help characterize what these characteristics mean in tangible and concrete ways that are more easily identifiable through examples in our work with autistic clients. For example, self-disclosure looks like sharing information or secrets about yourself with another person that you might not share with anyone. Self-disclosure and sharing personal information should be done bidirectionally so that trust can be established in the friendship. This includes keeping secrets, which requires you don't share information that the other person asks you not to tell others. These concrete and specific rules for friendship may need to be explicitly taught and reviewed in treating adults with autism.

Using self-disclosure, without it being reciprocated by the other person, is likely an uneven friendship and it may be risky to continue engaging, in a deeper way, with that person. The importance of a shared relationship is an essential element not to be overlooked when working with ASD clients (Laugeson, 2013). Working through how self-disclosure and other elements of friendship need to be shared, can help prevent some significant social issues that arise from clients being taken advantage of or used by others.

Validation and companionship are other characteristics of friendship that can be represented through specific acts of mutual understanding and demonstrations of care. Being fond of and "getting" one another is an important characteristic of friendships. Companionship also refers to a commitment to spend time together and being loyal through the process (Yau & Reich, 2018). Being a trusted companion looks like returning the friend's attempts to contact you and, while spending time together, focusing on the pleasure or enjoyment they are getting from the interaction.

Instrumental supports in friendship include practical and measurable actions that one takes to help another person (Morelli, Lee, Armn, & Zaki, 2015); for example, bringing food for a friend who is ill or giving a friend a ride to work because their car broke down. These concrete supports are easily identifiable and likely the most seamlessly provided by those with autism. Yet, if this is only being performed from one person to the other, the friendship is likely not shared and therefore runs the risk of being bad quality. In the research, many have demonstrated that although instrumental support is useful it does not have the same impact on well-being as do other supports that are more emotional in nature such as validation and conflict resolution (Morelli et al., 2015). This will likely present a challenge for people with autism who prefer direct, concrete demonstrations of care to abstract, affective methods for communicating their fondness.

Conflict resolution is the final but essential characteristic of friendship. It requires one to be able to disagree and argue with a friend while maintaining the integrity of the relationship. This is difficult for many clients with and without autism; but autistic clients have specific barriers when it comes to resolving a conflict. Due to dichotomous thinking tendencies, people with autism often interpret arguments or fights with others as indicators that the relationship should end or has already terminated (Laugeson, 2013). Understanding that these conflicts are actually signs of healthy and more intimate relationships is a starting point to then begin building the essential skills for resolving conflict. Most people struggle with this in relationships, and adults with ASD, although their approach to it may differ, are no different in how they can benefit from learning about best practices in working through conflict to maintain relationships.

Beyond the core characteristics of friendships that are important to learn about and to be able to identify in others, there are different levels of friendship that can help enhance one's exploration of social motivation. This speaks to the kinds of friendships the client has or is looking for. Some clients may have hundreds of acquaintances when combining both offline and online relationships, but perhaps only one or two good or best friends – most people have only one or two best friends. Therefore, working through the levels of friendship (Table 6.1) to help understand how social motivation will impact what kinds of relationships to target is a helpful step.

Using this information in counseling can help inform how we psychoeducate our clients. It can also guide conversations about qualities of friendship that clients currently have in their relationships and to help them identify what they're looking for in new ones. Lastly, it can be helpful in highlighting discrepancies for those who are engaging in relationships they believe to be of high quality but that could actually put them at risk.

Although not every ASD adult is the same, there is some interesting research identifying how their symptomology may impact insight into the quality of social interactions. Individuals with autism can commit common errors in making assumptions about the quality of their social interactions and relationships (Mazurek, 2014). In a nutshell, they tend to over- or underestimate this quality. Within the group of people who overestimate the quality of their social interactions and relationships there is the assumption that there is much more intimacy than exists. This can manifest itself in a sharing of personal information that is unexpected, unwelcomed or misused by someone who has not earned the trust or loyalty of the ASD adult. As it connects to another area of social communication, these adults tend to be less socially aware.

In underestimating the quality of social interactions and opportunities, the person believes they have a lack of or absolutely *no* experiences or people with whom to share social interactions. With more probing and obtaining third-party reports, this can often be proven wrong; even if the client has only one close friend, they've come to discount the quality of that relationship and equated their experiences to nothing. This leads to feelings of isolation and, in some cases, an over-identification with the idea that they cannot rely on anyone for interaction or support when needed (Mazurek, 2014).

Table 6.1 Levels of friendship

Type of friendship	*Characteristics*
Friendly interactions	A brief greeting such as "hey" or smiling, nodding or acknowledging a person passing by. This may include a stranger or less well-known classmate, neighbor, co-worker.
Acquaintance	Someone you see regularly and exchange information with briefly and superficially. For example, "Hey. How are you doing today?" without a long or significant response. This could include a person you sit next to in the office, see at your regular coffee shop or teacher.
Casual friend	A person who you know from a structured environment, such as school or work, that you engage in more meaningful conversation or spend time with both in and outside of that environment. This includes a person with whom you hang out with in groups with usual but not high frequency and are less likely to spend one-on-one time together.
Good friend	A person who you deliberately spend time with in planned social outings either individually or in small groups. This friendship is defined by higher levels of trust and frequency of time spent than in the previous levels of friendship.
Best friend	A person who you deliberately spend the most amount of time with, specifically in one-on-one settings. Characteristics of this relationship involve the highest levels of trust and sharing intimate secrets with one another.

Note
Information adapted from model presented in Garcia-Winner and Cooke (2011).

And, as you might imagine, when it comes social awareness, these kinds of clients tend to be hyper-aware. Social awareness will be explored at length in the next chapter.

Examples of how clients can present in treatment vary but here are some examples that can shed light onto how these social motivation variables become a priority in treatment. For those who assume high-quality interactions and relationships too early on or inaccurately, they can be easily influenced, manipulated or taken advantage of in ways that makes them much more socially and sexually vulnerable (Sullivan & Caterino, 2008). Clients who I've worked with have been robbed of money and computers, convinced to engage in activities they don't agree with and gotten involved in sexual situations they were not expecting. The deficit in accurately being able to assess their level of intimacy with another person and the assumption that they are good or best friends can lead to traumatic events. These are usually the result of victimization and inflicted by perpetrators who identify early on that the person is an easy target (Fisher, Moskowitz, & Hodapp, 2013). When a client becomes the victim of a violent or non-violet crime this is a priority in treatment and likely requires consultation with legal, financial, or other services.

On the other hand, for those who assume a lack of quality social interactions, and relationships, they are often left thinking the worst of other's intentions. Or in some cases they feel isolated to the extent that they believe no one can support them even though there is some objective evidence to suggest otherwise. These individuals are likely not at risk of victimization or harm inflicted by others, but instead they report low self-esteem, hopelessness and symptoms of clinical depression (Kato et al., 2013). With those who become severely depressed due to their isolation, they are at risk for self-harm and suicide.

Please be mindful that the above examples of those who over- or underestimate the quality of their social interactions and relationships are not the most common that are presented. But they can and do occur for even the most intellectually gifted and seemingly aware adults with ASD. Owing to the significant consequences of both being harmed by someone else or engaging in self-injury or death, it is clear to see why assessing one's quality of social interactions as it relates to social motivation is an important matter.

A final consideration in quantity and quality of social interactions and relationships is how to conceptualize and respond to those that live primarily or only online. Internet-based interactions, friendships and dating is a current norm and growing trend with the advancement of technology. Online social opportunities are endless and can be an incredibly helpful and connecting tool for adults with ASD who find it harder to connect with others in face-to-face environments. Interactions that occur either primarily or fully online can provide both a real and false sense of intimacy and closeness, which has benefits and barriers to many people.

The internet, which was aimed at connecting people worldwide, has evolved to be a primary vehicle for how people meet others to engage in different kinds of relationships. From online dating services to friendship circles and support groups, the internet has been able to provide new opportunities for socially isolated people to connect with others in a different way.

In research conducted with teens, scientists have discovered that several of the key quality indicators for offline relationships exist in online relationships (Yau & Reich, 2018). These online interactions can enhance contacts and allows space and time for emotional reactions to take place and be responded to. For people with lower social self-esteem, online relationships via social media platforms help them gain social capital from the experience and help reduce barriers that exist in other social opportunities (Steinfield, Ellison, & Lampe, 2008). Among the many ways younger or emerging adults are utilizing their online relationships effectively is to strengthen their newly formed and existing offline or face-to-face relationships with friends (Subrahmanyam,

Reich, Waechter, & Espinoza, 2008). For older adults, cognitive benefits in working memory and executive functioning have been reported for those who use social networking sites versus those who do not (Myhre, Mehl, & Glisky, 2017).

Based on these potential advantages of online friendships and relationships, it is important for practitioners to see their value even if it contradicts personal beliefs. This is true when working with caregivers of adults with autism who are concerned with them having little or no face-to-face friendships but hundreds to thousands of online "friends". But it could also be that these online connections are the social life-force for the person, so conveying displeasure or dissuading them from continuing could be harmful. It is easy to dismiss online relationships as lower in quality, and in some cases they might be. There are some specific ways that counselors and family members can help autistic adults look for the barriers and risks of online relationships.

Yet there are also barriers and significant problems with the kinds of interactions that online-only relationships yield. One barrier that can quickly transition to bigger problems is that without meeting someone in person, it can be difficult to verify their identity. There are technologies that can help people overcome this barrier through video chatting and calling options. But even with these precautions in place there are individuals and organizations that exist to take advantage of others by creating false identities, rushing a sense of intimacy and then coaxing money or other resources from vulnerable parties, which can easily snowball into major financial and personal safety issues (Patchin, 2013). These can be sophisticated operations that pay people to play in roles with matching pictures and video chat experiences who are taking advantage of others primarily for financial gain via psychological coercion. The act of creating a false identity and misleading someone else about this persona for the intended purposes of taking advantage of them for a particular resource is known as "catfishing" (Patchin, 2013). It is one of the main risks of engaging in fully online social relationships that do not eventually result in face-to-face interactions and in-person relationships.

Be mindful of your response to online social interactions and relationships as this may influence your reaction to a client with ASD who primarily engages in this way. If you convey your disapproval of this form of interaction and relationships, you certainly won't be the first or last person to do so, which could break down lines of communication and create a strain in your relationship. Assessing any potential risks or safety issues in a non-judgemental way is an important first step in addressing this in treatment. From there it may be necessary to intervene if safety is a concern. If it is not a concern, the next step could involve exploring and informing the client of the potential benefits and barriers of engaging primarily or solely in online relationships.

Clinical Interventions

As we've reviewed in this chapter, clients who are struggling with social motivation are likely to fall somewhere in the range of hyper- to hypo-motivated, which is when we usually see presenting issues arise from this autism symptom. Interventions that aim to regulate those who are extra-motivated, and increasing the motivation for those who are isolated and lonely, are presented. Once these are reviewed the case study depicts the story of Laura, whose desires to regulate social motivation and behavioral challenges were the primary targets in counseling.

Regulating Hyper-Motivation

In choosing the most effective clinical tools for helping clients who are socially hyper-motivated, the research supports the use of didactic instruction, self-monitoring and utilizing feedback from a social coach (i.e., trusted person in their life). I find it helpful to consider sequencing interventions in this order to scaffold the learning and application of these skills. If the client moves onto self-monitoring too quickly before having both the declarative and procedural knowledge provided in the instructional piece, they may be less likely to succeed in regulating their motivation.

When it comes to the selection of skills that will be important to teach in this first stage of regulating those who are overly motivated this can be dictated by (a) the most common errors the client engages in or (b) the most common errors most people with social deficits commit. For a more structured and directive approach, many practitioners select the latter option and for an approach that is more client-centered the former may work best. If you are presenting lessons based on either approach it's helpful to know about those that are most common for this clinical presentation. These broadly include non-reciprocal interactions in face-to-face conversations, electronic communication and initiating hang outs and get-togethers.

The good news is that several excellent, evidence-based tools are published and readily available to help instruct clients in the steps for avoiding the above errors and replacing them with better skills. For ecologically valid skill instruction, the best tools available come from UCLA's PEERS® program, where there are both trade books and manualized treatment resources to help improve these common errors in hyper-motivation. The *Science of Making Friends* (Laugeson, 2013) and the *PEERS® Young Adult Treatment Manual* (Laugeson, 2017) along with the electronic resources with online videos and iOS app have excellent clinical utility.

Integrating these well-validated tools into social skills instruction will be helpful and are bound to teach clinicians about more than they assumed to know about navigating tricky social situations. Since social skills are complex and nuanced, many counselors aren't sure exactly how to teach them and these tools are essential to overcome our own barriers. For example, for those clients who over-engage with their peers it's helpful to inform them and demonstrate ways to share conversations with detailed and sequenced rules. This also applies for online or electronic communication in which adults can learn rules about when and how often to contact others before it becomes off-putting and ineffective. One of the best rules for regulating a tendency to go overboard with contact online is the two-message rule. The rule states that if you contact a potential friend twice without a response, it's time to move on. This could allow the person to respond in their own time or if they do not respond than making attempts to another person who may reciprocate is best.

Once a client has learned about and acquired the skills to improve their social hyper-motivation, the next step is to help them accurately assess their change efforts. This should be done through a combination of self-monitoring and social coaching. Assessing change efforts from the perspective of the ASD adult themselves actively involves them in the process and improves self-awareness while the social coach requires third-party reporting that helps promote accuracy in the monitoring process.

To engage in the process of self-monitoring is to trust oneself to report as honestly as possible, even when results don't work in your favor. This often leads clients in therapy to over-report on their own outcomes and adults with ASD are not precluded from this phenomenon. However, one protective factor against this tendency among autistic clients is an interest in rule-following and brutal honesty. This is one reason in favor of self-monitoring for this population. In the process of self-monitoring with accuracy, it is helpful to encourage the client to choose a tool they will use to record their change efforts, so they can be analyzed in treatment. These tools can vary from traditional paper and pen journaling to the utilization of smart phone apps. As long as there is a clearly stated goal and direction for what is being monitored and how, many ASD clients comply with self-monitoring and benefit from it. One of the primary benefits is improved self-awareness, which can influence confidence or self-esteem and is one reason why a social coach can serve as a support person.

A social coach is a consistent person in the ASD adult's life who they trust and who is socially savvy. I typically inform clients that choosing a social coach is their decision so as to help them identify someone they feel comfortable with processing successful and challenging social situations. The person can be in their personal lives and include someone from their family, such as a parent, sibling, cousin, or even a good friend. Clients often have a tough time choosing someone from their lives to serve in this role depending on their goals. For those who are more focused on dating and romantic relationships, it may be uncomfortable or awkward to select a parent in this role. The hyper-motivated client is likely to think they have a trusted person identified early on and then this may result in a person who's not as consistent a coach as they'd hoped. The social coach is ideally available at least once a week to review skills and goals in an effort to brainstorm successes and errors they either witnessed or are hearing about from the client. They can also serve in the role of practice partner during weekly check-ins and ask the client to rehearse before applying the skills to others. This allows for an additional opportunity for feedback outside of therapy. The main goals of incorporating a social coach are to (1) include third-party assessment and reporting to improve accuracy in treating social motivation, and (2) to help generalize skills learned in counseling into the "real world".

Enhancing Hypo-Motivation

Socially demotivated clients have other identified goals in therapy: to more effectively engage in social interactions and relationships. In many cases, clients are looking for ways to decrease social isolation or improve their ability to socialize in situations that are essential for their success. This may result in a focus on enhancing skill deficits in the workplace, where socialization is part of or related to the job, or with family. Be mindful that after assessing a level of motivation that is lower than desired (i.e., the client is hypo-motivated instead of depressed) it's important to avoid imposing our own biases about how much socializing they should be engaged in. When other mental health issues have been effectively ruled out, respect the autonomy of our clients who are less motivated than others.

After a client's level of social motivation has been assessed as low, it's helpful to explore in what ways they are in fact motivated by social opportunities. If the socialization tends to result in a positive outcome in another area for which the client has higher levels of motivation this can be helpful. For example, one of my client's primary interests is movies. He loves science fiction movies about space exploration and adventure. He enjoys watching movies alone or with his best friend. His love for the movies drove him to seek out a job based on this interest and has been working in movie theaters for the past five years. This client has low social motivation as demonstrated by being satisfied hanging out with his best friend every other month, which is below average levels of social get-togethers for his age range. Yet, when it comes to work, he successfully engages in conversations with patrons and co-workers, which he truly enjoys. He seems to get his social quota met at work which leaves other areas of socialization, in his personal life outside of work, to be less important. Because he is motivated to keep the job he loves, social interactions and relationships with co-workers or supervisors are easier and more enjoyable for him.

If a client wants to enhance the frequency of social interactions and number of quality relationships, it may be helpful to identify and use extrinsic motivators (i.e., interests). These motivators can help to connect them with activities that get them involved in those interests and with other people at the same time. For these clients, identifying what warrants their social attention and maintenance is key for improving other areas of social communication, especially social cognition (Chevallier, Kohls, Troiani, Brodkin, &

Schultz, 2012). Therefore, it may be necessary for the client to identify groups online or in-person that come together, primarily for the purpose of engaging in the interest or activity. Joining interest-based groups based on intrinsic motivators for the ASD adult can be challenging to do if their interests are niche or rare. As counselors, it may be helpful to interpret how these rarer interests could be connected to mainstream or commonly shared interests. For example, if a client is interested in World War II, I might suggest a lecture or discussion at the local history museum. Even if the topic isn't on that particular war, the client may have never conceptualized that their interest in this historic event may help them connect with others who also enjoy history. Owing to dichotomous tendencies, this may not have occurred to the client and may provide the opportunity to improve their social motivation based on an intrinsic interest. In this role we can help serve as resource-locators and share information about community activities we're familiar with or that we find in research we conduct.

Case Example

Laura is a 19-year-old woman who is bubbly, gregarious and enthusiastic about starting counseling. She has experienced challenges in school and at home with behavioral issues that have created compulsive hygiene routines. These routines involve the application of makeup in layers, the insistence on changing hair styles throughout the day and asking the same question repeatedly. Her primary goal for therapy is to help her make and keep friends and get a boyfriend.

The family describes that Laura's history with her peers is sordid. In the beginning of new relationships, Laura can engage with others and get them interested in hanging out together. She's been able to do this successfully through activities based on her interests such as pottery class and the choral group she belongs to. During these group experiences, she meets a peer she likes, and they initially appreciate her enthusiasm and like her in return. She considers herself skilled at initiating friendships, based on a childhood friend she has, and dating, based on a brief romantic relationship.

After Laura spends more time with a potential friends or boyfriends, the dynamic rapidly shifts, which results in a strained relationship or complete rejection. Strains lead Laura to frequently get into conflicts or arguments with existing friends, which she tries to resolve but is often unsuccessful. She has been rejected multiple times because of her continued enthusiasm and insistence on interacting or hanging out with such frequency that the others begin to feel pressured and even harassed. Laura has earned a reputation in our group activities for texting or direct messaging her "friends" multiple times without a reply. Laura's mom has overheard other girls in these groups giggling and making comments about her being "obsessed" and "a creepy stalker".

In this case, it is important to work with both Laura and her mother, who is actively involved in parenting while Laura lives at home and completes her first few years of coursework at a community college. The relationship between Laura and her mom is strong; after learning about the value of a social coach, Laura immediately chooses her mother to serve in this role. Their closeness is a resource for helping her generalize skills but also needs to be attended to in case overreliance occurs. In treating Laura's hyper social motivation, involving her mother as social coach will be imperative, so her mother can serve to help Laura generalize the skills to the real world that Laura will learn in treatment. Therefore, Laura's mother will be provided with materials and offered conjoint sessions or consultative services as a supplement to Laura's therapy services.

Before conducting a formal assessment of social motivation, as provided by results from the Social Responsiveness Scale 2 results, a subjective assessment of the presenting issues can help a clinician hypothesize where Laura lands on this continuum. After considering both the formal objective and subjective assessment of Laura's social motivation it is determined she is hyper-motivated. This had led to a recent history of relationship rejection, including a break-up from a short-lived romantic relationship, and a decrease in social opportunities where they had previously existed (i.e., dance class). Laura can benefit from a combination of didactic social skills instruction, rehearsal and feedback from the clinician and social coach.

Ideally this would be provided in a group format, as this has been proven most effective for improving social skills for young autistic adults. Laura is able to join a local PEERS® group, which provides her with the opportunity to receive targeted treatment for improving ASD symptoms. Once she completes this treatment, Laura and her mother return for individual counseling to follow-up specifically to address her desire to socialize more than recommended in PEERS®. There are some issues that, even though they were addressed in this treatment, Laura still struggles to apply. Laura has a tendency to take the rules and instruction provided and exaggerate them; she can benefit from reviewing lessons specifically related to regulating her hyper-motivated behaviors in social situations.

The clinician focuses on the most common errors made by Laura, such as conversation hogging and the two-message rule in online or electronic communication (Laugeson, 2017). In order to best review these lessons, the counselor uses a combination of PEERS® videos and handouts to serve as reminders about the skills she learned. Laura seems to remember many of the lessons but then, when rehearsed to determine procedural knowledge, it is clear that the application of these skills can be improved with additional practice in session and opportunities in the real-world.

It is recommended that Laura engage in counseling once a week with her mother who can join sessions during the last 15–30 minutes. This time will include a review of the most important coaching feedback observed in counseling and ways that her mom can continue to coach her in other contexts. Her mother reports feeling uncomfortable with constructive feedback because she doesn't want to "give Laura low self-esteem or make her feel bad about herself'. The counselor reviews best-practice in social coaching, which ensures that the feedback provided starts with encouraging efforts or any successes and then goes on to ask open-ended questions about what Laura could have done differently. This can help shift coaching moments from punitive experiences to a collaborative growth process for Laura. It also may help Laura's mom be more motivated to provide her coaching since she previously viewed it as an adverse experience because of her belief that it was only about "correcting Laura".

Now that Laura's mom is ready to be actively engaged in social coaching, Laura can also be provided with additional tools for self-monitoring. The question is, how will Laura best be prepared to report on her level of social motivation through self-monitoring? The self-monitoring process can be individualized and for Laura this will include self-disclosure and keeping a social motivation log. One component of self-advocacy is self-disclosure, during which time a person can explain themselves to help other people understand them better and improve interactions. Laura chooses to partially self-disclose when interacting with others by making a brief statement such as "Just so you know, sometimes I get excited to hang out with you. If I message you too much, just tell me and I'll back off." In the process of self-disclosure, Laura lets the other person know she's self-aware of her "quirk" and gives them the chance to feel more comfortable being direct with her instead of automatically rejecting her. This does not guarantee that rejection won't occur but could prevent it from happening as frequently.

Lastly, Laura decides she wants to log her weekly level of social motivation as tracked by how many messages or texts she's sent her friends and checked how many times she broke the two-message rule. By monitoring the frequency of her attempts to contact others she can quantify how often this is happening and detect errors she might be committing in the process. She's also asked to track one social interaction or relationship during the week where she demonstrated an improvement or setback in social motivation, so this can be processed in session. This opportunity for feedback from the clinician can enhance the self-monitoring process by providing feedback and tweaks that improve what happens with Laura between sessions.

Laura waivers with how willing she is to respond to her mother's attempts at social coaching. When Laura has just experienced rejection, it is harder for her to successfully receive feedback because she is emotionally flooded. Therefore, in weekly session work with both Laura and her mom, it is helpful to establish some ground rules for when and how social coaching will be most productive. After collaborating, Laura decides on a code word she can use in the moment when her mom attempts to coach her and she's not emotionally ready. Due to her repetitious behavioral tendencies, it's important to establish with Laura that this code word can be used once to communicate her need for space but that when it is brought up at a later point it cannot be avoided with continued repetition of the code word. This helps give Laura a tool for managing her reactions and while not stigmatizing her when her social coach may be too intrusive for her taste.

Managing Laura's social motivation levels is a continued effort and work in progress since her hyper motivation levels have been years in the making and are tied to some behavioral repetition that can be addressed simultaneously. By focusing both on how she can best handle her behavioral compulsions and social motivation, Laura learns to effectively self-disclose in a way that helps others understand her actively-odd ways. She and her mother are also continuing to learn how to work through social coaching (a) during designated times of the week so Laura can prepare herself to accept and apply the feedback and (b) in a way that allows Laura to feel encouraged through the process.

References

Chevallier, C., Kohls, G., Troiani, V., Brodkin, E.S., & Schultz, R.T. (2012). The social motivation theory of autism. *Trends in Cognitive Sciences, 16*(4), 231–239. doi:10.1016/j.tics.2012.02.007

Chevallier, C., Molesworth, C., & Happe, F. (2012). Diminished social motivation negatively impacts reputation management: Autism Spectrum Disorders as a case in point. *PLoS ONE*, 7, e31107.

Constantino, J.N., & Gruber, C.P. (2016). *Social Responsiveness Scale – second edition (SRS-2) [manual]*. Torrance, CA: Western Psychological Services.

Demurie, E., Roeyers, H., Baeyens, D., & Sonuga-Barke, E. (2011). Common alterations in sensitivity to type but not amount of reward in ADHD and autism spectrum disorders. *Journal of Child Psychology and Psychiatry, 52*, 1164–1173.

Elsabbagh, M., Mercure, E., Hudry, K., Chandler, S., Pasco, G., Charman, T., ... BASIS Team (2012). Infant neural sensitivity to dynamic eye gaze is associated with later emerging autism. *Current Biology, 22*, 338–342.

Fisher, M.H., Moskowitz, A.L., & Hodapp, R.M. (2013). Differences in social vulnerability among individuals with autism spectrum disorder, Williams syndrome and Down syndrome. *Research in Autism Spectrum Disorders*, 7, 931–937. doi:10.1016/j.rasd.2013.04.009

Garcia-Winner, M., & Cooke, P. (2011). *Socially curious and curiously social: A social thinking guidebook for bright teens and adults*. Santa Clara, CA: Think Social Publishing.

George, R., & Stokes, M.A. (2018). Sexual orientation in autism spectrum disorder. *Autism Research, 11*, 133–141.

Goldberg, L.R. (1992). The development of markers for the Big-Five factor structure. *Psychological Assessment, 4*, 26–42.

Hobson, R., & Lee, A. (1998). Hello and goodbye: A study of social engagement in autism. *Journal of Autism & Developmental Disorders, 28*, 117–127.

Kato, K., Mikami, K., Akama, F., Yamada, K., Maehara, M., Kimoto, K., ... Matsumoto, H. (2013). Clinical features of suicide attempts in adults with autism spectrum disorders. *General Hospital Psychiatry, 35*, 50–53. doi:10.1016/j.genhosppsych.2012.09.2006.

Laugeson, E. (2013). *The science of making friends: Helping socially challenged teens and young adults*. New York: Wiley.

Laugeson, E. (2017). *PEERS® for young adults: Social skills training for adults with autism spectrum disorder and other social challenges*. New York: Routledge.

Mazurek, M.O. (2014). Loneliness, friendship and well-being in adults with autism spectrum disorders. *Autism, 18*, 223–232. doi:10.1177/1362361312474121.

Morelli, S.A., Lee, I.A., Armn, M.E., & Zaki, J. (2015). Emotional and instrumental support provision interact to predict well-being. *Emotion, 15*, 484–493. doi:10.1037/emo0000084.

Myhre, J.W., Mehl, M.R., & Glisky, E.L. (2017). Cognitive benefits of online social networking for healthy older adults. *The Journals of Gerontology: Series B, 72*, 752–760. doi:10.1093/geronb/gbw025.

Patchin, J.W. (2013). *Catfishing as a form of cyberbullying*. Cyberbullying Research Center. Retrieved from https://cyberbulling.org/catfishing-as-a-form-of-cyberbullying.

Silvia, P.J., & Kwapil, T.R. (2011). Aberrant asociality: How individual differences in social anhendonia illuminate the need to belong. *Journal of Personality, 79*, 1315–1332.

Steinfield, C., Ellison, N.B., & Lampe, C. (2008). Social capital, self-esteem, and use of online social network sites: A longitudinal analysis. *Journal of Applied Developmental Psychology, 29*, 343–445. doi:10.1016/j.appdev.2008.07.002.

Subrahmanyam, K., Reich, S.M., Waechter, N., & Espinoza, G. (2008). Online and offline social networks: Use of social networking sites by emerging adults. *Journal of Applied Developmental Psychology, 29*, 420–433. doi:10.1016/j.appdev.2008.07.003.

Sullivan, A., & Caterino, L.C. (2008). Addressing the sexuality and sex education of individuals with autism spectrum disorders. *Education and Treatment of Children, 31*, 381–394.

Yau, J.C. & Reich, S.M. (2018). Are the qualities of adolescents' offline friendships present in digital interactions? *Adolescent Research Review, 3*, 339–355. doi:10.1007/s40894-017-0059-y.

7 Enhancing Social Awareness

As children we begin to understand our place in social situations through the guidance of our parents or caregivers and our peers. In adulthood there is an expectation that we have learned about our place in the social landscape and mastered the best way to understand ourselves and others. In autism assessment and treatment, social awareness informs how a person understands their place in the social landscape and how they navigate it (Constantino & Gruber, 2016). The ability to become aware of our position in social situations requires the pre-requisite skill of self-awareness.

The construct of self-awareness is described in different terms across the social sciences. These include social self-efficacy and self-perceived social competence. Despite the use of different clinical or technical terms, self-awareness is viewed as a strong determinant of a variety mental health outcomes. Social awareness puts the construct of self-awareness into a context that narrows it more specifically to how someone views themselves in the social landscape. Even with this narrowing, social awareness is just one way to describe our ability to assess our social place.

Albert Bandura labeled this concept as perceived self-efficacy (Bandura, 1993). Others describe social awareness in terms of social self-efficacy and perceived social competence (Galanaki & Kalantzi-Azizi, 1991; Kolb & Hanley-Maxwell, 2003). Accuracy in social perception is a related concept that is referenced in the literature. In work on these analogous concepts, most researchers have found that with more accuracy in perceived social self-efficacy and competence the people are better able to manage their behavioral problems and successfully apply skills across different social situations. Yet, other research into these concepts argues that the human condition requires people to have positive illusory thoughts about themselves and how they fit in so that they can optimize well-being (Taylor & Brown, 1988). Therefore, when it comes to awareness about our social interactions and relationships, people are generally able to identify a few characteristics accurately, while maintaining some level of illusion about how we fit in socially.

We all have certain blind spots when it comes to being aware of our own strengths and weaknesses. When it comes to our challenges, many of us are shocked about how others interpret the way we interact socially. For example, one might have the perception that they are an effective listener because they practice skills they identify as being characteristic of such. When someone else speaks, they take in what the other person says by remaining quiet and not interrupting. Both of these things can be important to good listening, but these things on their own are rarely enough for someone else to feel heard and understood. When assessing from another perspective, this same person's friends or family members report that in conversation that person doesn't provide minimal responses neither do they make consistent or intermittent eye contact. The lack of these responses in combination with the others is what ultimately leads to them feeling unheard. When a person does not feel listened to or heard and the other person feels like they've done their best to provide a listening ear, this leads to confusion and frustration for everyone involved. The listener feels defeated ("I thought I was doing my best") while the speaker feels ignored ("All I wanted was their attention").

This exemplifies a common conflict that can arise in any relationship but may be more pervasive when one of the parties is diagnosed with autism and has impaired social awareness. Social awareness involves one's ability to assess the role we play in social interactions and relationships (Constantino & Gruber, 2016). This psychological skill requires a person to accurately assess where they fit in with different social groups or scenarios. When someone is high in social awareness it is easier to identify our own successes and errors in social situations, which some clinicians argue is required to be successful in relationships. Even though social awareness is different from self-awareness, the two are inherently connected. Better self-awareness is likely to result in more accurate social awareness (Mazurek, 2013). Understanding your role in the social landscape first requires the ability to identify one's own strengths and challenges. Yet the social sciences have determined that, for most people, especially in the area that they experience the most challenges, it is a struggle to accurately assess themselves.

Social scientists have made efforts to uncover what happens to both low and high performers in different domains when they assess their own abilities. The finding that is most important when conceptualizing clients is to understand that low performers, those who demonstrate lower skill levels in a domain, typically over-report their performance (Dunning, Johnson, Ehrlinger, & Kruger, 2003). They rate themselves better than their higher performing peers. The phenomenon that helps explain some of the reasons for which poor performers have little insight into their performance has been coined the Dunning-Kruger effect (Schlosser, Dunning, Johnson, & Kruger, 2013). At the beginning of their research on awareness, scientists hypothesized that both poor and top performers would have difficulties identifying their weakest areas of performance. As you can see, they discovered quite a different finding. They were not expecting top performers to under-evaluate how others perceived them and poor performers to over-evaluate how they perceive themselves.

The core symptoms of ASD typically lead autistic adults to perform poorly in the social realm. Because of their low performance in this area, they may be likely to over-estimate their skills in social interactions, which can lead to an additional challenge (Gillespie-Lynch et al., 2012). When someone is able to knowingly acknowledge their issues, other people they socialize with feel more comfortable. When a person is blind to their own challenges there is likely to be tension and, with time, conflict will likely arise. Therefore, the double whammy of (a) being a human who is (b) impacted by autism may make it more difficult to accurately self-assess. It will now be helpful to understand how impairments in social awareness specifically impact people with autism and implications for treatment.

Social Awareness in ASD

Social awareness deficits related to an ASD diagnosis describe specific core symptoms that are connected to the larger domain of social communication. Since this area of symptomology is considered one factor of social communication it will be referred to in that context throughout this chapter. To be eligible for a diagnosis of autism, a person needs to exhibit difficulties with reciprocating socially and emotionally and have challenges with integrating nonverbal communication into their repertoire (American Psychiatric Association, 2013). Social awareness is therefore the ability to pick up on or notice social cues that are often sensory in nature (Constantino & Gruber, 2016). When someone is unaware of how their lack of turn-taking in a conversation or misinterpretation of nonverbals in a relationship impacts other, this is typically where social awareness problems arise.

As discussed in Chapter 6, about social motivation, social awareness functions on a similar continuum. Clients with ASD may present with extraordinarily high (hyper) to low (hypo) levels of social awareness. One's level of awareness often is *influenced by* or can *directly influence* (the chicken or the egg analogy) co-morbid mental health issues. It is important to understand how this can present in counseling by highlighting the extreme ends of the continuum with the knowledge that most of the clients we will see in counseling fall somewhere in between. The reason this chapter (and others) takes this approach to understanding social awareness is because most risk is associated with the extreme, hyper, and hypo, presentations of the core social symptoms of ASD.

If you have already read Chapter 6 you know that we began by reviewing the overly (hyper) motivated clients first. When it comes to social awareness, we'll start with those who are less (hypo) aware. This is because being low in social awareness often comes with a high level of social motivation; when a client is socially hyper-motivated, they tend to be hypo-aware.

How this then translates into a client's clinical presentation is what we need to be assessing in treatment. A client who is hyper-motivated to socialize tends to make a lot of attempts at interacting or initiating relationships. In most situations the hyper-motivated client is not attending to how their skill performance may be impacting their ability to be successful in their attempts.

So, they continue to persist in new interactions or old ones without an accurate sense of how their performance is contributing to their social errors or failures. In these attempts, they often fail to realize that the skills they're applying are ineffective and are a prime cause of rejection. They may be keen to blame-seek or find other reasons to explain why social interactions and relationships fail. A lack of or deficit in social awareness is likely what continues to propel them to continuously make new attempts. If they were aware that their social performance was leading to these rejections, they may not be as willing to make additional, future attempts. Clients with different levels of social awareness are likely to present with co-occurring disorders that differ depending on whether they are hypo- or hyper-aware.

Autistic adults who are socially hypo-aware are those who are more likely to exhibit symptoms of hyperactivity, inattention and anxiety (Antshel, Zhang-James, & Faraone, 2013). Without a good sense of understanding of their role in social interactions, this leads them to bounce around from person to person in an effort to play the numbers game. This often translates to a logical model being applied to the social world, such as "the more people I try to socialize with, the better chance I have at being successful". This faulty logic leads to social errors that result in someone who repeatedly tries "too hard, too soon", pushes other people's limits and boundaries and are perceived as acting as if they're "all-over-the-place", flighty or even desperate. Others perceive these behaviors as anxious or hyperactive and it may be that clients are clinically presenting with these symptoms in addition to autism. Anxiety disorders and ADHD are two of the most common co-morbid conditions for people diagnosed with autism (Vohra, Madhavan, & Sambamoorthi, 2017). If social awareness levels are low, this may be a rationale to screen for clinical significance of anxiety or hyperactivity that can help inform treatment.

One reason to assess for this early on is that if symptoms of anxiety or hyperactivity aren't treated, skills training related to social awareness may not be feasible or realistic. Anxiety and hyperactivity can prevent effective learning and application of skills that would improve self-awareness in social circumstances (Laugeson & Frankel, 2010). Be mindful that for clients whose anxiety is the primary presenting issue, improving social awareness may be contradictory to improving their symptoms because it might enlighten them to the social challenges they exhibit and then fuel harmful anxious thoughts and behaviors.

Clients who are hyper-socially aware struggle with opposing co-occurring challenges related to isolation, loneliness and depression (Mazurek, 2013). Loneliness research defines the experience as a state of perceived disconnection from others that leads to difficulty finding meaning in one's life (Tiwari, 2013). Isolation is a state of complete or almost complete lack of connection from others that is more objectively defined through how much contact one experiences with others. Those who experience a lonely state of mind are often isolated, so there is an overlap between the two.

Yet, for some who's social awareness is inaccurate, they may report being lonely but are not socially isolated. These individuals may be around others with whom social contact is possible, but they are not able to take advantage of social opportunities to create meaningful connections. People with autism often have excellent memories that can include sensory experiences that they relive when recalling an event (Lorenz & Heinitz, 2014). When many of one's memories have themes of rejection, abandonment or bullying, these can feed one's desire to stay safe by disconnecting from others even when exposed to them. Alternatively, some autistic adults will be isolated or isolate themselves for similar reasons.

Imagine being regularly reminded and acutely aware of your deficits as the result of rejection throughout childhood and adulthood. The focus on the self in this presentation is to protect oneself and therefore avoid others. Yet, the intention of self-preservation can often lead to a consequence of such social isolation that significant depressive symptoms are a primary presenting issue. Low self-perceived social competence results in more depressive symptoms and is predictive of depressive symptoms in the future (Vickerstaff, Heriot, Wong, Lopes & Dossetor, 2007). Those who feel severely hopeless and helpless about the possibility of connecting with others in the social landscape can engage in self-harm and suicidal behaviors.

In fact, researchers report autistic adults are at a significantly higher risk of suicide when compared with the general population (Cassidy et al., 2014; Hannon & Taylor, 2013; Hedley, Uljarevi , Wilmot, Richdale, & Dissanayake, 2018; Segers & Rawana, 2014; Zahid & Upthegrove, 2017). Because of this it is our obligation as clinicians to assess for depression and suicidality among those clients who report higher levels of social awareness even if we consider this a potential treatment strength or resource. If hyper-social awareness leads to depression, the administration of assessments and interventions that directly address this life-threatening treatment concern. It's also important to consider how social-awareness can be improved for individuals with elevated awareness. This likely requires a focus on current, safe social supports and relationships that can be expanded upon, and avoiding too much emphasis on connecting with new people. New relationships can be unstable and if a depressed, hyper-aware client attempts to initiate them and experiences rejection this could be a tipping point that leads to the worsening of depressive symptoms and increases the potential for self-harm or suicide.

Several protective factors can be cultivated that either already exist in a person's life or can be added to prevent increased likelihood to become severely depressed and engage in self-harm or suicidal behaviors. One of these identified in research and clinical practice is to have clients engage with quality social supports when available and appropriate (Granello, 2010). The practice of recognizing loved ones in the client's life who can provide layers of support in critical times of need, helps clients learn about alternatives to what may seem like otherwise bleak or deadly outcomes.

Social supports can be a part of a lifesaving strategy for many clients who are suicidal because of the ability to help another person cope with their difficulties. In other clinical scenarios, social support can be more generally helpful because those who have relationships in which each person can rely on the other is linked to improved physical and mental health outcomes when dealing with life stressors (Bradbury & Karney, 2004). These health benefits are available to clients when they're able to identify the people in their lives with whom they can give and get social support. The reality is that social support is not one-dimensional or directional; it involves several components and requires reciprocity between two people who serve as supports to one another.

The dimensions of social support include instrumental and emotional types. Instrumental social support is the concrete help required to provide suggestions, give advice, or deal directly with problem solving. Emotional social support is provided through encouragement, affirmation and validation of one's experiences in the world (Devoldre, Davis, Verhofstadt, & Buysse, 2010). People with autism are typically accustomed to and comfortable with instrumental social support due to its concrete nature.

Many people with autism, and other classified disabilities, are accustomed to receiving a variety of supports provided to them. The kind of support that is provided is typically logistical, educational, and behavioral in nature. From an early age, the focus on getting therapy to aid with language needs, fine motor skills and academic learning can be all-consuming. Therefore, emotional support may end up taking a back seat to other priorities, especially when they don't appear to be as impairing as some other needs. A client with autism may clearly be able to identify the ways in which their family supports them financially or logistically, but it may be difficult for them to identify the abstract nature of how they receive emotional support.

One typical sign of autism is trouble expressing a full range of emotions. This can create a dichotomy of emotional expression that results in pronounced lability, with comfort expressing positive emotions or negative emotions but with little variation in between (APA, 2013). Emotional needs are often addressed when providing support for the autistic person if or when they have trouble coping with changes or transitions. Because of their different expression of emotional experiences, some people who could serve as social support may not be able to do so effectively because they aren't equipped with the skills or tools to do so.

Emotion coaching from a young age to help a child identify and regulate emotions can be an essential tool, yet many parents or caregivers aren't prepared to or are comfortable with this concept (Gottman, Katz, & Hooven, 1997). All this is included to say that, many times, adults with autism who come to counseling may not be accustomed to receiving emotional support from their loved ones despite years of receiving myriad other types of support. In other cases, the client who has been emotionally supported by their family members or caregivers may not be able to identify how or to process the experience of it.

Generally speaking, social support allows people in meaningful relationships the ability to be both the recipient and provider of help that is needed to live a healthy life. Although social support plays a central role in healthy relationship functioning it is complex and difficult to effectively provide (Rafaeli & Gleason, 2009). For autistic adults, the process of receiving and providing social support can often be riddled with the social communication issues mentioned above, which precludes them from reaping its benefits. Another part of social support is being able to be socially aware of who is valuable and who should be avoided in the process of providing and receiving support.

One of the risks of encouraging social relationships among people with autism is that in many cases they aren't aware of the other persons' intentions in that relationship. The deficit in perspective taking and theory of mind, discussed at length in Chapter 8, can result in the misidentification of a person as trusting and valuable. A person with autism often assumes that someone else's intentions match their own. If they are honestly interested and attracted to another person, their feelings are then projected, and it is assumed that these feelings are mutually shared (Kristen, Rossmann, & Sodian, 2014). Unfortunately, this leads them to being taken advantage of when they've mistakenly chosen to spend effort, time and resources supporting a person with bad intentions.

As clinicians we need to be comfortable aiding our clients in the process of accurately evaluating their relationships for the ones they can truly rely on for social support. Once we've helped them rule in those people in their lives who are valuable in this capacity, it is important to help them learn not only how to effectively receive emotional social support but to provide it. One of the best ways to help clients through this process is through social communication skill training. Clients with low social awareness often haven't been able to identify the strengths and challenges they have in listening to others, making them feel understood or communicating their own wants, needs or desires. This includes the process of working through conflicts and disagreements with others, which can be complicated but a necessary quality of good relationships.

By engaging in the process of learning about social supports, clients with autism can improve their social awareness in two ways. First, they gain an understanding of who they should (and should not) rely on and who will benefit by relying on them. Identifying how these relationships help them navigate the social world is a significant step towards social awareness. Second, they can explore their own strengths and challenges in social communication and relationships in order to better develop what they already do well and learn new ways of relating. In understanding how to best use their internal resources and apply tools they acquire through counseling and educational resources, problems in social awareness can be better managed.

Interventions for Treating Social Awareness Impairments

In assessing and planning to treat the social awareness cluster of social communication deficits with clients, it is critical to begin with the identification and treatment of any co-occurring conditions as a priority. Failing to recognize and treat the most common comorbid symptoms of debilitating anxiety, depression or interfering hyperactivity issues could be detrimental to the client with ASD (Vohra, Madhavan, & Sambamoorthi, 2017). In fact, if we do not sequence and pace treatment in a manner that prioritizes and spends time on these issues, any efforts towards improved social awareness may exacerbate these other conditions. Consider the hyper-socially aware client who is also socially anxious. If treatment began by focusing on identifying their most common strengths and challenges, the approach may inadvertently encourage them to ruminate on aspects of themselves they already fear negative evaluation about. Therefore, treating anxiety related to these fears and avoidance is a necessary preliminary step in sequencing of treatment.

Once primary diagnoses or co-occurring symptoms improve, treatment to enhance social awareness as a social communication tool can begin. The following interventions highlight how narrative therapy, video-based approaches and a specific cognitive behavioral strategy can be used to help people with ASD in counseling.

Storytelling

A starting point for exploring social awareness is through self-awareness. An approach to doing this can be to help the client create a narrative of their lives through creative expression. One benefit to utilizing creative and improvisational outlets is that this can also help manage anxiety and depression (Muller, Schuler, & Yates, 2008). Each client will differ in their preferred method of creative expression, but some common ways to creating a life story or narrative could be through written timelines, stories, poems, or songs. Alternatively, a client may decide to tell their life story through movement, such as dance or miming, or via visual art, such as painting or photography. This narrative should have a social focus that helps the client and clinician focus on what their story looks like as far as relationships, interactions, and how they've navigated different social situations are concerned. Be mindful that without a specific focus or prompt, this intervention may get lost in other details of the client's lives that could be important to learn about but may not be as relevant to social awareness as it could be. This is a helpful start to understanding social awareness so that the clinician can learn more about the client and segue naturally into examining the characteristics and roles the client has played socially.

To accomplish the goal of more closely examining one's characteristics in social situations, the clinician can elicit a conversation and create an accompanying list of the client's self-identified social strengths and challenges. The combination of processing this verbally with the visual aid of a list can be useful for a future step in this process. It may be that the client can respond to questions about this with some objectivity by identifying a few in both categories. In another subset of clients, they may only be able to identify their good social qualities, and these may or may not be perceived as such by others (hypo-aware). And with other clients who have faced more perceived rejection, identifying strengths will be harder (hyper-aware). Asking these questions, will help the clinician assess where the client is on the range of social awareness.

For clients who fall into the first subset, it will be helpful for them to use their social coach and other trusted people (i.e., counselor, siblings, close friends) to see their list and provide feedback. In this case, the process is likely to go best if the clinician has been able to meet with and train the social coach on the best methods for delivering feedback. In this ideal scenario, the social coach can provide constructive feedback, which includes encouragement of at least one strength that the client has included on their list by reflecting on an example of a time they've witnessed this. Following this up with corrective feedback is an important next step for clients with this level of social awareness so that they can learn about a difference in self and others' perception. Therefore, the social coach will then point out one way they have noticed the client faces challenges, and will gently guide them to understanding how this could be an opportunity for growth. Engaging in this gentle guidance can be done through Socratic questioning. For example, "Was there a time when ______ was a problem for you?". This gives the client the opportunity to respond and, if they don't, the social coach can provide an example of when they noticed it led to an issue that is relevant or important to the client. Many hypo-socially aware clients have effectively repressed memories of emotionally distressing experiences, so this may be required to help learn from previous mishaps or errors.

All of this can also be led by the clinician, especially when modeling for a social coach or if a social coach is not readily available. The disadvantage with this is that mental health professionals do not have exposure to a client's real-world interactions as much as a social coach would. But we can still serve in this role through concrete examples of interactions with others we observe, our own interactions, and through personal life examples reported by the client.

Video-Based Interventions

Another tool that can be used to improve social awareness is video feedback, which can lead to video self-modeling. With the technological access that most people have with smart phones, creating videos of oneself is easier than ever. One way to assess through video data is to have the client record themselves interacting with others at home in a natural setting. Obviously recording oneself is never as "natural" as you would hope for, but it can allow the client to see themselves in a "mirror" that aids them in identifying strengths and challenges they otherwise may not be able to. For example, if a client videos themselves having dinner with family and views it afterwards they may better be able to notice when they were taking over a conversation or seemed like they weren't listening. The mirror that a video recording can provide for the client can help paint an accurate picture of the successes and errors they demonstrate.

Video-modeling can be a complementary strategy and a step in treatment that helps with social communication skill training (Gelbar, Anderson, McCarthy, & Buggey, 2012). In the example above, the client is now aware of their social tendency to look down at their plate while others are talking and take over the conversation without asking questions to others. Now that they've identified these problems, counseling can help them learn how to provide intermittent eye contact and ask a family member a follow-up question. Learning these skills can be aided by the client recording himself practicing these skills in therapy or with the family during dinner. The video model can then be watched a few times before dinner or other social interactions to refine and master these skills. This strategy may also help clients who are more hyper-socially aware to see their strengths "in action" and can motivate them to join social activities where these skills can be effectively used to connect with others.

Bibliotherapy

One of the best extra therapeutic tools that can be used for clients who are hyper-socially aware is the use of bibliotherapy (Turner, 2013). Many clients who are overly concerned about how others are perceiving them, yet are not socially anxious, can benefit by having validating and affirming experiences. Learning about other adults with ASD who have been successful in a variety of social and professional settings is one way to accomplish this. Some clients are willing to read autobiographical accounts while others prefer watching videos or learning through movies. This can aid in the process of having clients learn about how to use their eccentricities and autistic mannerisms to their advantage through follow-up discussions and processing in therapy. In learning more about autistic people's lived experiences, a next step to bibliotherapy could be helping the client to connect with others who share their interests or ASD. Seeking out social support and recreational groups where clients can connect with others, with or without autism, can help them to best find their place or role in structured and semi-structured social situations.

In the aforementioned interventions, the preliminary ground work to developing a socially aware foundation is laid. Once this occurs, ongoing examination and disputation of old social patterns and tendencies can help monitor social awareness and deepen the social awareness work. There are several models for analyzing situations, identifying evidence and challenging assumptions in therapy. In Chapter 3, the positive psychology approach of journaling and disputation could be applied to enhancing social awareness if it were to focus on social interactions and relationships.

Cognitive Behavioral Assessment of Psychotherapy

Another model that can be useful to enhance social self-awareness is the cognitive behavioral analysis system of psychotherapy (CBASP). CBASP is an intervention that reports effectiveness for those with persistent mood disorders and personality or relationship issues (McCullough, 2015). In a guided and structured approach, this intervention asks the client to identify and analyze one distressing situation that has occurred within the last week. Once oriented to the process and practiced in session with the practitioner, in future sessions the client will complete a form that rates their satisfaction with the outcome of a situation of their choice. During the session, the clinician can take about 20 minutes of time to work through the CBASP model. During this time the client identifies the thoughts and behaviors exhibited that prevented them from getting the outcome they desired, which allows them to identify alternatives that would have been more helpful in getting the desired outcome. This concrete, evidence-based approach takes a scientifically sound, habitual process that can help develop an automatic process for the client to ultimately engage in. It can result in the client coming to session already having thought about and identified alternatives that they've then applied to a successful end. The ultimate goal for effective treatment is to have the client become their own therapist through fourth-order change, and through repetition of CBASP a more socially self-aware client who can work through solving their own problems is possible.

The following case study highlights these interventions and how they can be applied to help a client with hypo-social awareness issues and depression. Another component of this client's clinical picture is how the intersectionality of gender orientation and ASD can impact the direction of treatment. Terry's story as a gender non-conforming adult with autism hopes to convey how the individualization and sequencing of these interventions can result in positive treatment outcomes.

Case Example

Terry is a 32-year-old, autistic, gender non-conforming client who is presenting to counseling due to significant social isolation and overwhelming feelings of hopelessness about the future. Terry uses the pronouns they/their/them. Jordan is Terry's roommate and only friend, who they met at a local community support group five years ago urged them to counseling. Terry's roommate is worried about recent behaviors they're demonstrating which include not leaving the house for several days in a row and not having any other social support besides Jordan.

During the initial phone call with Terry to set up the intake, it is significantly challenging for them to provide substantial responses or secure an appointment. The counselor completes a brief self-harm and suicide assessment during the call and Terry explains that they are experiencing extreme lethargy and difficulty motivating themself to do much, but they have no plan or intention to take action to hurt or kill themselves. The extremely low level of motivation is likely a protective factor in Terry taking any action on their depressed state. In the same phone call, Terry asks if they're roommate, Jordan can join the initial session and that it might be helpful to get more information from their perspective. Terry reluctantly admits that Jordan is "better at this than I am" and the counselor explains that if they consent to them being involved that an arrangement for this can be worked out in the first session.

Upon meeting Terry, they present well-groomed and dressed, with a more masculine gender expression as marked by traditional men's clothing and physical appearance (i.e., short hair and some facial hair). Based on their physical appearance, it is clear to see why most people call Terry "him or he" when making assumptions about their gender. Even though Terry's affect is flat and they report low energy levels and mood, they are still able to demonstrate moments of relief through a smile or self-deprecating comment, which allows for them to seem appealing and approachable. It is easy to see that Terry is probably perceived as likeable to others even with the significant depressive symptoms they're currently experiencing.

In assessing Terry's history, it becomes clear how their social deficits during formative years led them to face social ridicule and rejection from peers. Terry reports their parents explained that they had autism around the age of ten even though they were diagnosed at seven years old. They were afraid of telling Terry earlier than this because they already "stood out" because "she was a tomboy". During school Terry didn't fit in well with the girls because of a lack of similar interests while the boys were somewhat accepting but never truly embraced Terry as part of their group.

Terry was smart and got along well with teachers, adults and older children at their school. They were able to survive by compensating for challenges in connecting to their peers by charming those in charge and flying under the radar just enough that the ASD symptoms weren't noticeable during earlier childhood. Terry's intellect and ability to relate to adults got them by until more peer interaction was required, at which point their social challenges caused concern and triggered an assessment at the school.

When Terry had to interact with peers they were ridiculed and bullied for being a teacher's pet or brown-nose. Terry was able to master group assignments and tried to teach other kids the right and wrong ways to do things, which gave them another reason to make fun of or harass Terry. This, in conjunction with their feeling misplaced between the girls and boys in their class, created more reason for Terry to face social challenges. Even after Terry learned about their diagnosis, which their parents were hoping could help them better understand themselves and navigate social relationships, they continued to have a hard time with peers. In addition to the discovery of their ASD diagnosis, Terry further explored their gender expression by changing their hair cut more drastically and dressing only in masculine clothing. The continued shift toward gender non-conformity provided more opportunities for Terry to get verbally bullied by peers at school as they all entered adolescence. Terry reports that throughout almost all middle and high school years they had one or two friends and that most social interactions with others were negative, so they found it "not worth it to even try". This pattern of retreating in order to avoid further rejection and ridicule continued on into young adulthood. During college, Terry sought counseling for the first time to help manage their depression because of two episodes of not being able to leave their room for three- to four-day long stretches.

After being treated for depression through medication management and brief therapy, Terry found acceptance in gender non-conforming groups they located, and found a community of others with whom they could connect and feel safer. Over the past eight years, Terry began to feel more comfortable with others and even sought out a relationship with one person romantically. The start of the relationship seemed to go well until an incident occurred, that they are confused about and unsure why it resulted in the other person breaking it off after just two months of dating. This occurred one year ago and both Terry and Jordan, their roommate, report their symptoms of depression, isolation and loneliness have increased significantly since then. The rejection in this relationship reminded Terry of the experiences they'd faced around the time of their diagnosis in childhood. They want to better understand how autism might be impacting their depression and social relationships.

In prioritizing Terry's treatment goals related to social awareness, addressing their depressive symptoms will be essential. After more mood stability is achieved, the ASD symptoms related to social communication and awareness can then be treated. Therefore, the first step in treatment should focus on alleviating symptoms of depression. It will be important to assess Terry's openness to psychotropic medical intervention that can complement therapy. After exploring Terry's feelings about psychiatric care, the counselor was able to clarify some of the research supporting this, which seemed to reassure Terry and they became open to seeing a local psychiatrist. Finding a practitioner who understands the needs of a gender non-conforming individuals is a must. In addition to this, medical intervention, talk therapy among adults with ASD is proven effective for treating depression. This should take a directive approach through cognitive behavioral interventions (CBT) that have been proven effective with this population.

The method of cognitive behavior analysis system of psychotherapy (CBASP) is a concrete tool that can help Terry examine weekly situations that are helpful and harmful for improving symptoms. Starting with this consistent, concrete approach is one that Terry takes to well and is able to explore one to two situations during each session. The combination of medical stabilization and talk therapy with a focus on building more helpful thoughts and behaviors to ameliorate their symptoms has improved Terry's symptoms of depression. Both Terry and Jordan have reported more energy, scheduled outings in public and improved sleep. CBT techniques to help ameliorate depressive symptoms can secondarily target social awareness goals. With CBASP, desired outcomes can shift from a focus on improving depression to social awareness and communication.

As Terry's depressive symptoms improve it is important to integrate interventions that will improve their self and social awareness. In order to understand their role in the social landscape, Terry will work with the therapist, Jordan and others in their life to create a narrative about their strengths and challenges. Terry is intellectually gifted and passionate about music. Their self-awareness narrative takes the direction of having them write and record a song about themselves. This improved self-awareness can help Terry understand how to utilize their strengths to connect with others socially and navigate around their challenges as best as possible. From here Terry is to share the narrative with trusted others in their life, like Jordan. Jordan is then able to better understand Terry and provide them with feedback about how they perceive their strengths and challenges. With third-party feedback about how others see Terry, they will be able to continue to grow in their self-awareness since the Dunning-Kruger effect will likely lead Terry to judge themself more poorly where other perceive them as quite strong. Remember that with higher performers, the tendency to judge more poorly is likely and this seems to apply to Terry.

As Terry's self-awareness improves, they will begin to embark on learning about other adults with autism. This can begin with models of individuals who have published memoirs, self-help guides or autobiographies with whom Terry can connect. The clinician suggests some resources, such as Temple Grandin's *Thinking in Pictures – My life with Autism*, John Elder Robison's, *Switched On: A Memoir of Brain Change and Emotional Awakening*, or David Finch's, *The Journal of Best Practices*. From these resources, Terry reports learning more about how autism can function as an advantage and the ways in which they will be able to use their interests and abilities to connect with others socially and professionally. Terry appreciated how embracing John Elder Robison is of neurological differences, how David Finch used his humor to connect to his spouse, while Temple created a successful career out of her interest in animals. These success stories helped instill hope for Terry and learn specific ways in which they can build on their attributes to improve their life in similar ways.

Terry is also recommended to research information about individuals who identify as LGBT-ASD. Recent research suggests that autistic adults report increased gay, lesbian, bisexual and asexual orientations and decreased heterosexuality (George & Stokes, 2018b). Gender identity and orientation differences are also found among people diagnosed with ASD when exploring rates of gender dysphoria and comparing them with non-ASD adults (George & Stokes, 2018a). Providing psychoeducation and references to research could be helpful for Terry since they are intellectually curious. This may also help to contextualize and affirm their experience as a gender non-conforming individual who is aiming to improve self- and social-awareness.

Through the combined efforts of processing weekly situations in counseling, seeking feedback from Jordan and self-exploration through bibliotherapy and learning about others like them, Terry is finally able to solidify what might have led to the recent break-up and other social relationship strains. They are unsure of how to successfully both give and get social support from their relationships. This is highlighted through feedback from Jordan and Terry's parents. For many years, Terry has identified a few trusted people on whom they rely, but they do not understand how to communicate their needs consistently. This leaves their loved ones and caregivers frustrated that Terry "won't let me in" and "I try to support Terry, but they are so closed off". In times of crisis, Terry will finally relent and ask for help but waits until a breaking point to do so, which is frustrating to others. In return, Terry is not attending to when their loved ones need support from them. Without the ability to lean on others for support nor understand when others need to lean on them, Terry's relationships have been stunted. Now, armed with this awareness of how social relationships can improve by added social support, Terry can learn how to improve this skill.

In order to enhance their social support, Terry engages in skills training, which improves their ability to show understanding (empathy) to others when they demonstrate signs of distress. They also learn how to communicate, through self-disclosure, to others about this challenge and how the other can send them signs when they need support. Terry's social communication in expressing themselves when distressed can improve through focused social skills training as they navigate how to manage a disagreement or recover from an argument with a loved one. As Terry continues to learn more about themselves, by gaining social awareness, their prognosis improves. Terry is now able to identify when depressive symptoms may be worsening, ask for help from others and be available to loved ones when they need support.

References

American Psychiatric Association. (2013). *Diagnostic and statistical manual of mental disorders* (5th ed.). Arlington, VA: Author.

Antshel, K.M., Zhang-James, Y., & Faraone, S. (2013). The comorbidity of ADHD and autism spectrum disorder. *Expert Review of Neurotherapeutics*, *10*, 1117–1128.

Bandura, A. (1993). Perceived self-efficacy in cognitive development and functioning. *Educational Psychologist*, *28*, 117–148.

Bradbury, T.N., & Karney, B.R. (2004). Understanding and altering the longitudinal course of marriage. *Journal of Marriage and the Family*, *66*, 862–881.

Cassidy, S., Bradley, P., Robinson, J., Allison, C., McHugh, M., & Baron-Cohen, S. (2014). Suicidal ideation and suicide plans or attempts in adults with Asperger's syndrome attending a specialist diagnostic clinic: A clinical cohort study. *The Lancet Psychiatry, 1*, 142–147.

Constantino, J.N., & Gruber, C.P. (2016). *Social Responsiveness, Scale – second edition (SRS-2) [manual]*. Torrance, CA: Western Psychological Services.

Devoldre, I., Davis, M.H., Verhofstadt, L.L., & Buysse, A. (2010). Empathy and social support provision in couples: Social support and the need to study the underlying process. The *Journal of Psychology, 144*, 259–284. doi:10.1080/00223981003648294.

Dunning, D., Johnson, K., Ehrlinger, J., & Kruger, J. (2003). Why people fail to recognize their own incompetence. *Current Directions in Psychological Science, 12*, 83–86.

Elder Robison, J. (2016). *Switched on: A memoir of brain change and emotional awakening*. New York: Random House.

Finch, D. (2012). *The journal of best practices: A memoir of marriage, Asperger syndrome, and one man's quest to be a better husband*. New York: Simon and Schuster.

Galanaki, E.P., & Kalantzi-Azizi, A. (1999). Loneliness and social dissatisfaction: Its relation with children's self-efficacy for peer interaction. *Child Study Journal, 29*, 1–22.

Gelbar, N.W., Anderson, C., McCarthy, S., & Buggey, T. (2012). Video self-modeling as an intervention strategy for individuals with autism spectrum disorders. *Psychology in the Schools, 49*, 15–22.

George, R., & Stokes, M.A. (2018a). Gender identify and sexual orientation in autism spectrum disorder. *Autism, 22*, 970–982. doi:10.1177/1362361317714587.

George, R., & Stokes, M.A. (2018b). Sexual orientation in autism spectrum disorder. *Autism Research, 11*, 133–141. doi:10.1002/aur.1892.

Gillespie-Lynch, K., Sepeta, L., Wang, Y., Marshall, S., Gomez, L., Sigman, M., & Hutman, T. (2012). Early childhood predictors of social competence of adults with autism. *Journal of Autism and Developmental Disorders, 42*, 161–174

Gottman, J.M., Katz, L.F., & Hooven, C. (1997). *Meta-Emotion*. New York: Routledge.

Grandin, T. (2006). *Thinking in pictures: My life with autism*. New York: Vintage Books.

Granello, D.H. (2010). The process of suicide risk assessment: Twelve core principles. *Journal of Counseling & Development, 88*(3), 363–371. doi:10.1002/j.1556-6678.2010.tb00034.x.

Hannon, G., & Taylor, E.P. (2013). Suicidal behaviour in adolescents and young adults with ASD: Findings from a systematic review. *Clinical Psychology Review, 33*(8), 1197–1204.

Hedley, D., Uljarević, M., Wilmot, M., Richdale, A., & Dissanayake, C. (2018). Understanding depression and thoughts of self-harm in autism: A potential mechanism involving loneliness. *Research in Autism Spectrum Disorders, 46*, 1–7.

Kolb, S.M., & Hanley-Maxwell, C. (2003). Critical social skills for adolescents with high incidence disabilities: Parental perspectives. *Exceptional Children, 69*, 163–180.

Kristen, S., Rossmann, F., & Sodian, B. (2014). Theory of own mind and autobiographical memory in adults with ASD. *Research in Autism Spectrum Disorders, 8*, 827–837. doi:10/1016/j.rasd.2014.03.009.

Laugeson, E.A., & Frankel, F. (2010). *Social skills for teenagers with developmental and autism spectrum disorders: The PEERS treatment manual*. New York: Routledge, Taylor & Francis Group.

Lorenz, T., & Heinitz, K. (2014). Aspergers – Different not less: Occupational strengths and job interests of individuals with Asperger's syndrome. *PLoS One, 9*, e100358

Mazurek, M.O. (2013). Loneliness, friendship and well-being in adults with autism spectrum disorders. *Autism, 18*, 223–232. doi:10.1177/1362361312474121.

McCullough, J.P. (2015). *CBASP: A distinctive treatment for persistent depressive disorder: Distinctive feature series*. New York: Routledge Taylor/Francis.

Muller, E., Schuler, A., & Yates, G.B. (2008). Social challenges and supports from the perspective of individuals with Asperger syndrome and other autism spectrum disabilities. *Autism, 12*, 173–190. doi:10.1177.136236130786664.

Rafaeli, E., & Gleason, M.E. (2009). Skilled support within intimate relationships. *Journal of Family Theory & Review, 1*, 20–37.

Schlosser, T., Dunning, D., Johnson, K.L., & Kruger, J. (2013). How unaware are the unskilled? Empirical tests of the "signal extraction" counterexplanation for the Dunning-Kruger effect in self-evaluation of performance. *Journal of Economic Psychology, 39*, 85–100. doi:10.1016/j.joep.2013.07.004.

Segers, M., & Rawana, J. (2014). What do we know about suicidality in autism spectrum disorders? A systematic review. *Autism Research*, 7(4), 507–521.

Taylor, S.E., & Brown, J.D. (1988). Illusion and well-being: Psychological perspective on mental health. *Psychological Bulletin, 103*(2), 193–210.

Tiwari, S.C. (2013). Loneliness: A disease? *Indian Journal of Psychiatry, 55*, 320–322. doi:10/4103/0019-5545.120536.

Turner, N.D. (2013). Bibliotherapy and autism spectrum disorder: Making inclusion work, *Electronic Journal for Inclusive Education, 3*.

Vickerstaff, S., Heriot, S., Wong, M., Lopes, A., & Dossetor, D. (2007). Intellectual ability, self-perceived social competence and depressive symptomatology in children with high-functioning autistic spectrum disorders. *Journal of Autism & Developmental Disorders, 37*, 1647–1664.

Vohra, R., Madhavan, S., & Sambamoorthi, U. (2017). Comorbidity prevalence, healthcare utilization and expenditures of Medicaid enrolled adults with autism spectrum disorders. *Autism, 21*, 995–1009. doi:10.1177/1362361316665222.

Zahid, S., & Upthegrove, R. (2017). Suicidality in autistic spectrum disorders: A systematic review. *Crisis: The Journal of Crisis Intervention and Suicide Prevention, 38*(4), 237.

8 Building Social Cognition Skills

Alison Bourdeau and Ali Cunningham Abbott

Humans are social animals who ultimately seek connection, companionship, and belonging with one another. As social beings, we have automatic, neurological processes occurring on a constant basis which help us communicate and cooperate with others (Harari, 2015). One of these processes helps us interpret how other people experience us, which then allows us to respond accordingly. This happens in almost all of our daily interactions from brief, watercooler conversations with co-workers to the deeper conversations we have with clients. In fact, some of these happen so automatically we aren't consciously aware of the thought processes involved until they're pointed out.

Think back to the last conversation or social interaction you had with someone in a work or casual social setting. While interacting in this scenario you were automatically, unconsciously wondering (a) if the person or people you were interacting with enjoyed the time with you, and (b) if they'd want to repeat a similar experience in the future. In fact, as I write this book, I'm experiencing this same process because I'm hoping that (a) you are enjoying the guide (or at least finding it useful), and (b) wondering if you would read something of mine again or this would lead to us collaborating in the future. Even though writing a book isn't the most social endeavor, it still has me applying social thinking skills to determine if it will be as successful as I hope. This is how much social cognition is infused into the automatic processes of our human experience, because, ultimately, in most of our personal and professional efforts we seek out connection, approval, and belonging in our social groups.

This allows us to understand how others are experiencing us and if we should invest time and energy into doing this again. Most of us assume that others should be able to interpret *a lot* about us by reading between the lines of the messages sent. And this works for many people who can easily take another person's perspective. Yet, for those who are neurodiverse this can be a struggle (Sperry & Mesibov, 2005). People with autism and other neurological differences fall into this category because of a deficit in cognitive processing that impacts social thinking.

Social cognition (or thinking) is the ability to interpret and adapt to changes in different social interactions, circumstances and environments. As discussed in Chapter 7, if social awareness is understanding our role in the social world, social cognition is the ability to identify and interpret the changes in that social environment as they occur, as well as manage your own responses to those changes (Constantino & Gruber, 2012). So much of social thinking requires us to pick up on covert clues that people intentionally or unintentionally communicate to one another. The social cognition subscale of the Social Responsiveness Scale-2 examines an individual's ability to pick up on the subtle social nuances of social communication that are not explicitly stated. The manual for this describes social cognition as being able to think and interpret in reciprocal exchanges and behaviors. The questions within this particular subscale all relate to the ability to identify these subtle shifts within reciprocal interactions and make the adjustments needed in order to successfully maintain interactions and relationships.

The differences in responses across environments can be challenging for individuals with ASD, as distinguishing the subtle shifts in expectations across settings can be complex. Individuals with ASD can have deficits in social cognition, which has implications for effective social interactions and overall social competence. It is estimated that anywhere from 70–90% of communication is nonverbal, and the communication that is verbal is often not explicit or direct (American Speech-Language-Hearing Association (ASHA), 2018). If someone has challenges in reading social cues and nonverbal communication, there will certainly be an impact in the ability to identify social rules for engagement. Humor in the form of sarcasm, idioms, and exaggerated statements made in jest can be misinterpreted or overlooked by this population. The very nature of social communication is often in opposition with the manner in which the autistic brain processes the world (Baron-Cohen, 2002). Due to social conventions, individuals tend to use "white lies" or nonverbal messages to communicate in order to avoid discomfort or confrontation and to nurture and maintain social relationships. This can prove to be confusing for autistic adults who may not communicate in this manner. Furthermore, it can lead to misunderstandings, miscommunications, and disruptive circumstances in school, work, and leisure activities.

Adults with ASD without deficits in intellectual functioning will experience challenges in the ability to develop and maintain social relationships (Howlin, Goode, Hutton, & Rutter, 2004). In fact, they report similar social outcomes to their ASD and intellectually disabled peers. If their ability to understand and process intellectually is average to above average, what is causing these similar results? Understanding how social intelligence and thinking is impacted is one of the keys to assessing where the client's level of social cognition is and to planning interventions for improving this deficit.

This lack of connectedness has implications for overall quality of life, with these individuals experiencing higher levels of depression, isolation, and loneliness than their neurotypical (NT) peers (Kirby, Baranek, & Fox, 2016). As discussed in previous chapters, the neurodiversity movement developed the term "neurotypical", and it first appeared in 1994. It refers to individuals without a developmental disorder such as autism or exhibiting typical neurological development. This term had been adopted by the autism community in order to refer to those without autism. In more recent times, the advent of the neurodiversity movement has brought forth another moniker, neurodivergent (ND). This shifts away from the idea that those with autism have atypical brain development and supports the idea that there is room in society for different types of thinkers. The important message here is that autistic people are different than most, not less than.

Social cognition includes various skills such as interpreting nonverbal cues, taking another person's perspective, recognizing emotional responses, showing understanding, and solving social problems (Laugeson & Ellingson, 2014). If there is a deficit within the individual's ability to replicate any of the aforementioned elements, there will be an impact on their ability to socially communicate with success. While this might not be noticeable initially, over time this deficit becomes more obvious, which is generally why the maintenance of social relationships can be more challenging than just the initiation. The strategy of masking or camouflaging is often utilized by the individual in order to blend in or fly under the social radar. Individuals with ASD utilize strategies such as behavioral observation and mimicking in order to have an understanding of what is socially acceptable behavior. The challenge is that while the individual might possess the declarative knowledge of social interactions, it is with the procedural knowledge that the proverbial wheels fall off (Bellini, 2008).

Social cognition, like social motivation and awareness, is part of the social communication domain of autism but also warrants its own focus in treatment. Let's see how social motivation, social awareness and social cognition connect. Individuals that have challenges in social cognition will demonstrate high to low levels of social motivation and awareness. The intersection of these can manifest in a few different presentations.

How social motivation and awareness connect to social cognition reflects how and when a person is paying attention to cues that will allow them to shift directions within the interaction in order for it to be successful. Autistic people are likely stuck looking at a situation from their own perspective, which prevents them from considering how others are perceiving the same event or interaction. The following scenario is an example of a challenge that can arise when challenges in social motivation and social cognition coincide.

One example is that the client's parent frequently contacts them to see if they've hung out with a new friend or socialized lately. As a result of this "hounding", the client may be more befuddled and frustrated because they can't understand why their parents are interfering in this way. From the parents' perspective, they are concerned that due to low motivation their adult child is isolated or lonely and from the client's perspective they don't want to be bothered. It is not part of the client's automatic process to pause and consider why their parent might be concerned and interfere. This is a complex cognitive task that requires deliberate practice and action on the client's behalf. A similar principal is likely to occur as a result of the intersection of low levels of social awareness and social cognition deficits.

In low levels of social awareness, clients will typically struggle to understand why they are being rejected even after they've made multiple attempts at building relationships. These are the clients who tend to face rejection frequently but may not face as many negative mental health consequences because they're not aware of their role in the process. They may blame others or circumstances for their rejection, an indicator that they have low social awareness. Yet, it is also likely an indicator of moderate social cognition impairment. When the client is unable to take the perspective of the people in the circumstance to see what their impression is of them, this is a deficit in social thinking. In this way, social awareness and social cognition levels will impact one another.

For many who have mild ASD symptoms there may not be an obvious indication that there is a disability present. This is why this presentation of ASD falls under the category of invisible disabilities, like many other mental health disorders. There is no visible or obvious indication to others, so aberrant behaviors will often cause individuals to react negatively through rejection because of a lack of awareness of their differences. Visible disabilities allow others to be aware of more obvious challenges during an interaction. This is not the case with ASD, and this often has negative implications for the individual. Social errors are less tolerated and explicit instructions on how to change course are not taught in adulthood. Being caught in this "social purgatory" can lead to a higher risk of suicidal thoughts, behaviors, and completion (Cassidy, Bradley, Bowen, Wigham, & Rodgers, 2018). Understanding social cognition and how its deficits impact individuals with ASD is critical to the development of appropriate treatment to target areas for intervention and prevention of self-injurious and suicidal behaviors.

Our clients with ASD may be making authentic attempts to connect with others without considering the others' perspective and they likely don't even realize this is occurring. Without the knowledge of this, some clients will isolate, and the safety within that isolation will reinforce itself. Without specific, targeted interventions to mitigate these deficits, they can go largely unchecked. This isolation and low social engagement can lead to depression. Takara and Kondo (2014) found that adults with atypical ASD traits and depression are at a higher risk of suicide. The importance of social connectedness cannot be understated. Adequate social cognition skills are necessary for engaging successfully with others. So, when these skills are impaired, social connectedness is negatively impacted.. Because clients with ASD have inherent social cognition impairments, it is important to understand the origins of this from a neurological perspective as well as the interventions that can help improve this deficit.

Perspective Taking and the Theory of Mind

The Theory of Mind (ToM) is the understanding of an individual that their perceptions of events differ from those of others who are experiencing the same event. This theory has been researched to a great extent to better understand how this cognitive difference presents itself in individuals with ASD. The Theory of Mind describes the mental function of perspective taking that has been well-documented as a cognitive deficit for many people diagnosed with ASD (Baron-Cohen, Leslie, & Frith, 1985). In some of the literature this has been named "mind blindness", which describes the impairment people with Theory of Mind deficits face when they attempt to interpret what others are thinking (Senju, Southgate, White, & Frith, 2009). For most people this is an innate ability. For people with autism, it is not.

Instead, social thinking is an ability that can be developed with deliberate treatment that targets it. In reviewing the current outcomes of research related to ASD and ToM, it is clear that further attention to social cognition needs to be given to adults (Baron-Cohen, 2002). The need for interventions for adults past the age of 30 is critical, as many of them have "fallen through the cracks" and have not been able to benefit from earlier interventions due to issues of access or age of diagnosis. The following are some of the clinical methods for assessing Theory of Mind among people with autism.

The Reading the Mind in Eyes Test (RTMIET) (Baron-Cohen, Jolliffe, Mortimore, & Robertson, 1997) was developed to help identify social thinking deficits. At the time, researchers believed there were no tests in existence that were sensitive enough to detect the subtle cognitive differences that are common with mild forms of autism spectrum disorder. In some literature this is also referred to as high functioning autism (HFA). A common sentiment within the autism community at the time was that there might be a "perceived social competence" for adults with mild ASD, or those who had received the earlier used diagnosis of Asperger syndrome or HFA (Greenberg, 2017). This can lead to gaps in treatment and the right support to improve the skill sets for adults who don't have moderate to severe symptoms.

Kleinman, Marciano, and Ault (2001) took the RTMIET-R one step further by including a verbal auditory component in assessment. The authors incorporated perception that required participants to identify emotions through verbal intonation. This required them to focus not on *what* you say but *how* you say it. Utilizing the two stimulus modalities of visual and auditory testing, they developed the "Mental State Voices Task". The individuals were given pictures of male and female eyes and asked to choose from a set of words what they felt the corresponding emotional state was. The authors stated that there were psychometric issues with the initial test. The first version had issues with having a forced choice between two options, leaving too narrow a range of scores.

This narrow range of scores caused ceiling effects, which led to a decreased sensitivity to detect individual differences and a loss of power. It also had issues with being able to distinguish individuals with what the authors considered the "broader phenotype" or "lesser variant" and individuals with AS/HFA (Lamport & Zlomke, 2014). Additional issues related to the items themselves, having basic and complex mental states, items that related specifically to eye gaze, and having the two words be semantic opposites. Adjustments were made in all of these areas for the revised test, and it was indicated that the adjustments increased sensitivity in the instrument.

The combined purpose of assessments such as this are to look into the subtle elements of social skills such as social cognition, and identify competence and areas in need of further intervention. These assessments were utilized mainly in research, and in later years a tool was developed in order to look at the various elements related to social skills, and to identify areas of challenge to apply specific interventions. The SRS-2 is the tool that emerged from this earlier research, and, unlike the former tools mentioned, this one has more utility in both research and clinical settings.

Baron-Cohen, Wheelwright, Hill, Raste, and Plumb (2001) believed that deficits are masked due to the learning of compensatory strategies. The use of such compensatory strategies such as "masking" or "camouflaging" can lead others to believe that the individual with ASD is now asymptomatic. In reality, deficits persist across the lifespan, and can change depending on the complexity of the social environment at different developmental stages (Magiati, Tay, & Howlin, 2014). Put plainly, an individual with a diagnosis of ASD is not cured, but they may at different stages of their lives receive the needed interventions to have deficits shift to less significant levels of impact. Some believe this is due to the use of masking and camouflaging that can be applied for those clients with fewer social awareness deficits.

Social Cognition Interventions

While a variety of interventions exist, interventions that are evidence-based and ecologically valid should be utilized whenever possible. The rationale for this is to avoid taxing out one's frustration tolerance for interventions. Within this population there is a potential to color similar experiences with a broad brush, and this can be both helpful and hurtful to the counselor navigating treatment of different clients with autism. The use of interventions that are evidence-based provides the practitioner with information regarding efficacy, reliability, validity, and replicability (Wong et al., 2013). Therefore, these should be your broad-brush stroke interventions while considering how you sequence and individualize simultaneously. This is a big task, which is why we recommend the utilization of manualized treatment, such as PEERS® and other resources as a starting point.

In Chapter 4, you learned about how assessment and treatment planning can be informed by the SRS-2 in both research and clinical practice. The social cognition subscale of the assessment is where this clinical piece is put into practice. It provides specific insight into perceptual deficits, which helps us determine the point at which to provide explicit instruction and more directive interventions.

Social cognition is most likely improved over the course of social communication skills treatment or training. You've also learned about the ideal conditions through which clients can improve their social skills in Chapter 5. Therefore, as clients learn new ways of communicating, they are simultaneously improving social thinking. Improving social cognition cannot happen in a vacuum, but instead can be intentionally integrated at any point through individual counseling and group treatment scenarios. In individual counseling settings, the practitioner should focus on having the client take their perspective in the immediate interactions they have during sessions, while in group formats, the clinician is able to get the client to take a variety of perspectives from peers in treatment. One positive aspect about promoting social cognition is that it can be clearly addressed through process and practice in therapy.

Practicing Perspective-Taking

Interventions that provide the opportunity for individuals with ASD to immediately practice and rehearse newly acquired social skills with peers leads to greater generalization (Laugeson & Ellingsen, 2014). As mentioned earlier, generalization is often at the heart of successes and also errors. Generalizing a learned skill from the clinical setting to the outside social context is a benefit, but over-generalizing the skill to two different social scenarios where it is not the same can be an error. Individuals with ASD benefit from explicit instruction with opportunities for behavioral rehearsal for mastery that are contextually relevant. This needs to be done in a multitude of contexts in order to ensure that the individual has the requisite skills in a variety of social scenarios. Traditional approaches to intervention do not necessarily account for individuals with auditory processing deficits or challenges with social cognition. These challenges are not unique to individuals diagnosed with ASD but can significantly impact the efficacy of efforts by counselors.

The utilization of modeling, behavioral rehearsal, video examples, and non-examples, and the introduction of both proactive and reactive skills in conjunction with a caregiver/spouse component provide a comprehensive program for individuals with ASD. One such program that exists is known as the Program for the Education and Enrichment of Relational Skills for Young Adults (PEERS®), and was developed at the UCLA Semel Institute for Neuroscience and Human Behavior (Laugeson, 2017). This model utilizes the principles of cognitive behavioral therapy (CBT) with the goal of improving social functioning for young adults with ASD and other social difficulties. The PEERS® program includes all of the evidence-based methods of social communication skills training reviewed in Chapter 5.

These methods take the learning from abstract to concrete and provide opportunities for in-vivo corrective feedback. The goals of the program are to teach young adults how to develop and maintain social and romantic relationships, and also to navigate and manage conflicts and rejection by their peers (Laugeson, 2017). Social thinking questions provide an opportunity for an individual to reflect on the perspective of others within a social interaction. This is important in order to make the connection between their behavior and the feedback.

The following three questions are a part of the PEERS® curriculum and are utilized across the 16-week intervention.

1. What was that interaction like for [name]? What could they have been feeling or thinking during the interaction?
2. What did [name] think of you during the interaction?
3. Is [name] likely to want to interact with you again?

As you can see from the above questions, the intent is to guide the individual to break down elements of the interaction and to attempt to take the perspective of the individual within that specific element of the interaction. The three areas examined within these questions are the other individual's perspective, their thoughts on the person, and if it will re-occur. Each of these questions provides an opportunity to identify social errors, provide corrective feedback, and brainstorm alternative social behaviors. While the questions were designed as a part of an intervention for individuals with ASD, any individual with challenges in identifying social cues can benefit from this targeted style of Socratic questioning. There are alternate interventions to PEERS® that can be adapted and utilized with individuals with ASD. While not specifically developed for this population, the creative and expressive elements of these narrative approaches have connections to many of the visual approaches utilized in their formative years.

Showing Understanding

The skill of demonstrating empathy and understanding to others is one that allows us to directly connect deeply to others. This is the next vital step to effectively taking another person's perspective because it is the manifestation of the social thinking process that we can then communicate to others (Devoldre, Davis, Verhofstadt, & Buysse, 2010). Adults with autism are effectively able to learn the skill of showing understanding to others when it is explicitly instructed through social communication skills and relationship treatment (Cunningham, Sperry, Brady, Peluso, & Pauletti, 2016). This has been done through ASD specific intervention and counseling strategies that psychoeducate clients about how to do this effectively (Laugeson, 2017; Guerney & Ortwein, 2008; Gottman & Silver, 2015).

Based on the resources and literature about demonstrating empathy, some helpful steps can aid our clients in acquiring this skill through counseling. The client first needs to be able to answer the social thinking questions in the initial intervention above; showing understanding needs to be scaffolded or sequenced after the client can adequately identify another person's perspective. From there, the following steps can be taught and practiced with the client to enhance their empathic communication:

1. Listen for the other person's feelings. (For example, "Gosh, I'm so annoyed right now I could just scream.")
2. Reflect back those feelings. (For example, "You seem really frustrated.")
3. Ask follow-up questions, continue to listen, maintain gaze aversion. (For example, "What did they do to annoy you?" while making intermittent eye contact.)
4. Let the person know how you can be there for them, *if* they want it. (For example, "I can see you're still upset. Is there anything I can do to help?")

Steps to helping clients learn how to show understanding can be found in a variety of treatment resources and will need to take the client's context into consideration. Is the client struggling most with showing appreciation to their family members, co-workers, a friend or partner/spouse? It's likely that if they're unable to do it in one relationship that they'll struggle in others due to challenges with generalization. It is helpful to understand the differences in showing understanding to others in different relationships and contexts. With a co-worker, showing understanding may not require as much attention to the emotional state they're experiencing, whereas, with a parent or spouse, the client may need to learn how to connect to the emotional process their loved one might be feeling.

Creative Therapies

Expressive arts interventions such as therapeutic storytelling utilize a more narrative approach and can be adapted to assist the individual tell a social story from another person's perspective. This technique shares elements of social stories. Social stories are a widely used intervention for younger individuals with ASD as a means to provide a visual awareness of scheduling, dealing with trauma, and also to prime for upcoming events and transitions (Myles, Trautman, & Schelvan, 2004). Therapeutic storytelling can be adapted in this manner to provide an awareness of another individual's perspective in different situations. The story can be developed and read collaboratively, and then it would be beneficial to incorporate the social thinking questions as part of the process in order to evaluate the individual's level of awareness.

Photo-therapy is another useful tool that has ties to strategies utilized with children with ASD (Teti, Cheak-Zamora, Lolli, & Maurer-Batjer, 2016). In formative years, photos are utilized in a variety of ways, one being to give the individual an awareness of their own facial expressions. Having photos of the individual in various stages of expression provides an opportunity to label and discuss. Another useful strategy is to incorporate images of social scenarios. These can be evaluated by the client, and the clinician can follow up utilizing the social cognition questions. This type of intervention gives the clinician insight into where the social cognition deficits lie, and where to provide further assistance in understanding.

When working with individuals on the autism spectrum, it is important to understand that it will likely require you as the counselor to step out of the traditional role that you might be used to. Utilizing role play, behavioral rehearsal, video modeling, and social cognition questions all seek to appeal to the learning and processing style of this population. Another area in which you might have to provide feedback is with hygiene. The idea of presumed competence and how masking and developmental age play a role also have a connection to the hygiene of adults with ASD. There is an assumption by a certain age that an individual has an awareness of what is acceptable in relation to dress, cleanliness and behavioral habits related to hygiene. If an individual is not specifically taught appropriate behaviors when young, there is an assumption that they will be able to pick it up from surrounding peers. But this requires a solid basis in perspective-taking and social cognition.

What if this individual has deficits in the ability to perceive social cues, or feedback that is not explicitly stated? This individual will likely have gaps in this area. And as the individual ages, there is an assumption that they must be making a conscious choice to behave in a manner contrary to social norms, or that it should be someone's else's responsibility to inform them. What if there is no one to tell them? What if they live alone, or have a caregiver that does not know? You can see how this situation can be avoided for quite some time due to other's feelings of discomfort and the individual with ASD suffering the social consequences. Something such as poor hygiene has the ability to impact an individual's social and romantic relationships, as well as employment options (Myles & Southwick, 1999).

As a counselor, there is a unique opportunity to provide this corrective feedback in a manner that is respectful and explicit. Deficits in this area can provide a significant barrier. Without feedback from the counselor related to this, any interventions regarding social interactions are bound to be challenging. Let's see how these social cognition impairments and therapeutic interventions can assist Samantha improve her ability to relate to others and meet her life goals.

Case Example

Samantha is a 25-year-old female who comes to counseling due to challenges developing social relationships. She indicates that she often feels lonely but doesn't know how to meet people. Samantha reports that she has historically had challenges in connecting with peers, with increasing intensity when she entered middle school. Samantha reports that she found the transition from her small elementary school to a large middle school overwhelming, and keeping track of all of her classes and assignments was a consistent challenge. She assumed that others felt the same way she did, so never sought out help to assist her with her challenges. When asked who she connected with, Samantha said that she enjoyed her art teacher and would often eat lunch in the teacher's room. She indicated that she generally felt that it was easier to communicate with adults as opposed to her peers, they seemed to accept her more and be willing to listen regarding her interests. She stated that when she tried to talk with other girls in her class, they seemed to like her, but then they would stop speaking to her all of a sudden without providing a reason why.

She tried to follow what the trends were in terms of what she wore and what music and shows she followed, but as soon as she caught on to what was "cool", it would change. She would try to communicate with others regarding her special interests, and they would either laugh at her or get tired of listening. Her frustration in trying to keep up with the trends led to her feeling isolated and depressed. She explained that it felt like middle school was a game with rules, but that the rules constantly changed. She had a hard time keeping up with what others liked, and it ultimately became exhausting. Between trying to keep up with the social rules and trying to stay on task at school, she would regularly come home and "melt down" as her mother called it. She said she simply felt worn out and depleted from trying to be someone that others liked, the perfect student, the "cool" kid; it all just was too much for her to maintain.

In high school, things increasingly worsened. She reported feeling even more isolated, as she did not relate to the other girls in her grade. She found it even more difficult to keep up. Her "melt downs" shifted from a more external expression to a more internal one. She reported that it was at this time she began experimenting with self-harm, as a way to "numb her feelings' and "let it all out". She was able to hide this for some time by wearing long sleeves, but when she continued this style into the warmer months, her mother became curious. When her mother discovered the cuts on her arms, she brought her to a counselor to assist with the self-harm and feelings of depression. Samantha stated that her counselor was "all right" but didn't feel as if she got much out of the sessions. The counselor wanted her to talk about her feelings, and she didn't feel comfortable doing so. She said that when she talked about the situations that caused her pain, she re-lived them in a way, and that was unpleasant. She also stated that the counselor didn't tell her what she should do, and instead asked her what she thought she should do, which was confusing. She told her mother that "if I knew what I was supposed to do differently, I wouldn't be here". Frustrated by the lack of progress within counseling sessions, her mother brought Samantha to the doctor to get medication for her depression. Samantha indicated that the medication helped somewhat, although she did feel "dull around the edges" most of the time. Her social interactions didn't increase, but she did stop the cutting, as she didn't want to go back to counseling.

At the age of 25, Samantha reports that she still finds it incredibly hard to meet people, and experiences feelings of anxiety before any type of situation that will require socialization. Since she left the school environment, she isn't even sure where you go to meet people. She indicates that her attempts to engage people in conversations don't work out, and she has given up trying for the most part. She indicates that she is close with her mother and younger sister and relies upon them as her social support. She stated that they both just "get me".

Samantha reveals that she struggles to connect with people at work as well. She has been working at the same office job for two years and enjoys her duties. She is an office assistant and is responsible for filing and other activities related to office organization. While she is often commended for her ability to complete her duties efficiently, she has not moved up to a higher position. She would like to be an office manager but did not get a promotion last time she qualified for one. She indicated that she wasn't sure why and that her employer didn't give her an explanation. When asked about what she dislikes about her work, she reports that she thinks there are way too many meetings, which she feels takes from her the ability to complete her tasks in a timely manner. She stated that she thinks the other people in the office waste too much time talking and don't follow company policies. She has reported several co-workers to human resources for infractions of company policy and feels frustrated that nothing seems to happen as a result of her reports. She does not enjoy the break room or company parties and tends to avoid them. She indicated that she has no friends at her current job, and no longer makes attempts to connect with her colleagues.

She has previously been diagnosed with both generalized anxiety and depression. While medication has helped her with mood and stress, it has not helped her figure out why developing relationships is so hard for her. She indicated that it seemed like the doctors were more concerned with medicating the symptoms than helping her figure out why she has such difficulty connecting. They seemed to be under the impression that the symptoms were causing the challenges in connecting, as opposed to the reverse. Upon her mother's suggestion, she was evaluated by a clinical psychologist and diagnosed with mild, autism spectrum disorder. She wasn't sure about this diagnosis. From what she understood about autism she pictured kids rocking and flapping and not talking; that certainly wasn't her.

She did some research online and found out that it was a spectrum disorder, with some individuals having a milder presentation. This seemed to be a better fit and explained how she has felt throughout her life. In particular, the aspects of social communication connected with her experiences growing up. She stated that she "just doesn't get people" and wished there was a set of instructions on how to make friends. She reports that counselors ask her a lot of questions she doesn't know the answers to and feels like they should have the answers since that is what she came for. Samantha informs the practitioner that she really didn't think more therapy could help, but her mom encouraged her to go and so she's giving it another try.

Through this clinical picture, it is clear that Samantha has a valuable story to tell. Therefore, the counselor wants to honor her requests for her goals in therapy, which appear to be (1) to learn skills for making friends, and (2) allowing her to take ownership of the process. This will require the counselor to adjust to the issues she's had with too many process questions; she needs to be able to air her concerns and then get some concrete steps how to move forward successfully.

In order to help her meet these goals, which Samantha agrees to, the counselor works with her to explain the best ways to make new friends, utilizing materials in the book *The Science of Making Friends* (Laugeson, 2013). This incorporates learning social skills lessons through reading and video modeling, which includes social thinking questions. Since she lives in an area where social skills groups are not available, this resource, along with individual counseling, is the next best alternative to helping her learn concrete steps for relationships. It is also how she can develop opportunities to practice what she's learned with the counselor. A weekly schedule of lessons to learn is created and Samantha agrees to have her mom included in brief, weekly conjoint sessions, where she learns about how to best support Samantha as her social coach.

As social skills are learned and rehearsed in individual therapy and with Sam's mom, the three social thinking questions are utilized repetitively in sessions and in video instruction. This allows for the client to move from perspective taking as an intentional act to more of an automatic one, which requires a lot of repetition (Turner-Brown, Perry, Dichter, Bodfish, & Penn, 2008). The counselor plans to integrate social thinking questions four to six times throughout each weekly session. Sam's mom is coached on how to repeat these questions between sessions when she observes her social successes and challenges.

In working with Sam, the counselor learns about her excellent creative writing skills and has even read a recent blog that was published describing her experience as autistic woman. Given this strength and interest, the counselor and Sam explore narrative storytelling as a part of her ability to reframe autism and her social challenges. She has developed several short stories about her life that shift her experiences of rejection and misunderstanding others' intentions into touching and humorous writings. Additionally, the feedback she receives from her family and others who read and comment about her material online helps her to see how her actions are influencing others. She develops a nice community of online followers and has a sense of connectedness to other women who share some of the struggles she's written about. Through social communication skill building and her creative expressions, Samantha is able to improve perspective taking and reports better relationships with work colleagues and the possibility of some emerging friendships.

Within this chapter, the topic of social cognition was examined as a construct and case study highlighting how deficits in this area might present for a counselor. Taking the time to conceptualize this case is important in order to determine the best possible interventions. Different interventions were identified for working to improve social cognition deficits for a range of clients with ASD. Some interventions have been specifically designed for this population while other interventions are more general in nature, with adaptations that address the needs of autistic clients. The key is to identify the areas of strength, the client's ability to think socially, and to develop a treatment plan to improve those areas where the client can benefit from additional skills.

References

American Speech-Language-Hearing Association. (2018). Retrieved from: www.asha.org.

Baron-Cohen, S. (2002). The extreme male brain theory of autism. *Trends in Cognitive Sciences, 6*, 248–254.

Baron-Cohen, S., Jolliffe, T., Mortimore, C., & Robertson, C. (1997). Another advanced test of theory of mind: Evidence from very high functioning adults with autism or Asperger syndrome. *Journal of Child Psychology and Psychiatry, 38*, 813–822.

Baron-Cohen, S., Leslie, A.M., & Frith, U. (1985). Does the autistic child have a "theory of mind"? *Cognition, 21*, 37–46.

Baron-Cohen, S., Wheelright, S., Hill, J., Raste, Y., & Plumb, I. (2001). The "reading the mind in the eyes" test revised version: A study with normal adults, and adults with Asperger syndrome or high-functioning autism. *Journal of Child Psychology & Psychiatry, 42*(2), 241–251.

Bellini, S. (2008). *Building social relationships: A systematic approach to teaching social interaction skills to children and adolescents with autism spectrum disorders and others with social difficulties.* Shawnee Mission, KS: Autism Asperger Publishing.

Cassidy, S.A., Bradley, L., Bowen, E., Wigham, S., & Rodgers, J. (2018). Measurement properties of tools used to assess suicidality in autistic and general population adults: A systematic review. *Clinical Psychology Review, 62*, 56–70

Constantino, J.N., & Gruber, C.P. (2012). *Social Responsiveness Scale – 2.* Los Angeles, CA: Western Psychological Services.

Cunningham, A., Sperry, L., Brady, M.P., Peluso, P.R., & Pauletti, R.E. (2016). The effects of a romantic relationship treatment option for adults with autism spectrum disorder. *Counseling Outcome Research and Evaluation*, 7(2), 99–110. doi:10.1177/2150137816668561.

Devoldre, I., Davis, M.H., Verhofstadt, L.L., & Buysse, A. (2010). Empathy and social support provision in couples: social support and the need to study the underlying process. *The Journal of Psychology, 144*, 259–284.

Gottman, J.M., & Silver, N. (2015). *The seven principles for making marriage work: A practical guide from the country's foremost relationship expert.* New York: Crown Publishing.

Greenberg, D. (2017). Asperger disorder: Gone but not forgotten. Retrieved from: www.psychiatrictimes.com/psych-congress-2017/asperger-disorder-gone-not-forgotten.

Guerney, B.G., & Ortwein, M. (2008) *Mastering the mysteries of love: Relationship Enhancement® program for couples, leader's guide.* Frankfort, KY: Relationship Press.

Harari, Y.N. (2015). *Sapiens: A brief history of humankind.* Canada: Signal Books.

Howlin, P., Goode, S., Hutton, J., & Rutter, M. (2004). Adult outcomes for children with autism. *Journal of Child Psychology and Psychiatry, 45*, 212–229. doi:10.1111/j.1469-7610.2004.00215.x.

Kirby, A.V., Baranek, G.T., & Fox, L. (2016). Longitudinal predictors of outcomes for adults with autism spectrum disorder: Systematic review. *OTJR Occupation, Participation and Health, 36*(2), 55–64. doi:10.1177/1539449216650182.

Kleinman, J., Marciano, P.L., Ault, R.L. (2001). Advanced theory of mind in high-functioning adults with autism. *Journal of Autism and Developmental Disorders, 31*, 29–36.

Lamport, D., & Zlomke, K. (2014). The broader autism phenotype, social interaction anxiety, and loneliness: Implications for social functioning. *Current Psychology, 33*(3), 246–255. doi:10.1007/s12144-014-9210-0.

Laugeson, E.A. (2013). *The science of making friends: Helping socially challenged teens and young adults.* San Francisco, CA: Jossey-Bass.

Laugeson, E.A. (2017). *PEERS® for young adults: Social skills training for adults with autism spectrum disorder and other social challenges.* New York: Routledge, Taylor & Francis.

Laugeson, E.A., & Ellingsen, R. (2014). Social skills training for adolescents and adults with autism spectrum disorder. In: F. Volkmar, B. Reichow, & J. McPartland (Eds.), *Adolescents and adults with Autism spectrum disorders.* New York: Springer.

Magiati, I., Tay, X.W., & Howlin, P. (2014) Cognitive, language, social and behavioural outcomes in adults with autism spectrum disorders: A systematic review of longitudinal follow-up studies in adulthood. *Clinical Psychology Review, 34*, 73–86.

Myles, B.S., & Southwick, J. (1999). *Asperger syndrome and difficult moments: Practical solutions for tantrums, rage, and meltdowns.* Shawnee Mission, KS: Autism Asperger Publishing.

Myles, B.S., Trautman, M.L., & Schelvan, R.L. (2004). *The hidden curriculum: Practical solutions for understanding unstated rules in social situations.* Shawnee Mission, KS: Autism Asperger Publishing.

Senju, A., Southgate, V., White, S., & Frith, U. (2009). Mindblind eyes: An absence of spontaneous theory of mind in Asperger syndrome. *Science, 325*, 883–885. doi:10.1126/science.1176170.

Sperry, L.A., & Mesibov, G. B. (2005). Perceptions of social challenges of adults with autism spectrum disorder. *Autism, 9*, 362–376.

Takara, K., & Kondo, T. (2014). Comorbid atypical autistic traits as a potential risk factor for suicide attempts among adult depressed patients: A case–control study. *Annals of General Psychiatry, 13*(1), 33. doi:10.1186/s12991-014-0033-z.

Teti, M., Cheak-Zamora, N., Lolli, B., & Maurer-Batjer, A. (2016). Reframing autism: Young adults with autism share their strengths through photo-stories. *Journal of Pediatric Nursing, 31*, 619–629.

Turner-Brown, L.M., Perry, T.D., Dichter, G.S., Bodfish, J.W., & Penn, D.L. (2008). Brief report: Feasibility of social cognition and interaction training for adults with high functioning autism. *Journal of Autism and Developmental Disorders, 38*, 1777–1784. doi:10.1007/s10803-008-0545-y

Wong, C., Odom, S.L., Hume, K., Cox, A.W., Fettig, A., Kucharczyk, S., … Schultz, T.R. (2013). *Evidence-based practices for children, youth, and young adults with Autism Spectrum Disorder.* Chapel Hill: The University of North Carolina, Frank Porter Graham Child Development Institute, Autism Evidence-Based Practice Review Group.

9 Working with Behavior Challenges

Elisa Cruz-Torres and Ali Cunningham Abbott

A primary worry for many autistic clients is that their uniqueness, eccentricities or sense of self will be challenged or changed in treatment. This concern may be well-justified when clients have received messages over their lifespan that attempt to diminish their desires or punish them for certain needs. Behavioral differences, or autistic mannerisms in the literature, among people with autism often leave them standing out among others and creates a target for them to be isolated or rejected. This leads people with autism to feel as though *simply being themselves is the problem*. I encourage you to pause, let that sink in and allow yourself to reflect on the feeling this elicits. It'll be important to come back to in order to deepen our empathic responses to our clients who are struggling with how their innate interests and behaviors lead to challenges in their lives.

As practitioners, we need to be clear in our approach to behavioral challenges that it is our hope to support the client in changes they identify, or those that are making a clear, negative impact in helping them meet other goals. Sometimes this involves the counselor directly, kindly and with compassion pointing out behavioral challenges they and others notice that the client might not be as aware of. Clients with whom I've worked with have often come with clear, concrete goals they want to improve about their behaviors, such as sleep hygiene or study habits. But in most instances, there are nuances about their behaviors that have caused them problems but are more complex to address. Examples of this could be helping them understand why it's a challenge to complete a group task at work without a fight or the potential benefits of not staring at attractive co-workers due to a history of harassment reports. These are just some examples of challenges that result from characteristically repetitive behaviors and restricted interests that will come up when counseling adults with autism.

Whether clients have an extensive or brief history of negative feedback about the way they navigate the world or the extent of their interests, it is important for practitioners to be aware that when broaching the topic of behavioral challenges with clients this can trigger an understandably resistant response. The aim of this chapter, therefore, is to provide a review of traditional and newer approaches that are established, evidence-based and emerging practices in promoting behavioral skill development and building flexibility among adults with ASD.

Restricted and repetitive behaviors and thoughts (also referred to as "sameness behavior") are among the original characteristics documented in autism and continue to be core elements of its clinical presentation (Kanner, 1943; APA, 2013). Individuals with ASD may have obsessions with numbers, letters, and/or confined interests and compulsions to repeat and perform behaviors that are rule-governed or self-stimulatory, such as tapping of surfaces and arranging objects (CDC, 2018). These symptoms often appear to overlap with characteristics frequently associated with obsessive compulsive disorder (OCD). While obsessions and compulsions are common and often associated with distress, compulsions are more frequently exhibited by adults with ASD than obsessive behaviors (McDougle et al., 1995; Tani et al., 2012). It has been proposed that "obsessions require an awareness of and ability to articulate intrusive thoughts and ideas" (McDougle et al., 1995). Therefore, individuals with ASD with better intellectual functioning may be more capable of acknowledging and communicating these thoughts, which may deepen social withdrawal and isolation (Tani et al., 2012). It is important to note that repetitive and restrictive behaviors are usually experienced over the lifespan. While age-related improvements among individuals with autism have been reported, it is not effective to rely on the passage of time to improve restrictive interests and repetitive interests. Without an understanding of how ASD symptoms change from adolescence to adulthood and the provision of appropriate services to support these transition periods, it is likely that adults with autism will exhibit symptoms of other disorders, which can complicate treatment and prognosis (Chowdhury, Benson, & Hillier, 2010).

Additionally, during the transition of adolescence to adulthood, higher cognitive abilities may include awareness and stigma of diagnosis and social deficits leading to increased feelings of anxiety, isolation and loneliness, exacerbating ASD-related deficits. A closer examination of co-occurring mental health issues may help prevent the attribution of behavioral challenges solely to ASD-related symptoms. Ultimately, multidimensional approaches that use efficacious and appropriate interventions and supports for individuals is a more well-rounded and appropriate plan for treating both ASD symptoms and co-occurring psychiatric conditions. (Chowdhury, Benson, & Hillier, 2010). Treatment approaches for individuals with ASD with co-morbidities who are actively seeking therapy, should aim not to cure the disorder, but to maximize potential and improve quality of life.

When compared with neurotypical peers, individuals diagnosed with autism spectrum disorder (ASD) share similar lifespans; however, attaining and maintaining a satisfactory quality of life is impacted by ASD symptoms (Howlin, 2000). People with ASD may experience a wide variety of obstacles and challenges in their lifetimes, difficulties that can be far-reaching and range from deficits in the ability to live independently to difficulties regulating emotions (Jang & Matson, 2015; Tani et al., 2012). Additionally, various forms of psychopathology and challenging behaviors, such as anxiety, obsessive-compulsiveness and avoidance are also commonly presented in the ASD population (Jang & Matson, 2015). Alone, these conditions can be problematic. Coupled with an ASD diagnosis, however, symptoms may become exacerbated and manifest in more behavioral challenges and clinically significant impairments (Jang & Matson, 2015; Bruggink, Huisman, Vuijk, Kraaij, & Garnefski, 2016). When considering how these impairments can impede treatment plans and goals, it becomes even more critical that a thorough evaluation be conducted to provide the opportunity for accurate and differential diagnosis, as detailed in Chapter 4.

Co-occurring mental health issues can be overshadowed by more salient characteristics of autism, which can minimize the focus in addressing these more covert thoughts and behaviors that may also be hindering an individual's ability to respond appropriately in various social situations (Kerns et al., 2016). For example, symptoms such as obsession, compulsions, and repetitive behaviors overlap in ASD and OCD. Avoidant and isolative behaviors inherent as a child may be deemed a result of social skill deficits. If inadequately treated in childhood, these behaviors may gradually worsen over time and manifest into social phobias and anxiety that become more detrimental as the individuals enter adulthood (Jang & Matson, 2015). Coupled with communication deficits inherent with an autism diagnosis, one's ability to accurately express thoughts and to describe mental states and experiences are often hindered, therefore complicating the processes of devising effective behavioral interventions (Leyfer et al., 2006).

Cognitive and behavioral inflexibility may hinder the ability to appropriately apply coping skills and emotionally regulate thoughts and feelings. Symptoms of excessive worry, apprehension, and emotional dysregulation may suggest an anxiety process that is exaggerated and maladaptive among some individuals with ASD (Kerns et al., 2016). For example, confusion resulting from exposure to new environments and personal relationships can lead to an agitated, bewildered state (Howlin, 2000). Even with an inherent lack of social awareness, these poor coping skills can be stigmatizing and distressing, creating an aversion to social situations, promoting a heightened sense of phobias, excessive fear and anxiety (Howlin, 2000; Kerns et al., 2016; Tani et al., 2012).

One researcher and clinician describes one model for conceptualizing how cognitive processes and behavioral problems function to compound the likelihood that adults with ASD will face anxiety or depression (Gaus, 2011). These are commonly reported symptoms by autistic adults and the model provides a guiding framework that therapists can utilize when considering the range of factors that can impact the assessment and treatment planning processes for this population. A model for understanding how thoughts and behaviors connect to several presenting clinical issues is helpful. Adults with autism face challenges in processing information about others, the self and non-social information. With the deficits in perspective taking (others), self-competence and social awareness (self) and executive functioning (non-social information) the cognitive differences set the stage for the development of mental health issues such as anxiety and depression.

Beyond the cognitive challenges, behavioral deficits in self-management and social skills compound these issues that eventually lead to issues with mood and anxiety. From odd or stereotypic mannerisms to being perceived as rude while having poor hygiene, these behavioral issues are often those that result in rejection and isolation from others. What results from these behavioral problems is poor social support and chronic stress (Gaus, 2011). Experiencing these difficulties in an ongoing basis is what helps precipitate and perpetuate depression and anxiety among this population.

What follows is a description of a scientific approach that is rooted in decades of empirical research supporting its efficacy in promoting skills and reducing maladaptive behaviors with various persons on the autism spectrum.

Applied Behavior Analysis

Applied Behavior Analysis (ABA) stems from the science of behavior that is based on the belief that to improve a human condition, treatment must focus on the behavior itself (Skinner, 1938/1966, 1953). To clarify, a causal relation is confirmed between a target behavior and the stimuli preceding the behavior (antecedent) and immediately following it (consequence). Upon the confirmation of this relationship, one can determine the function of behavior and set out to manipulate the antecedent and consequential stimuli to promote the desired change in behavior (Cooper, Heron, & Heward, 2007).

By understanding the laws of behavior and how the manipulation of antecedents and consequences in one's environment can predictably change individual responses, one can plan and control for these variables within therapeutic programs aimed at promoting positive changes (Skinner, 1938/1966). Traditionally, ABA incorporates naturalistic and structured intervention techniques across a variety of settings and specifically aims to improve socially significant behaviors (Cooper, Heron, & Heward, 2007). That is, not only are problem behaviors targeted for reduction, procedures are also used to build more appropriate, functional skills that are important to the client and his/her significant others. ABA has decades of scientific research establishing and validating its effectiveness in treating individuals diagnosed with autism and is a psychotherapeutic approach recommended by the US Surgeon General for individuals with other mental disorders and mental health problems (Kazdin, 1996; Skinner, 1938/1966; Surgeon General, 1999; Wong et al., 2013)

The practice of ABA evolved from laboratory work with animals in the 1940s and 1950s to its application in building useful skills with people with developmental disabilities and the psychiatric disorders emerging during the 1950s and 1960s (Skinner, 1938/1966; Bijou, 1957). This work laid the foundation for understanding how to study and change behavior for typically developing individuals. The work then branched out to include those with varying disorders in both natural (home) and structured (school or clinic) settings (Bijou, 1996; Lovaas, 1987; Morris, Altus, & Smith, 2013; Risley, 2001). In these settings, children with autism had their first exposure to improving behavioral challenges through training sessions specifically aimed at reducing problem behaviors or learning new behaviors.

Over the past three decades, with continued growth of evidence in the use of ABA to promote positive behavior changes among a variety of individuals, the demand for services has accelerated rapidly. And not surprisingly, to date, no base of ABA recipients is larger than those with ASD (Behavior Analyst Certification Board, 2018). Due to the use of ABA first being implemented in the treatment of individuals with intellectual disabilities and autism, and with increased funding in autism research, individuals diagnosed with ASD have the largest body of evidence demonstrating the effectiveness of ABA and, therefore, have received the most recognition in its application (Behavior Analyst Certification Board, 2018).

As the evidence in its effectiveness strengthens and demand for services increase, approaches utilizing ABA methodologies continue to grow and evolve. These interventions aim to promote, support, and maintain positive behaviors, while reducing maladaptive behaviors. In its contemporary application, ABA therapy focused on building a positive therapeutic relationship with clients as a foundational ethical imperative (BACB *Professional & Ethical Compliance Code for Behavior Analysts*, 2017). Having a strong rapport with clients is essential to effective behavioral therapy.

This is important to note because ABA has been criticized for (a) focusing more on behavioral gains than personal development, and (b) using physically and emotionally harmful methods for improving behaviors. When observing some ABA strategies, such as discrete trial training, people have considered the strategy for frequently reinforcing children and adults for doing "the right thing" with food or snacks akin to training domestic animals. In these instances, observers and critics perceive ABA as paying more attention to the acquisition of behaviors over helping the person with their growth and development.

Criticisms about the use of physically harmful techniques are not unfounded due to a few cases that have been publicized to help families avoid institutions where these practices have been used. These are examples in which practitioners have used aversive techniques to attempt to reduce problem behaviors that have resulted in serious injury and even death. *These, of course, are not the kind of behavioral strategies or procedures we are suggesting practitioners ever apply*. Behavioral approaches that utilize punishment-based techniques to manage problem behaviors are only allowable when the "dangerousness of the behavior necessitates immediate use of aversive procedures" and is executed in a limited way in the least restrictive manner possible (BACB, 2017, p. 13). All professionals who are overseen by this board and other clinicians who have additional ethical and professional obligations (ACA, APA) are discouraged from utilizing ABA strategies and other behavioral procedures that use punishment. It is important to understand that most practitioners will utilize reinforcement above and beyond punishment techniques and will do so from a place that prioritizes the client's wellbeing and the therapeutic relationship.

Next, we will include an introduction of therapeutic approaches that have advanced the field of behavior analysis. Each method described will include strategies and interventions that can be implemented by professionals working together as part of a multi-disciplinary team in supporting young adults with ASD who are exhibiting symptoms beyond those related to ASD traits. To learn more about ABA and its impact in the autism community, the following resources are recommended:

- The Behavior Analyst Certification Board at www.bacb.com/about-behavior-analysis/
- Cambridge Center for Behavioral Studies at https://behavior.org/
- Association of Professional Behavioral Analysts. (2017). *Identifying Applied Behavior Analysis Interventions* [White paper]. Retrieved November 8, 2018 from Behavior Analyst Certification Board: www.bacb.com/wp-content/uploads/APBA-2017-White-Paper-Identifying-ABA-Interventions1.pdf

Positive Behavior Support

Expanding on the elements of ABA by incorporating its core elements, positive behavior support (PBS) comprises targeted assessments and individualized interventions that are designed to promote skills that maximize independence, improve quality of life and prevent problem behaviors (Carr et al., 2002; Schall, 2010). As a practice, PBS promotes the belief that people with disabilities should be given the opportunity to be included in everyday life activities in the same setting with others without disabilities (Carr et al., 2002). The PBS approach aims to identify strategies that are not only valuable to the recipient, but also utilizes assessments that are individualized to promote the development and implementation of interventions that are ecologically valid.

A functional behavior assessment (FBA) is best-practice for identifying the purpose of a problem behavior. Through observation and data collection, one can predict when the problem behavior will occur and identify the environmental conditions that are reinforcing or maintaining it (Cooper, Heron, & Heward, 2007). Before making adjustments to the environment based on the results of an FBA, it must first include, at minimum, an operational definition of the problem behavior, descriptions of the antecedent factors that predict the occurrence and non-occurrence of the behavior, and descriptions of the consequential factors that are maintaining the problem behavior. To obtain this information, a collection of interviews and questionnaires from caregivers and direct observations of the individual are collected and recorded.

Results from an FBA help guide the development of a support plan by describing strategies that are efficient in their delivery, relevant to the individual, and effective in meeting the function of the problem behavior. When considering possible functions of behavior, one must think about the intended consequence of that behavior. That is, what is the behavior leading to or achieving for that person? The four common functions contributing to both adaptive and maladaptive behaviors are attention, escape, tangible, and automatic/sensory (Cooper, Heron, & Heward, 2007). Table 9.1 provides a brief description of each.

Once the function(s) of the problem behavior is/are hypothesized, more appropriate behaviors meeting the function are selected and interventions to promote these alternative behaviors are identified. The PBS plan also details (1) who will implement the strategies and how often; (2) how crisis emergencies will be handled; and (3) how data will be collected to monitor and assess progress. Proactive and consequential strategies and modifications designed to promote the new behavior(s) and prevent the occurrence of the problem behavior are also described. The inclusion of established treatments is essential to the PBS approach. What follows is a review of some of the evidence-based practices (EBP) deemed effective for adults (18–22 years old) with autism who may also have co-occurring conditions.

Reinforcement

A basic, and arguably the most important, concept of behavior analysis is the understanding that consequences are the strongest determinants in shaping behavior change. By presenting a positive consequence (i.e., adding something that the individual desires) or withholding a negative consequence (i.e., removing something undesirable or aversive from the individual's environment) after

Table 9.1 The functions of behavior

Function	*Why?*	*When?*
Attention	Allows access for a desired person or interaction	Occurs any time during social interaction
Escape	Eliminates the need for unwanted interactions or activities	Occurs when an activity is too boring, hard, or disliked
Sensory	Stimulates a pleasure zone in the brain or body	Occurs most likely when excited or nervous, but could happen any time
Tangible	Allows access to preferred items or activities	Occurs when an activity or item is desired

Source: Cooper, Heron, and Heward (2007).

the individual engages in a behavior, the principle of reinforcement affirms that the future frequency of that behavior (i.e., responses preceding these types of consequences) will be strengthened or maintained. This understanding provides the foundation for utilizing PBS interventions.

Once the function of a problem behavior has been determined, we aim to change the consequences maintaining that behavior. After identifying what is reinforcing the behavior, a PBS plan will include the provision of a rich schedule of reinforcement for the replacement behaviors, while no longer providing reinforcement for maladaptive behaviors, effectively increasing the frequency of the appropriate behavior. For example, the differential delivery of reinforcement for an individual, who enjoys receiving attention from others, can be effective in reducing/eliminating undesirable behaviors, such "bad hygiene" (Figure 9.1).

Let's say an FBA indicates the function of "infrequent showering and not putting on deodorant" is avoidance of a non-preferred activity. A schedule of reinforcement might include initially focusing on increasing the number of times attention is provided, as well as how it is delivered. Giving specific praise when he engages in the desirable behavior(s) (e.g., "You smell really good today!") and reducing the frequency and magnitude of attention when no deodorant is applied or shower is taken (e.g., providing a brief, soft hello versus an energetic greeting) will ultimately lead to an increase in "good hygiene" behaviors. This, of course, is contingent on the individual finding attention, such as praise, to be valuable and a desirable consequence for his showering and putting on deodorant.

Reinforcement is a foundational evidence-based practice that is largely used in conjunction with most other evidence-based practices. It has been used in multi-component treatment packages to improve a variety of skills in adults with ASD, such as employment outcomes (Hendricks, 2010; Kemp and Carr, 1995; Schall, 2010), extinguishing phobic avoidance (Shabani & Fisher, 2006), reducing maladaptive behavior (Roth, Gillis, & Reed, 2014), as well as teaching proactive sexual education (Tullis & Zangrillo, 2013).

Antecedent-Based Intervention

Due to the various characteristics of ASD, individuals can find it challenging to navigate daily responsibilities, understand social and behavioral expectations, and successfully complete various tasks. Antecedent-based interventions (ABI) are an evidence-based practice used to modify one's environment to change or shape his/her behavior. Typically, an FBA is first conducted and,

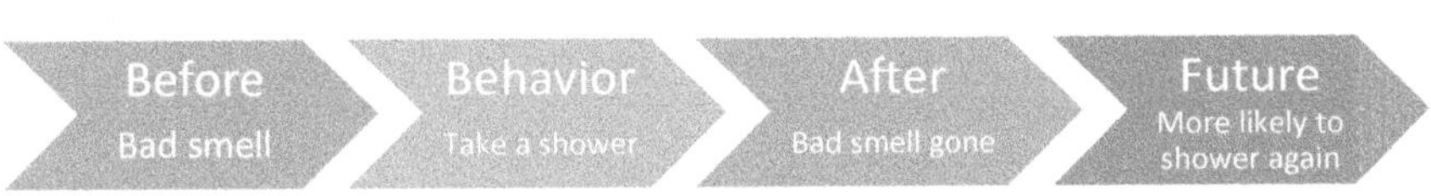

Figure 9.1 Negative reinforcement.

once the maintaining conditions are identified, ABIs are designed and implemented to meet the function(s) of the target problem behavior by modifying the environment, providing choices, and using motivating items before the occurrence of the problem behavior. Common examples of these proactive strategies include modifying activities or materials and enriching the environment with visual supports, schedules and routines for adults with ASD.

An example is provided in Figure 9.2 for the individual working on increasing his or her "good hygiene" skills but needs visual reminders.

These interventions can help individuals in understanding rules, routines, or expectations in educational and vocational settings, promoting independence and reducing stress and anxiety (Schall, 2010; Shabani & Fisher, 2006; Wong et al., 2013). Opportunities for choice-making in activities or materials emphasize the importance in respecting an individual's autonomy (Schall, 2010; Wong et al., 2013). Understanding motivating factors can minimize frustrations while using strengths and interests to promote competence and feelings of accomplishment. The delivery of reinforcement is often used in conjunction with ABI strategies.

Behavioral Skills Training

The goal of a PBS approach is to teach a new behavior that serves the same function as the problem behavior, inevitably extinguishing and replacing it. Behavioral skills training (BST) is an EBP that has been effective in promoting new targeted behaviors, such as vocational, communication, and social skills, among high functioning adults with ASD (Burke, Andersen, Bowen, Howard, & Allen, 2010; Dotson, Leaf, Sheldon, & Sherman, 2010; Laugeson, Gantman, Kapp, Orenski, & Ellingsen, 2015). BST packages consist of instruction that is delivered didactically, using verbal and written materials to enhance teaching. This instruction is followed by the modeling of the steps of the target intervention. Modeling can be done in vivo or with the use of video demonstrations. Individuals are then given the opportunity to practice

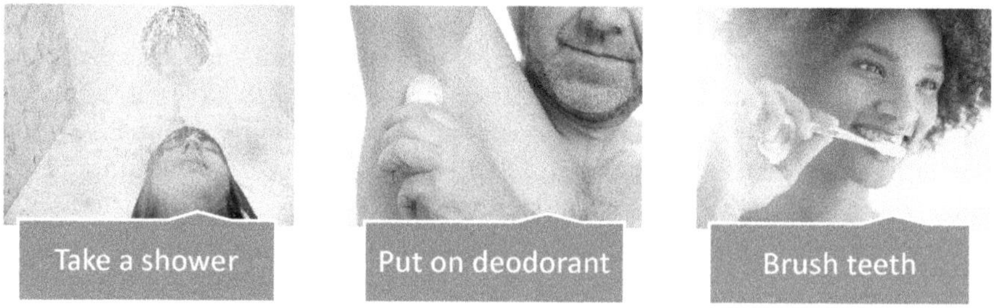

Figure 9.2 Good hygiene visuals.

Photos ©Getty Images, artwork by Camila Massu (shower), Michael Heim (deodorant), and Tetra Images (toothbrush).

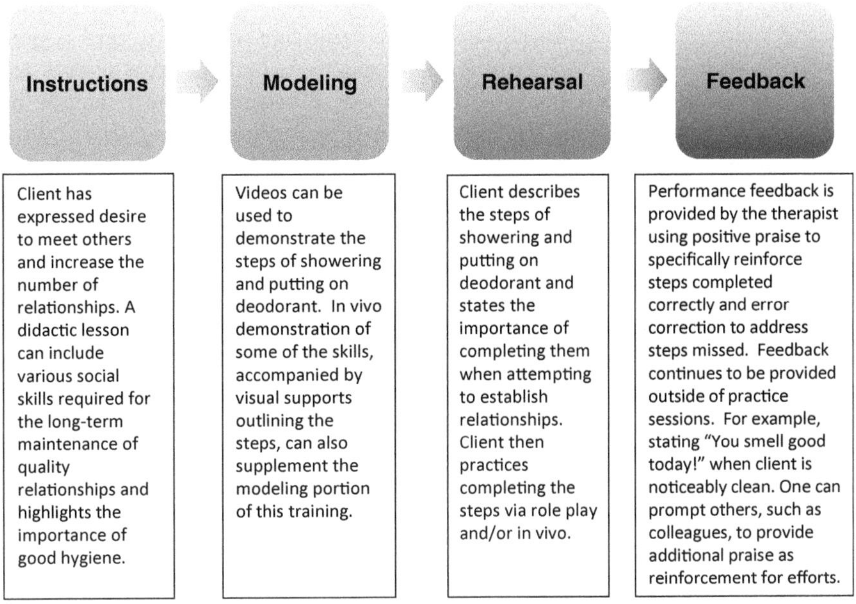

Figure 9.3 Behavioral skills training steps.

Source: Author created.

implementing the steps and are provided with immediate feedback on their performance. If the individual can teach another person to complete the skills they learned, then the BST can be considered successful.

Let's take our friend who is learning "good hygiene". A BST package, that includes reinforcement and ABI strategies, might look like Figure 9.3.

Contextual Science of Behavior

As ABA continued to evolve, researchers sought to dig deeper and analyze more non-traditional basic assumptions of human conditions. While it was recognized that thoughts, emotions, and beliefs are part of "psychological activity" that contribute to the contingencies shaping one's behavior (Hayes, Barnes-Homes, & Roche, 2001; Skinner, 1974), research and practice within the scope of ABA continued to focus on publicly observable human conditions and ignored the impact these recognized private events had on the function of behaviors (Skinner, 1974; Zettle, Hayes, Barnes-Holmes, & Biglan, 2016). Contextual Behavioral Science is a branch of behavior analysis that seeks to understand how functional, contextual approaches to language and cognition influence verbal interventions across a variety of areas.

Studying the function of overt behaviors stemming from these private events led contextual behavioral scientists to branch away from behavior analysis and delve into the examination of how language, emotions, and cognition shape human behavior. From this perspective, such internal events are parts of an organism that provide meaning or function to the behavior or response that emerges from the relationships established among them. This interrelationship supports the behavior analytic understanding that the three-term contingency (antecedent-behavior-consequence) applies even to events that are private – they are variables that can be manipulated to influence behavior.

This functional contextual account for determining the "cause" of behaviors examines the contexts in which private experiences are evoked and how these contexts affect the relationship between those internal events and other behaviors (Zettle, Hayes, Barnes-Holmes, & Biglan, 2016). Examining these non-traditional basic assumptions (such as mindfulness) as they relate functionally to their environmental contexts provides a more pragmatic perspective of the impact that thoughts, emotions, and cognition exert on overt behaviors. While traditional behavior analysis views behavior as distinct from thoughts and feelings, proponents of CSB practices recognize that understanding private behavior is essential to addressing overt activity (Zettle, Hayes, Barnes-Holmes, & Biglan, 2016).

To learn more about the utilization of CSB for adults with ASD, see:

- Association for Contextual Behavioral Science at https://contextualscience.org/
- Zettle, R.D., Hayes, S.C., Barnes-Holmes, D., & Biglan, A. (Eds.). (2016). *The Wiley Handbook of Contextual Behavioral Science*. West Sussex, UK: Wiley

Cognitive Behavioral Therapy

During the 1980s, a second-wave of behavior therapies began to establish themselves as valid treatments addressing common mental health issues such as depression and anxiety. Although the effects of environmental stimuli on behavior continued to be important, thoughts, perception and interpretations about these stimuli were becoming an increasing focus. Drawing on cognitive psychology and behaviorism, Cognitive Behavioral Therapy (CBT), focuses on what the client thinks in order to then alter the problems he/she is presenting (Kazdin, 1996). Moving beyond traditional psychotherapeutic approaches, which focus on the analysis of past events and how they negatively impact thoughts and actions, CBT practitioners work with clients to study and identify private events, alter the irrational cognitions that are creating and sustaining maladaptive behavior and/or negative mood states, and aim to replace them with thoughts, statements, and expectations to better manage unpleasant emotions and dysfunctional behaviors (Benjamin et al., 2011;

Binnie & Blainey, 2013; Kazdin, 1996; Spain, Sin, Chalder, Murphy, & Happe, 2015).

Recognizing emotion regulates human behavior socially, behaviorally and psychologically, CBT aims to promote emotional regulation by identifying the intrinsic and extrinsic processes that allow one to monitor, evaluate, and modify emotional reactions to reach a goal (Hartman, Urbano, Manser, & Okwara, 2012; Mafesky & White, 2014). This goal-oriented approach encourages individuals to, not only reduce undesirable symptoms, but identify specific and measurable goals they would like to reach. For example, a therapist will work to replace a client's self-defeating assertions (e.g., "I can't make a friend") with thoughts that promote positive outcomes (e.g., "I can learn ways to make and keep a friend"). This approach looks at how thoughts, emotions and behaviors are interrelated and how their effect on the core beliefs of all humans helps improve emotional regulation, promoting the development of appropriate coping strategies.

CBT has been shown to be effective in treating a variety of disorders in children, adolescents, and adults in the general population, with promising outcomes in reducing anxiety and managing anger among individuals with ASD (Binnie & Blainey, 2013; Hartman, Urbano, Manser, & Okwara, 2012; Paxton & Estay, 2007; Spain et al., 2015). However, it has been proposed that the social cognition deficits and cognitive inflexibility inherent in the ASD population influence their ability to think, feel, and behave in a manner that makes it challenging to identify and conceptualize their own thoughts and feelings, as well those of others, modify personal beliefs, and evolve within social contexts of their environment (Gaus, 2011; Hartman, Urbano, Manser, & Okwara, 2012). Coupled with frequent negative life experiences (such as social rejection and employment failures), negative perceptions about themselves, their future and the world around them become reinforced, producing more deviant behavior disturbance (Gaus, 2011). Uncontrolled outbursts, aggression and self-injurious behaviors, while often perceived as defiant, may likely be due an inability to effectively cope with emotions resulting from overstimulation or stress (Mafesky & White, 2014).

In working with individuals with ASD, it is critical clinicians distinguish between symptoms that have evolved from maladaptive thinking from core ASD deficits. For example, social communication difficulties should be distinguished from social anxiety, the need for sameness and routine differentiated from OCD-related symptoms, or social anxiety from a social/communication deficit (Binnie & Blainey, 2013). Following an appropriate and accurate assessment process, CBT intervention goals are then aimed at reducing the co-morbid psychiatric symptoms. For example, proponents of CBT for use with the ASD population suggest that its application in reducing symptoms of depression and anxiety requires an increase in social and coping skills (Gaus, 2011).

As previously mentioned, social communication difficulties inherent in individuals with ASD may impair their ability to identify and describe their own feelings and emotions. These deficits may pose a challenge in the utilization of traditional cognitive interventions, which often require journaling of thoughts and self-evaluation of implemented strategies. The following approaches are suggested modifications of traditional CBT protocols in using this approach with adults with ASD: (1) increase the use of visuals to support methodology; (2) describe distinctive features of emotions; (3) develop goal outcomes that are individualized; (4) build and strengthen emotional intelligence; (5) highlight the importance and development of targeting skills that specifically target replacement behaviors; (6) speak slower and decrease the amount of jargon used, be more direct in identifying underlying thoughts (Paxton & Estay, 2007; Spain et al., 2015). These suggestions still align with the structured methodology that includes clearly identified goals for treatment when using CBT; however, a less Socratic approach that includes a more direct and flexible style would likely be more beneficial when working with individuals with ASD. To learn more about the utilization of CBT for adults with ASD, please use the following resources:

- The Beck Institute for Cognitive Behavior Training at https://beckinstitute.org
- Gaus, V. (2019). *Cognitive-Behavioral Therapy for Adults with Autism Spectrum Disorder: Second Edition*, New York: Guilford Press. Accompanying reproducible materials available for download at: www.guilford.com/add/forms/gaus.pdf

Going beyond the traditional CBT approach of restructuring thoughts to alter feelings, a third wave of behavioral and cognitive therapy approaches emerged combining techniques from CBT with strategies promoting acceptance and mindfulness. These therapies focus on how a person connects and relates to their thoughts in order to build acceptance of acquired emotions and motivate one to develop stronger regulation skills. The primary shift from traditional CBT to third wave approaches is a deliberate move away from labeling behaviors as maladaptive or dysfunctional. Instead they move toward an acceptance of behaviors as neither "good nor bad" and describe all behavior as a natural part of the human condition that we can learn to move through and beyond to create healthier choices and outcomes. The third wave approaches we will review next are dialectical behavior therapy, acceptance commitment and relational frame theory.

Relational Frame Theory

The first of the third-wave approaches to be highlighted is Relational Frame Theory (RFT). As a behavioral theory which draws on a several well-established behavioral principles, such as stimulus equivalence and multiple exemplar training, RFT is rooted in the understanding that humans exist in a world that is constructed in language that has been shaped by their past experiences. Through language and cognition, humans develop meaning about the events we experience in life based on how we communicate and think about them (Fletcher & Hayes, 2005).

In early childhood, language training interactions explicitly teach relationships between objects and words, as well as through identification of objects when their names are heard. Through a history of differential reinforcement of various responses (i.e. naming, identifying), language is acquired, developed, and maintained and relational training evolves into development of relational responding (Hayes et al., 2001). Through life events, words acquire meaning that reflect the quality of those experiences. For example, if as a young child, one experiences sea sickness after being on a boat, that individual might develop an aversion to all floating vehicles. Signs of anxiety may appear during a discussion about a cruise or a fishing trip, even if he has never been on a cruise or participated in a fishing trip. The derived relation between "boat" and "cruise" has emerged as a result of the previous aversive event and signs of anxiety can present themselves even without any direct experience with the novel item or event. From the RFT perspective, derived relations influence the development of psychopathology. They impact one's ability to separate the process of thinking from established thoughts and internal events, leading to an inability to regulate thoughts, feelings, and emotions and "being in the moment" (Fletcher & Hayes, 2005).

The utilization of RFT with individuals with ASD has largely focused on the remediation of language and social skills deficits, such as making appropriate requests and building perspective-taking skills (Murphy, Barnes-Holmes & Barnes-Holmes, 2013; Rehfeldt, Dillen, Ziomek, & Kowalchuk, 2007). However, RFT has been implemented to address psychological concerns that typically fall outside the scope of behavior analysis, such as anxiety, depression and self-awareness (Relational Frame Theory, n.d.). Implications for practice in using the RFT approach with clients with ASD and co-morbid diagnoses indicate the importance of understanding that the development of relational frames requires experience with distinct relations. Because individuals with ASD tend to have more limited background knowledge and experiences, basic relational units must first be established through multiple training opportunities (Dymond & Roche, 2013). For example, to build simple contextual control of if–then relations, a therapist can implement I-YOU trials (e.g., If I [therapist speaking hypothetically] have a red shirt and YOU [client] have a black shirt: Which shirt do I have? Which shirt do you have?). From here, more complex deictic relations can be built, such as HERE–THERE and NOW–THEN.

Due to deficits in empathy and an inability to understand another person's perspective, explicit training can promote perspective-taking, improving social cognition and theory of mind outcomes (Dymond & Roche, 2013). Additionally, focusing on the instruction of skills that result in the development of untaught skills can promote generalization to a variety of daily environments and situations. Finally, targeting these relations may help in identifying some of the maladaptive, distressing thoughts that are controlling one's behavior and in building new relations that promote security and a stronger sense of self (Barnes, Grannan, Lovett, & Rehfeldt, 2012).

To learn more about RFT, see:

- Resources for Learning RFT at https://contextualscience.org/resources_for_learning_rft
- Hayes, S.C., Barnes-Holmes, D., & Roche, B. (Eds.). (2001). *Relational Frame Theory: A Post-Skinnerian Account of Human Language and Cognition*. New York: Plenum Press.

Acceptance and Commitment Therapy

A second third-wave approach based on modern behavioral psychology is Acceptance and Commitment Therapy (ACT). ACT is a treatment approach that aims to create psychological flexibility by applying mindfulness and acceptance strategies with commitment and behavior change strategies (Harris, 2018). The underlying philosophy of ACT is based on the notion that pain and suffering are natural and unavoidable conditions for humans, and, like RFT, language and cognitions control our experiences and shape our behaviors (Harris, 2018). Expanding on B.F. Skinner's work addressing verbal behavior (i.e., an aspect of ABA that teaches language by focusing on the idea that words are meaningful when the function of their use is discovered), the ACT approach aims to accept the private events that have fostered psychological difficulties, identify the painful thoughts, feelings, and beliefs that have formed, and then manipulate them so one can move toward a richer, more meaningful life (Harris, 2018).

The ACT model, also known as a hexaflex, promotes psychological flexibility by encouraging the recognition and acceptance of inevitably painful situations and teaches mindfulness skills as an effective way to address and cope with these private events. The goal is to encourage action that leads to positive results. The hexaflex is comprised of six core processes.

Acceptance: Involves the active awareness of private events and a mindful choice to allow them to happen rather than avoiding them.

Cognitive Defusion: Aims to decrease the fixation or strength of thoughts and feelings by attempting to alter their undesirable functions and how one reacts or interacts to those private events.

Being Present: Promotes active, non-judgemental contact with the environment to experience what is happening in the moment without predictions or assessments about the future.

Self-as-Context: Fosters defusion and awareness in building an understanding that an individual is not his/her thoughts, emotions, or experiences; there is a self outside of privately occurring events.

Values: Recognizes humans are guided by the standards and ideals they hold; incorporates acceptance, defusion, and being present with exercises and techniques leading to a life consistent with values.

Committed Action: Connects behavior change efforts and contact with psychological challenges to concrete, desirable goals (Harris, 2011).

ACT has proven to be an effective model in treating a variety of psychological disorders, such an anxiety, depression, OCD, and social anxiety (Association for Contextual Behavioral Science; Pahnke, Lundgren, Hursti, & Hirikoski, 2014) and, because it is not a specific set of techniques, is applicable for use in both individual and group sessions, classroom, clinical and workplace environments, and other settings and populations (Association for Contextual Behavioral Science). Currently, research in the utilization of the ACT protocol with the ASD population is scant. However, research incorporating ACT into a skills training at a special school setting led to decreases in stress, hyperactivity, and emotional symptoms and increases in prosocial behaviors for adolescents and young adults with ASD (Pahnke et al., 2014). Another significant outcome was the high level of satisfaction reported by the students.

Due to rule-governed behaviors, experiential avoidance when faced with aversive situations, and psychological inflexibility when problem-solving, the non-judgemental and accepting approach of ACT with individuals with ASD can be beneficial in reducing various symptoms. For instance, by explicitly targeting skills in social situations, such as identifying and accepting self-critical thoughts while also being mindful of the appropriateness of a conversation, he/she can potentially improve social skills and generalize coping skills. Additionally, developing and practicing acceptance and mindfulness strategies and behavior change procedures can also be helpful in building different perspectives, an area that is often problematic for the ASD population (Pahnke et al., 2014). To learn more about the ACT model, including training opportunities see the following resources:

- ACT overview, workshops and training, visit: www.actmindfully.com.au
- Harris, R. (2008). *ACT Made Simple: An Easy-to-Read Primer on Acceptance and Commitment Therapy*. Oakland, CA: New Harbinger Publications
- Harris, R. (2009). *The Happiness Trap: How to Stop Struggling and Start Living: A Guide to ACT*. Boston, MA: Shambhala Publications

Dialectical Behavior Therapy

Initially developed to treat emotional regulation difficulties exhibited by persons with Borderline Personality Disorder, Dialectical Behavior Therapy (DBT) utilizes mindfulness, interpersonal effectiveness, emotion regulation, and distress tolerance aimed at reducing negative emotions that impede the ability to meaningfully connect with others, to liberate and increase a sense of control over one's life (Hartman et al., 2012). As suggested in the name, the underlying principle of DBT is dialectic – balancing of opposites. This approach seeks to avoid the "all-or-nothing" thought process and promotes the idea that two seemingly opposite perspectives can be true at the same time. The foundational dialectic of DBT is acceptance and change. That is, DBT goes beyond traditional CBT, which solely focuses on the steps required for change, and teaches the client to first accept their current situation and then recognize the need to change behaviors to improve their quality of life (Hartman et al., 2012).

The first step of the DT model validates the individual's experiences and coping mechanisms currently in place. During this mindfulness training, individuals learn how to observe, describe, and be a part of their environment without suppressing or giving control to emotions. The second step involves interacting with others while getting one's own needs met, maintaining interpersonal relationships and one's own self-respect. Here, the balance between personal needs and the demands of others is promoted. During the third step of the DBT model, clients learn to recognize, interpret, and experience emotional symptoms without judgement or suppression. They then learn to take the opposite action in response to emotionally overwhelming situations with the goal of replacing the unproductive emotion with a more effective one. Finally, clients learn strategies aimed at promoting distress tolerance. That is, clients acquire skills that encourage a willing engagement to deal with a reality that might be painful, but promote the recognition that pain evolves into suffering when there is an unwillingness to first accept that it exists (Hartman et al., 2012).

Several adaptations of the DBT model have proven to be effective for a variety of disorders such as bipolar and depression, populations with moderate to severe emotional dysregulation and/or suicidal behaviors (Hartman et al., 2012). It is clear, a critical component of regulating emotion is having the ability to differentiate between emotions, understand the antecedents triggering them, describe the significance of their physiological impact, and use coping skills to determine what emotion should be expressed and how (Hartman et al., 2012). Due to sensory and communication challenges and executive function deficits, individuals with ASD are at a disadvantage in developing this level of self-awareness; however, proponents of DBT assert that, with the proper adaptations, individuals on the higher end of the autism spectrum or those diagnosed with Asperger's Syndrome, could benefit from the DBT approach. Because the DBT approach recognizes that one's behaviors have served a purpose (and may still do), clients are validated and empowered in thinking they can have a positive effect on their own lives and in the choices they make. This is especially powerful for adolescents and adults with ASD who may be accustomed to society focusing primarily on their deficits, asserting they need the assistance of others to be successful.

Clinical trials and treatment outcomes in the use of DBT with the ASD population are scant (Mafesky & White, 2014); however, as this approach continues to be explored with this population, recommendations for implementation have been suggested. Some of the specific adaptions include the use of visual supports to enhance the DBT approach in recognizing, understanding, and expressing one's emotions. For example, worksheets or scale systems identifying various degrees of emotions supplemented with visual depictions can help to concretize the concept of emotion. Additionally, modeling and role-play activities can capitalize on the visual strengths of clients with ASD while providing an opportunity to practice skills in a protected environment. Social skill deficits and lack of social reciprocity may hinder a client's ability to successfully participate in the reciprocal nature of DBT. Focusing on social skills training and integrating perspective-taking strategies can help increase understanding and ability to read others' emotions and accurately respond to them. Integrating client interests can help build connection with others and promote engagement. Finally, individualized feedback to address non-compliance may be altered to minimize distress in a client with ASD who might shut down or avoid participating. Therapists may instead address such issues utilizing a group format to analyze "hypothetical" situations. Including family members, contriving situations with group leaders, and the inclusion of a variety of exercises in both clinical and natural settings can help in maintaining and generalizing acquired skills. Finally, it is important to recognize that, while regulatory skill deficits are inherent in the ASD population, clients prescribed psychoactive medications may experience increased dampening of emotional responses, complicating the treatment process (Hartman et al., 2012). To learn more about the utilization of DBT, see the following resources:

- DBT – Linehan Board of Certification at https://dbt-lbc.org
- Linehan, M.M. (2015). *DBT Skills Training Manual*. New York: Gilford Press
- McKay, M., Wood, J.C., & Brantley, J. (2007). *The Dialectical Behavior Therapy Skills Workbook: Practical DBT Exercised for Learning Mindfulness, Interpersonal Effectiveness, Emotion Regulation, & Distress Tolerance*. Oakland, CA: New Harbinger Publications

From the evidence-based behavioral interventions recommended above, we hope that when addressing the myriad behavioral challenges your clients face you can adhere to one or more of these models. If we continue to focus on integrating what they're already good at, with what they can learn to do to better their lives we can help them effectively achieve behavioral goals. It is not about changing their sense of self, but it is about improving their sense of worth through behavioral changes they're willing to commit to. When treating the autistic mannerisms that can cause problems in our client's lives, we need to validate inherent needs, interests, and desires, while exploring new ways they can acquire skills that will help them meet their goals and improve quality of life.

Case Example

Natalie is a 38-year-old, gay woman who is a talented professional artist and is currently seeking her master's degree in fine arts. She is successful in her career as a painter, private art teacher and even specializes in providing lessons for children with learning differences. Natalie has experienced a lot of success in her work. Where she struggles is in personal relationships and intrapersonal issues, which have resulted in a series of bad relationships and disordered substance use. Recently, Natalie completed a 60-day stay in residential treatment after she was hospitalized for alcohol poisoning when she went on a drinking binge to deal with a break-up. While in treatment, she was assessed and received the diagnosis of autism spectrum disorder. She was referred to outpatient treatment from her residential provider because of the counselor's experience treating adults with autism who aim to improve their relationships.

Upon meeting Natalie, it is clear that she identifies strongly as a recovering alcoholic and found support in that community to help her maintain sobriety. The overdose episode led her to examine how her drinking had escalated over the last 10 years from a casual drinker in her early twenties to heavy drinking to help her navigate new social situations, such as dating. During treatment she was educated about how repetitive behaviors are connected to her new autism diagnosis and she's reluctant to accept this conceptualization of her alcohol use. She tends to embrace that alcohol use is a problem and insists that she will be able to remain sober "forever". Her commitment to this goal is steadfast and a resource in counseling. Yet, her resistance about the ASD diagnosis and how engaging in repetitive behaviors to handle emotional distress are areas to be mindful of as treatment progresses.

In assessing more about Natalie's relationship history, she reports having at least 10 serious relationships in the last eight years. Before she turned 30, Natalie indicated she was so focused on school and her career that she was uninterested in dating and described herself as asexual. When she turned 30, she explains that a "light bulb" went off and she didn't want to be alone forever, so she began dating one of her adult students. This student had been making romantic and sexual advances towards Natalie for several months before she agreed to go out with her and pursued her first romantic relationship. During this first, short-lived, relationship Natalie learned that she only liked to go on dates with her girlfriend on Friday or Saturday nights, not both. She also discovered that her girlfriend's interest in watching reality television agitated her to the point that she made frequent comments to dissuade her from watching. This example of this first relationship and others that followed, revealed a pattern in Natalie's relationships. The pattern is that she finds girlfriends in convenient situations (work, school, etc.) who seek her out and when she responds with specific rules for their relationship and finds something annoying about them, the relationship ends abruptly and mostly in anger. The result has left Natalie feeling like a failure in relationships and exacerbated her need to deal with the turmoil in her relationships and break-ups by drinking.

Since Natalie is resistant to the autism diagnosis she received during her in-patient substance use treatment, it will be important to explore some of the cognitive process surrounding this reaction. This first step in working with Natalie's behavioral challenges will have her take on an investigative frame of mind in examining the evidence for such a diagnosis. She reacts well to this strategy because it allows her to be in control of applying a concrete lens to processing the diagnosis and understanding how it may actually help her moving forward. The practitioner should be mindful not to impose their beliefs about autism onto the client, but instead have her weigh the pros and cons of understanding herself through this framework. This will also help the counselor assess Natalie's flexibility and willingness to shift from one position to another.

With this approach Natalie does successfully demonstrate flexibility by accepting that autism may be an accurate description of her issues. The clinician should then reflect on how they processed her demonstration of flexibility as an indicator of health and progress. Sharing the feeling associated with this shift, for example "Your willingness to explore this possibility with me as your guide makes me hopeful about our work together" may also help strengthen the therapeutic relationship. It can also help serve as a model for communicating feelings and a corrective experience in her relationship history in which the clinician reinforces the efforts she's making. Through processing and reflecting on this achievement, Natalie and the counselor find it important to identify that gaining more flexibility overall will be a helpful goal for treatment. This first step of getting client buy-in and validating their experience is key to moving forward with changes in other behaviors.

As Natalie moves through treatment stages, the counselor helps her become mindful of the different cognitive and emotional process she experiences when she wants to insist on sameness and resist change. This is actively practiced in session with Natalie during which the clinician will sporadically engage in something that is (a) unexpected or (b) bothersome to her so she can apply distress tolerance and emotional regulation skills in these opportunities. With practice, Natalie is able to begin identifying her thought processes ("I hate that she's doing this" or "I do not want this to happen right now") and emotional responses (i.e., anger). From this initial step of mindful awareness, Natalie agrees to acquiring new skills to help regulate her frustration during these times. She readily applies some simple progressive muscle relaxation exercises into her self-care routine and creates a plan for taking a pause or a break when her frustration escalates beyond a certain point.

Concurrently, Natalie and the clinician explore the characteristics of healthy romantic and sexual relationships through psychoeducation and analysis of her history. She discovers that in many of these instances she hasn't even been authentically interested in most of the women with whom she's engaged in relationships. Instead, she realizes that her thoughts about turning 30 and desire "to be loved and accepted" led to her going along with advances made by others, which resulted in toxic relationships with women who she didn't like. Her restricted interest about being in a relationship contributed to the cycle that she is motivated to break. This helps create a treatment goal related to acquiring new behavior and communication skills.

The counselor helps equip Natalie with new skills for setting boundaries in a variety of relationships across settings in her life. She learns how to decline someone's advances or sexual pressure and how to express interest in someone she actually finds appealing. This is accomplished via the steps of behavior skills and social communication training with instructional steps, behavior rehearsal, feedback and homework assignments. In an effort to begin generalizing this skill, she begins by creating a disclaimer with her clients at work that she can use to start the relationship with professionalism. She also begins trying to start conversations with new women she meets at art events or non-work-related social outings. It is important for her to date someone who is sober so she finds that before and after support group meetings she can practice these skills, even if it doesn't lead to the ultimate goal of establishing a romantic relationship. Her more rigid thought process has her following the one-year of sobriety before dating rule so she's able to use this as a resource in practicing these new skills in a safer, more comfortable context. The therapist reminds Natalie of this in order to reinforce how autistic mannerisms can often be a strength.

As Natalie continues individual, outpatient treatment it is evident that she has made gains in both becoming more behaviorally flexible as she continues to challenge previously steadfast beliefs to try new ways of handling her frustration and anger. She reports several instances during which others' actions have made her mad but with mindfulness and relaxation techniques her tendency to have outbursts has decreased. Natalie also has been able to maintain professional boundaries with her students; when one admirer persistently asked her out, she was able to decline while maintaining the teacher–student relationship that had never worked out for her in the past. As she prioritizes her sobriety from alcohol and other substances, she hasn't engaged in romantic relationships yet but looks forward to the potential. With continued efforts towards flexibility in her intrapersonal processes and interpersonal relationships, Natalie is finding satisfaction in her community of sober supports and a sense of self that she reports not feeling secure about before.

References

American Psychiatric Association. (2013). *Diagnostic and statistical manual of mental disorders: DSM-5*. Washington, DC: American Psychiatric Association.

Association for Contextual Behavioral Science. (n.d.). Retrieved from: https://contextualscience.org/.

Barnes, C.S., Grannan, L.K., Lovett, S.L., & Rehfeldt, R.A. (2012). Behavior analytic interventions for individuals with Autism spectrum disorders. *Psicología, Conocimiento y Sociedad*, *2*(1), 27–53

Behavior Analyst Certification Board. (n.d.). Retrieved from: www.bacb.com/about-behavior-analysis/.

Behavior Analyst Certification Board. (2017). *Professional & ethical compliance code for behavior analysts*. Retrieved from www.bacb.com.

Benjamin, C.L., Puleo, C.M., Settipani, C.A., Brodman, D.M., Edmunds, J.M., Cummings, C.M., & Kendall, P.C. (2011). History of cognitive-behavioral therapy (CBT) in youth. *Child and Adolescent Psychiatric Clinics of North America, 20*(2), 179–189. doi:10.1016/j.chc.2011.01.011.

Bijou, S.W. (1957). Patterns of reinforcement and resistance to extinction in young children. *Child Development, 28*, 47–54.

Bijou, S.W. (1996). Reflections on some early events related to behavior analysis of child development. *The Behavior Analyst, 19*, 49–60.

Bruggink, A., Huisman, S., Vuijk, R., Kraaij, V., & Garnefski, N. (2016). Cognitive emotion regulation, anxiety and depression in adults with autism spectrum disorder. *Research in Autism Spectrum Disorders, 22*(1), 34–44. doi:10.1016/j.rasd.2015.11.2003.

Binnie, J., & Blainey, S. (2013). The use of cognitive behavioural therapy for adults with autism spectrum disorders: a review of the evidence. *Mental Health Review Journal, 18*(2), 93–104.

Burke, R.V., Andersen, M.N., Bowen, S.L., Howard, M.R., & Allen, K.D. (2010). Evaluation of two instruction methods to increase employment options for young adults with autism spectrum disorders. *Research in Developmental Disabilities, 31*(6), 1223–1233. doi:10.1016/j.ridd.2010.07.023.

Carr, E., Dunlap, G., Horner, R.H., Koegel, R.L., Turnbull, A.P., Sailor, W., Anderson, J.L., Albin, R.W., Koegel, L.K., & Fox, L. (2002). Positive behavior support: Evolution of an applied science. *Journal of Positive Behavior Interventions, 4*(1), 4–16.

Centers for Disease Control and Prevention. (2018). Autism Spectrum Disorders (ASDs). Retrieved from: www.cdc.gov/ncbddd/autism/signs.html.

Chowdhury, M., Benson, B.A., & Hillier, A. (2010). Changes in restricted repetitive behaviors with age: A study of high-functioning adults with autism spectrum disorders. *Research in Autism Spectrum Disorders, 4*, 210–216.

Cooper, J.O., Heron, T.E., & Heward, W.L. (2007). *Applied behavior analysis* (2nd ed.). Columbus, OH: Merrill/Prentice Hall.

Dotson, W.H., Leaf, J.B., Sheldon, J.B., & Sherman, J.A. (2010). Group teaching of conversational skills to adolescents on the autism spectrum. *Research in Autism Spectrum Disorders, 4*(2).

Dymond, S., & Roche, B. (2013). *Advances in relational frame theory: Research and application*. Oakland, CA: New Harbinger Publications.

Fletcher, L., & Hayes, S. (2005). Relational frame theory, acceptance and commitment therapy, and a functional analytic definition of mindfulness. *Journal of Rational-Emotive and Cognitive-Behavior Therapy, 23*(4), 315–336.

Gaus, V. (2011). Cognitive behavioural therapy for adults with autism spectrum disorder. *Advances in Mental Health and Intellectual Disabilities, 5*(5), 15–25.

Hartman, K., Urbano, M., Manser, K., & Okwara, L. (2012). Modified dialectical behavior therapy to improve emotion regulation. In C.E. Richardson & R.A. Wood (Eds.), *Autism spectrum disorders*. New York: Nova Science Publishers.

Hayes, S.C., Barnes-Holmes, D., & Roche, B. (2001). *Relational frame theory. A post-Skinnerian account of human language and cognition*. New York: Kluwer Academic.

Harris, R. (2011). Embracing your demons: An overview of acceptance and commitment therapy psychotherapy. Retrieved from: www.psychotherapy.net/article/Acceptance-and-Commitment-Therapy-ACT#section-the-goal-of-act.

Harris, R. (2018). Acceptance and commitment therapy training. Retrieved from: www.actmindfully.com.au/about-act/.

Hendricks, D. (2010) Employment and adults with autism spectrum disorders: Challenges and strategies for success. *Journal of Vocational Rehabilitation, 32*(2), 125–134.

Howlin, P. (2000). Outcome in adult life for more able individuals with autism or Asperger syndrome, *Autism, 4*(1), 63–83.

Jang, J. & Matson, J.L. (2015). Autism severity as a predictor of comorbid conditions. *Journal of Developmental and Physical Disabilities, 27*(3), 405–415. doi:10.1007/s10882-015-9421-9.

Kanner, L. (1943). Autistic disturbances of affective contact. *Nervous Child, 2*, 217–250.

Kazdin, A.E. (1996). Developing effective treatments for children and adolescents. In E.D. Hibbs & P.S. Jensen (Eds.), *Psychosocial treatments for child and adolescent disorders: Empirically based strategies for clinical practice* (pp. 9–18). Washington, DC: American Psychological Association.

Kemp, D.C. & Carr, E.G. (1995). Reduction of severe problem behavior in community employment using an hypothesis-driven multicomponent intervention approach, *Journal of the Association for Persons with Severe Handicaps, 20*(4), 229–247.

Kerns, C.M., Rump, K., Worley, J., Kratz, H., McVey, A., Herrington, J., & Miller, J. (2016). The differential diagnosis of anxiety disorders in cognitively-able youth with autism. *Cognitive and Behavioral Practice, 23*, 530–547.

Laugeson, E., Gantman, A., Kapp, S., Orenski, K., & Ellingsen, R. (2015). A randomized controlled trial to improve social skills in young adults with autism spectrum disorder: The UCLA PEERS program. *Journal of Autism & Developmental Disorders, 45*(12), 3978–3989. https://doi.org/10.1007/s10803-015-2504-8.

Leyfer, O.T., Folstein, S.E., Bacalman, S., Davis, N.O., Dinh, E., Tager-Flusberg, H., & Lainhart, J.E. (2006). Comorbid psychiatric disorders in children with autism: Interview development and rate of disorders. *Journal of Autism & Developmental Disorders, 36*(7), 849–861. doi:10.1007/s10803-006-0123-0.

Lovaas, O.I. (1987). Behavioral treatment and normal educational and intellectual functioning in young autistic children. *Journal of Consulting and Clinical Psychology, 55*, 3–9.

Mafesky, C.A. & White, S.W. (2014). Emotion regulation: Concepts & practice in autism spectrum disorder, *Child and Adolescent Psychiatric Clinics of North America, 23*(1). doi:10.1016/j.chc.2013.07.002.

McDougle, C.J., Kresch, L.E., Goodman, W.K., Naylor, S.T., Volkmar, F.R., Cohen, D.J., & Price, L.H. (1995). A case-controlled study of repetitive thoughts and behavior in adults with autistic disorder and obsessive-compulsive disorder. *The American Journal of Psychiatry, 152*(5), 772–777

Morris, E.K., Altus, D.E., & Smith, N.G. (2013). A study in the founding of applied behavior analysis through its publications. *The Behavior Analyst, 36*, 73–107.

Murphy, C., Barnes-Holmes, D., & Barnes-Holmes, Y. (2013). Derived manding in children with autism: Synthesizing Skinner's verbal behavior with relational frame theory. *Journal of Applied Behavior Analysis, 38*(4), 445–446.

Pahnke, J., Lundgren, T., Hursti, T., & Hirikoski, T. (2014). Outcomes of an acceptance and commitment therapy-based skills training group for students with high-functioning autism spectrum disorder: A quasi-experimental pilot study. *Autism, 18*(8), 953–964.

Paxton, K. & Estay, E.A. (2007) *Counselling people on the autism spectrum: A practical manual*. London and Philadelphia: Jessica Kingsley Publishers.

Rehfeldt, R.A., Dillen, J.E., Ziomek, M.M., & Kowalchuk, R.K. (2007). Assessing relational learning deficits in perspective-taking in children with high-functioning autism spectrum disorder. *The Psychological Record, 57*(1), 23–47.

Relational Frame Theory. (n.d.). Retrieved from: www.actmindfully.com.au/up images/rft_simplified.pdf.

Risley, T.R. (2001). Do good, take data. In W.T. O'Donohue, D.A. Henderson, S.C. Hayes, J.E. Fisher, & L.J. Hayes (Eds.), *A history of the behavioral therapies: Founders' personal histories* (pp. 267–287). Reno, NV: Context Press.

Roth, M.E., Gillis, J.M., & Reed, F.D.D. (2014). A meta-analysis of behavioral interventions for adolescents and adults with autism spectrum disorders. *Journal of Behavioral Education, 23*, 258–286. doi:10.1007/s10864-013-9189-x.

Schall, C.M. (2010). Positive behavior support: Supporting adults with autism spectrum disorders in the workplace. *Journal of Vocational Rehabilitation, 32*, 109–115. doi:10.3233/JVR-2010-0500

Shabani, D.B., & Fisher, W.W. (2006). Stimulus fading and differential reinforcement for the treatment of needle phobia in a youth with autism. *Journal of Applied Behavior Analysis, 39*(4), 449–452. doi:10.1901/jaba.2006.30-05.

Skinner, B.F. (1953). *Science and human behavior*. New York: Macmillan.

Skinner, B.F. (1938/1966). *The behavior of organisms: An experimental analysis*. New York: Appleton-Century. (Copyright renewed in 1966 by the B.F. Skinner Foundation, Cambridge, MA).

Skinner, B.F. (1974). *About behaviorism*. New York: Knopf.

Spain, D., Sin, J., Chalder, T., Murphy, D., & Happe, F. (2015) Cognitive behaviour therapy for adults with autism spectrum disorders and psychiatric co-morbidity: A review. *Research in Autism Spectrum Disorders, 9*, 151–162.

Surgeon General. (1999). *Mental health: A report of the Surgeon General*. Retrieved from: https://profiles.nlm.nih.gov/ps/retrieve/ResourceMetadata/NNBBHS.

Tani, M., Kanai, C., Ota, H., Yamada, T., Watanabe, H., Yokoi, H., … Iwanami, A. (2012). Mental and behavioral symptoms of person's with Asperger's syndrome: Relationships with social isolation and handicaps. *Research in Autism Spectrum Disorders, 6*, 907–912.

Tullis, C.A., & Zangrillo, A.N. (2013) Sexuality education for adolescents and adults with autism spectrum disorders. *Psychology in the Schools, 50*(9). doi:10.1002/pits.21713.

Wong, C., Odom, S.L., Hume, K., Cox, A.W., Fettig, A., Kucharczyk, S., … Schultz, T.R. (2013). *Evidence-based practices for children, youth, and young adults with Autism Spectrum Disorder*. Chapel Hill: The University of North Carolina, Frank Porter Graham Child Development Institute, Autism Evidence-based Practice Review Group.

Zettle, R.D., Hayes, S.C., Barnes-Holmes, D., & Biglan, A. (Eds.). (2016). *The Wiley handbook of contextual behavioral science*. West Sussex, UK: Wiley.

10 Promoting Independence

We all make assumptions. As people, we have expectations of one another based on life experiences, preferences, and biases that dictate what we assume about others. We expect that children need and benefit from a lot of guidance and supervision, so they can learn to navigate the world. Our assumption is also that by the time children become adults they'll require less support and launch into independence successfully. When adults don't gain independence and still require significant support after the time that our societal norms dictate they *should*, it is considered a failure to launch (Kins & Beyers, 2010).

As mental health practitioners, we make assumptions about clients. These assumptions usually include the expectations of coming to session on time, being able to pay for services and, hopefully, being motivated for change and engaged in therapy. When clients do not meet these expectations, we experience a range of reactions from minor frustration if these are minimal to termination of services when they're egregiously violated. Recognizing the values we may anticipate, expect for or hope from others is an essential step in acknowledging our attitudes towards what we favor and dislike. In counseling, the values we uphold can be in conflict with the social or cultural factors of the client (Sue & Sue, 2016). One example of our values is that as counselors we often value when our clients embody individual insight and are actively willing to take their own steps towards problem-solving. This value excludes the consideration of external or environmental factors that could contribute to understanding the root of one's presenting problems. When taking on this value we could elicit helping the client and others to create systemic solutions that may be essential to addressing their presenting issues.

Acknowledging when our counseling values conflict with the characteristics or values of our clients is necessary to practicing in an ethically responsible and competent manner. If we are unable to identify and accept that these values have the potential to be barriers in connecting with and helping clients, we are failing. We are responsible to state these aloud and declare what we will do differently to avoid having our assumptions hinder our ability to do good work. One of the reasons I practice from an integrative approach is that I can prioritize systems theory in my work, which is a way I can actively resist a counseling or therapy value of viewing the individual client as the primary agent of change. It is in this declaration that I intentionally attempt to avoid the pitfalls of the individualistic focus we trend towards as a person living in the United States and as a mental health counselor.

In my case as a professor and counselor, I tend to assume that in high school or undergraduate work, every student learned about or was exposed to Carl Maslow's hierarchy of needs. Maslow's theory prioritizes physiological, basic needs as the foundation or bedrock of the self while more advanced needs build on this and can only be attained through personal growth and development (Maslow, 1970). The basic physiological needs he identified are food and shelter. Once a person has these in place, they can go on to meet their safety, belonging, and higher order psychological and creative needs. Decades of research has supported Maslow's foundational theory about needs; it is now widely accepted that the physical and protective needs of having sufficient food and shelter are essential to both mental and physical health (Maslow, 1970). All this is to say that without having these basic needs in place, psychological health and growth on one's own or through therapy are not likely to be achieved.

In teaching the master's level course, *Social and Cultural Foundations of Counseling*, this theory is not one that is explicitly reviewed in readings, but it is one that I come back to when discussing some of the socio-economic and class barriers that our clients can face. When many people picture someone living in poverty whose basic needs are not being met, they tend to make assumptions about deficiencies within the person that has led them to their circumstances. This assumption fails to recognize the external and systemic factors contributing to joblessness, homelessness, and poverty.

Individuals with autism are not precluded from the realities of systemic issues that result in under- or unemployment, living in poverty, having limited access to healthcare and facing housing problems. Due to systemic and individual issues that people with autism face, estimates of how much it costs to support a person with autism across their lifespan ranges from 1.4 to 2.4 million dollars. The largest costs for adulthood include supportive living arrangements, medical care and productivity loss (Buescher, Cidav, Knapp, & Mandell, 2014). To fulfill the basic needs of food and shelter, it is safe to say that employment or any form of income is essential to achieving independence. Unfortunately, current data about employment, housing, and other aspects of life that help one to achieve independence are currently lacking for the general population and much worse for those diagnosed with autism.

In exploring how to most effectively counsel adults with autism it is vital to assess various aspects of their lives. This chapter will review the current state of autistic independence related to employment, education, housing, and other areas of life. When one or more aspects of adult independence are not in place, it will be necessary to help our clients connect with supportive resources. A review of commonly available resources to support the autistic adult's journey toward gaining independence will also be offered.[1]

The Current State of Autism in Adulthood

As more children have been identified and diagnosed with autism spectrum disorder, these youths grow into young adults and, eventually, older adults, during which time they are faced with the challenge of getting their basic needs met. The transition from late adolescents to young adulthood is a particularly high-risk stage of life for family members and their autistic teens and adults (Smith, Greenberg, & Mailick, 2012). The major changes that occur during this stage, including leaving well-known environments, such as home and school systems, are compounded for a person with autism. One reason they may face more distress is likely due to their symptomology related to change; many autistic people are simply more averse to it (APA, 2013). Change contradicts the preference for and/or insistence on sameness or routine.

Parents of people with autism also report experiencing higher levels of anxiety during this period. Much of this is understandable when considering the bleak landscape of options or resources available beyond school age (Lounds, Seltzer, Greenberg, & Shattuck, 2007). In the years-long search for adult services that their loved one can benefit from, family members and the autistic adults are now faced with the realities of entering into this system, which is under-resourced and leads to many poor outcomes.

Drexel University has taken the lead in researching and reporting on current trends in the autistic adult's life outcomes through the Life Course Outcomes Research Program. They've taken existing and new data from those who access disability services across the majority of states in the US to broadly identify the primary outcomes for adult independence. The aim is to gain a better understanding of the lives of these individuals as compared with the general population and subgroups within the ASD and developmental disability (DD) community (Roux, Rast, Anderson, & Shattuck, 2015, 2017). The National Autism Indicators Reports (NAIR) gathered data from both a targeted group of adults across the lifespan 18–64 and young adults, to assess a variety of outcomes across domains.

The following is a summary of some important reported outcomes for adults with ASD using state services according to performance in the workplace, school, housing, social participation, and other services that adults get access to:

- *Employment*: 14 percent reporting having a paid position in the community; about half participated in an unpaid activity, while 27 percent reported no work or day-time activities.
- *Educational Attainment*: About 33 percent of adults with ASD receive education in a college setting; 70 percent of ASD college students enroll in community colleges.
- *Housing or Living Arrangements*: About half of the adult ASD population lives with family, a parent or other relative; 60 percent of these adults

receive some paid in-home supports, leaving 40 percent without support while living with their relatives. Twenty-seven percent lived in group homes with other people with disabilities.

- *Social and Community Participation*: A significant majority of adults (80 percent) reported monthly outings for shopping, dining, or running errands mostly seeking out rides from family members or friends to get around. Most adults reported having a friend who was not a service provider or family member, while approximately 40 percent reported feelings of loneliness.
- *Access to Healthcare*: Between 44 and 64 percent of adults had received psychiatric treatment for at least one mental health issue and experienced disruptive behaviors that resulted in medical care through medication management and other services.

A consistent point from the National Autism Indicators Reports and other research emphasizes that the experiences in adolescence and earlier childhood dictate later outcomes in young and older adulthood. Poor outcomes during and after high school increase the risk for poor outcomes later in life (Buescher et al., 2014; Lavelle et al., 2014). This potentially sets young adults up for ongoing struggles if the skills required for adulthood aren't a primary focus in schools and education settings (Smith, Maenner, & Seltzer, 2012; Taylor & Seltzer, 2012). This requires programs to integrate programming that helps teens get training on non-academic subjects, which can be difficult to achieve in a typical K-12 model. The integration of teaching independence and soft skills is difficult for educators to realistically accomplish due to demands from the systems they work in that emphasize academic and other educational goals as priorities.

One important note about the data collected through NAIR, is that information gathered is from adults with ASD who seek state services and are likely to have more moderate to severe needs. Those who become eligible for state funded services need to meet certain criteria for eligibility for those who are in most need, which helps justify the allocation of funds. But this also speaks to the limitations of those whose outcomes are reported because adults with mild ASD who are not as impaired may not be included in these data (Roux et al., 2015, 2017). Other researchers have specifically targeted this group of autistic adults who report results that have a few but not many differences compared with their more impaired ASD peers.

Adults with mild autism symptoms and normal intellectual functioning have been assessed to determine quality of life in different domains of life from social to employment satisfaction. The reality is that many of these adults are disadvantaged, even with recent improvements in resource availability and access to support (Howlin & Moss, 2012). Generally speaking, less than 20 percent of autistic adults report good to very good life outcomes. About half of those participating in research were employed, 25 percent had at least one friend and fewer than 15 percent experienced a long-lasting romantic relationship (Howlin & Moss, 2012). For autistic adults who do create long-lasting relationships and have children, anecdotal and empirical evidence indicates they demonstrate a healthy parenting approach and strategies (Rutter, 2011). Those who are in the minority can be successful in gaining independence through employment and social relationships.

The community and environment where our clients live have the potential to significantly influence adult outcomes. For example, adults with ASD who were raised in a cohesive, religious community reported better outcomes in employment, relationships and life satisfaction (Farley et al., 2009). These environmental factors from employment systems, family dynamics, parenting style, social support and others may help determine the potential for success among adults with mild ASD.

Many autistic people's outcomes are determined by logistics and circumstance. For example, geographic location, resource availability, training and preparation for both the autistic individual and the systems they are involved in are major influences in getting much needed help. This requires clinicians to be prepared not only to help clients make individual, symptom changes but also to work in consultation and collaboration with other professionals in surrounding systems. Models of consultation are important to explore in determining what supplements to counseling to provide in a sustainable way.

The consultee-centered consultation (CCC) model provides a helpful framework for working on mental health issues in community settings (Newman & Ingraham, 2017). When working with this client population, consultation can often be executed in order to help resolve work-related issues. Consulting with job coaches, managers, and co-workers is possible to help strengthen their knowledge base and assist them in being best prepared to solve problems they may be facing with the client as a result of autism or another co-occurring clinical issue. Therefore, the practitioner's ability to connect effectively with support people in their client's lives is important for successful treatment and independence outcomes.

Counseling autistic adults will be about striking a balance between treating clinical issues and coordinating services or resources alongside them. This part of our work will be to help clients manage logistical aspects of their lives in arranging educational supports, gaining employment skills or navigating transportation systems. In helping adults with ASD achieve their potential it is imperative that we are at least familiar with, if not expert in, the services and resources available that help clients with their goals for independence.

Services and Resources

The currently dreary state of independence during adulthood for autistic people has forced systems and institutions all over the world to take a hard look at important gaps that need to be filled. The anticipation of larger numbers of adults requiring services has been predicted by researchers and professional organizations alike (Gerhardt & Lanier, 2011; Autism Speaks,

2018). Over the last few decades, researchers, advocacy organizations, and individuals have worked tirelessly to lobby and fight for increased funding and resources to be allocated to adult services (Advancing the Future for Adults with Autism, 2018). In some of the literature, warnings have been issued to government officials as to an impending increase of adults requiring services and funding that is not available.

Given the limited adult services available, there are additional burdens on family members to take on caregiving, financial, and energetic resources that can be hard, if not impossible, to sustain over a lifespan. Some research suggests that services that are currently available are well-intended but likely not adequate in part because they do not align with young adults' and parents' priorities and do not offer the essential types of services they need to support the transition to adulthood (Sosnowy, Silverman, & Shattuck, 2018). Many parents worry about their adult children outliving them and other family members, imagining their autistic adult being without adequate support in older adulthood.

So, where do families and autistic adults turn to help them with planning for adulthood and the future? Although there are improvements that need to be made, there are services specifically designed for adults with ASD, or developmental disabilities, through federal and local government funded programs. Additionally, there are private and non-profit organizations that have emerged in recent years to help meet the demands that the government has not been able to provide. The information provided in this chapter will review the types of services and examples that are available at the national, regional or state level for accessibility to most practitioners. Additionally, I will highlight select services in certain areas of the country that provide unique, innovative and quality programming that can serve as models and could be suitable for families or adults who are able or willing to relocate or travel for services.

Given how many different kinds of programs exist, how do we understand what programming is right for our clients? Relying on a referral list from national organizations can be one place to start to begin gathering information. National resources for autistic adults can be located on the following websites:

- Autistic Self Advocacy Network, http://autisticadvocacy.org
- Autism Society of America, www.autism-society.org
- Autism Speaks, Resources by Stage ("Young Adults" and "Adults") or Audience ("Person with Autism"), www.autismspeaks.org/directory

It is best practice to network and familiarize oneself with service providers so that you can confidently connect clients to these services. Often times this requires us to conduct community visits and directly interact with professionals who work for these local service providers. Therefore, taking time to attend resource fairs, share a meal with local providers or accompany clients and their family members to a site visit may be required to stay informed about best fit and availability of services. This might also include inviting service providers into counseling sessions with clients (with consent, of course) when topics arise in their lives that are related to an aspect of their independence, and impacts their mental health. For example, when a client is at risk of losing their job because of a challenging behavioral issue or social deficit, it can be essential to collaborate with a vocational coach who can get exposure to how employment and clinical goals align. These professionals can also serve to help generalize any skills-based goals as an additional resource in the client's life.

Employment Programs and Services

Employment options for adults with autism range from traditional job placements to more restricted settings such as sheltered workshops. Within this range the employment possibilities include vocational training programs, volunteering, internships, part-time work and competitive employment. Placement in different employment programs will range depending on ASD symptomology, cognitive functioning and abilities. For example, our clients with mild to moderate impairments are not likely to be placed in a sheltered workshop setting. Sheltered workshops are viewed by professionals as the least desirable type of employment program due to historically low levels of engagement, activity, or enrichment for those who attend (Gill, 2005; Gerhardt & Lanier, 2011). But it is important to understand the full landscape of disability employment programs to understand what may be appropriate for different clients. Given how many employment options are available in a location, clients may be referred by others to programs that aren't a good fit for them but might be one of only a few choices.

Any employment program that excludes people from the general population or has people completing menial tasks that don't promote growth or make a meaningful contribution to society are dehumanizing. Many states and local programs have moved away from this type of employment programming, but when providing referrals and connections to clients please consider ruling out any options like this. This is when connecting and networking with the local providers will inform your ability to parse out productive from unproductive employment programming.

Now that there's an understanding of what kind of programs to avoid in the employment programming landscape, let's explore other options that are available. Education is fundamentally connected to the kinds of employment options our clients are eligible for. Given that approximately 50 percent of adults with autism are eligible to hold higher degrees, it's important to explore a range of different employment experiences (White et al., 2016). Additionally, employers report that although degrees are required to meet basic employment needs, they are most interested in seeing job candidates who have practical and applicable experiences. Therefore, having a history of pre-employment volunteering, internships or part-time work opportunities is important to begin in late childhood and adolescence.

Author and autistic adult advocate, Temple Grandin, strongly encourages parents to start employment-related tasks and routines with children from a young age. From her own experience, she attributes success to her neighborhood jobs such as delivering newspapers and mowing lawns. She reports this early work contributed to a strong work ethic as an adult (Grandin & Duffy, 2008). Research on integrating employment opportunities and skills early in life supports that these people can have slightly improved outcomes in post-secondary employment (Roux et al., 2013).

Educating parents on the importance of starting chores at home and completing tasks for others is one way to encourage skills related to employment later in life. No matter when pre-employment skills become a focus, there is likely to be an opportunity for the autistic child, teen or adult to volunteer doing something they're interested in. It may also help the person be less averse to work when they are invested in the choice-making process. This can be a challenge when suggestions by a caregiver, counselor, teacher, or peer are rejected. Actively engaging the adolescent, young or older adult in the process of selecting a volunteer or employment option, is likely to result in more enjoyment and buy-in.

Due to the lack of good employment outcomes in adulthood, and the partial attribution of this pertaining to a lack of preparation and skills among people with autism, more funding is being allocated to pre-employment training beginning earlier on in education (IACC, 2018). The earlier pre-employment and employment skills are included in educational programming, the more the potential for attainment of skills is improved. There are several programs that incorporate employment practices in educational settings, including Project SEARCH and TEACCH Supported Employment (Rutkowski et al., 2006; TEACCH Supported Employment Program, 2013). Even though these are some of the most popularly utilized programs in the K-12 system they typically begin around the age of 14.

Some researchers and practitioners argue that this is not early enough and it hasn't demonstrated enough positive outcomes in research or real-world outcomes (i.e., improved employment rates in adulthood). Other technology-based programs have been recently developed and are emerging as best practice to help with job training skills in a virtual environment. The inclusion of virtual-reality job interviewing, vocational training and navigating social work interactions started in publicly funded programs such as Vocational Rehabilitation (VR).

One recently developed and researched program is JobTIPS. This web-based program focuses on finding and keeping a job and is accessible to many without requiring in-person services that may not be readily available or offered depending on one's geographic location (Strickland, Coles & Southern, 2013). Resources are being spent to improve and implement job training programs that are as accessible as possible. Once young adults are no longer eligible to receive services as students of the public education system, other services are then available.

Support in traditional employment settings is available via federal funding, which provides vocational rehabilitation services for those who meet eligibility requirements (Fleming, Del Valle, Kim & Leahy, 2012). These services typically aid constituents in securing work, maintaining it and continuing to receive other government benefits. The Division of Vocational Rehabilitation (VR) in each state employs rehabilitation counselors who help adults build résumés, complete job applications, prepare for interviews and navigate complicated job-related tasks. From the start of the employment search to maintaining an existing job, rehabilitation counselors can play a vital role (Office of Special Education and Rehabilitative Services, OSERS, 2017). It is important to note, that this support is vital for the employment success of many autistic adults, but many VR divisions are under-resourced and therefore some people can be on a waiting list for long periods of time. During these waiting periods, some become demotivated, isolated, and even depressed due to lack of daily activity and productive purpose.

Private efforts to support employment opportunities for people with autism have become more popular as industries and social entrepreneurs have begun to understand how employing autism can serve as a business advantage. Retail companies were among the first to see the potential for those with autism and other disabilities in their workforce through employment programs, for example at Walgreens stores nationwide. More recently, technology companies broadly and publicly recruit people with autism for specialty positions in large companies, such as Microsoft and SAP. Smaller organizations have also spearheaded social entrepreneurial models to employ those with autism in other industries, such as car washes (Rising Tide) or as chocolatiers and retail workers (Chocolate Spectrum). These businesses have served as models to help train others who want to create autism-friendly business-hiring practices with a manualized and practical way to do so. The innovative programming being developed in the private sector gives promise to an improved employment landscape for adults with autism.

The following are employment resources made available locally and nationally. For additional information, please visit:

- Rehabilitation Services Administration (Vocational Rehabilitation Services), www2.ed.gov/about/offices/list/osers/rsa/index.html
- The Autism Advantage and Rising Tide U, https://theautismadvantage.com/
- Autism Speaks Employment Toolkit, www.autismspeaks.org/tool-kit/employment-tool-kit

Post-Secondary and Adult Education

For some adults with ASD, education beyond their federally mandated K-12 degree or certificate is not a possibility nor an interest. As the educational system evolves and obtaining a bachelor's degree becomes a more common requirement for entry-level positions, these autistic adults without higher educational degree will face challenges with employment options. Since education and employment are integrally connected in that one is usually required for another, it's important to understand what kinds of educational programs are in place to help support higher education and employment training programs.

Some people with autism will complete high school with traditional diplomas and be eligible for different levels of educational attainment (White et al., 2016). Others, who are primarily in special education classes throughout their K-12 education, will complete with an alternative diploma that does not make them eligible for further education in typical higher education settings. Those students are provided with an opportunity to receive educational services in a high school setting until the age of 22, at which point they are no longer eligible for this type of educational programming. Many young adults with ASD transition from the school system to the postsecondary system, from one funding stream to another.

Best practice for young adults with autism who are transitioning from one educational program to another includes them in environments where they might not historically have had access. The development of non-degree seeking programs within community, state, and private college and university settings has grown in recent years (Anderson & Butt, 2017). These academies or certificate programs vary in design but create specialized trainings and workshops in the college environment. Some programs offer their students the ability to audit degree-seeking classes and provide residential services on campus as well. Academy and certificate programs often enrich the autistic adult's knowledge related to work, relationships, daily living skills, and independence overall. Therefore, these educational programs go beyond the typical scope of schooling and incorporate life skills that are not deliberately taught in other academic settings.

Many academy and certificate programs exist, one of which is located at Florida Atlantic University, the Academy for Community Inclusion (ACI). This program allows students to audit college classes, earn certificates and take custom-designed, life skills courses. Programs such as this are funded by government programs and therefore accessible to a range of people.

Community or state colleges – their name or designation can differ depending on location – also provide educational opportunities that adults with autism may benefit from. This more affordable, less competitive, and smaller setting can lend itself to a more appealing and less daunting transition to education beyond high school (Anderson & Butt, 2017). Vocational programs, also known as trade and industry fields, that are offered in these settings can often be a good fit for autistic adults who choose to obtain work in different professions such as healthcare technicians, engineering, mechanics, maintenance and cosmetology. The benefit in this option is that the student can also seek associates or bachelor's degrees in specialized areas such as medical coding, digital animation, or paralegal work. The practical implications of seeking a degree or training in such programs usually reflect real-world, employability needs in growing industries.

Community colleges also provide student accessibility or disability services which support students with autism in their academic needs at this level of education. The services students are offered typically include the procurement of academic accommodations through the Americans with Disabilities Act (ADA), help with navigating interactions or communications with professors or peers, and technology to overcome barriers (ADA, 1990). The types of services are available to students with autism through accessibility services. Services do vary based on the institution, so it is important to know about the variety of programs available to clients. Yet, even when we have done research and identified local community or state college programs that offer good educational opportunities for adults with autism, this still may not be the best fit for our clients.

The final option for adults with autism in their search for educational attainment is the traditional route that many diploma-receiving, high school graduates take: attending a university to obtain a bachelors, masters or doctoral degree. Young autistic adults may have excelled academically in their K-12 careers. Some are well-prepared with high GPAs, strong standardized test scores and a résumé of extracurricular activities or internships that make them strong candidates for competitive university settings. Therefore, going to a college or university setting can be the best educational choice.

Attending college as a traditional student, one who goes directly from high school to college without one or more gap years, has its benefits and challenges for many, including those with ASD. One benefit is that adults who are seeking professional degrees and plan on seeking higher degrees will be able to do so sooner and can start the process as early as possible. This can help the student with ASD complete the required degrees alongside their neurotypical peers and can stimulate and motivate them toward goal attainment and achievement (Morris, Brooks, & May, 2003). Another benefit is that students with ASD in these environments can be included in opportunities that most other college students have experiences with. Inclusive experiences for autistic adults in these settings can help enhance their ability to connect with others, learn at an above average level and remain competitive in the job market (Gerhardt & Lanier, 2011). Since the ability for anyone to attend a college or university is a privileged position, the young adult with ASD who seeks this educational option can benefit from the privileges associated with obtaining a higher education degree.

There are also well-documented challenges that some adults with ASD face in a typical college or university setting. The difficulties they encounter may not be academic in nature and usually have more to do with transition issues, organization and the mastery of daily living skills. The major change from high school to college student causes significant mental health issues for many who attend (Auerbach et al., 2018). This is reflected in the preponderance of students who seek counseling and psychological services at universities.

In 2018 the World Health Organization surveyed almost 14,000 college students, 31–35 percent of them reported experiencing recent or lifetime disorders including depression, mania, generalized anxiety, panic disorder, and substance use disorders (Auerbach et al., 2018). Given the symptomatic criteria of the insistence on sameness and routine, the changes that are inherent in the process of going to college compounds the stress that ASD students face. This can make the transition issues that are hard for most college students, more challenging for adults with autism.

Organizational skills are necessary to help manage the multiple demands of going to school and other responsibilities. This stage of life requires the ability to cognitively organize oneself including scheduling, the prioritization of academic versus social demands, and managing time spent in leisure activities. This is clinically referred to as executive functioning, and autistic adults often have deficits in this area of cognition (Mandell & Ward, 2011). Executive functioning skills aren't fully developed in the brain until a person's mid-20s, so for neurotypical young adults this is already impaired. This is one of the reasons why thinking in consequential terms and predicting short or long-term effects of actions is hard to do in early adulthood. For autistic adults who are attempting to organize and plan life as a college student, support from counselors, coaches, tutors or family members can be essential to their success.

A significant percentage of college or university students live on campus or in student accommodations. This includes living in college dormitories, student housing or local apartments where other students commonly reside. For most in this transitional age, it is the first time they've lived away from caregivers or family, which requires them to manage tasks they may not have otherwise *had* to do. It is important to acknowledge that there is a learning curve in the process of mastering the daily living skills required for a person who is living independently for the first time.

Many adults with autism do not naturally learn or acquire the skills to be successful doing laundry, attending to hygiene, or preparing a meal (Gerhardt & Lanier, 2011). These daily tasks can be difficult to learn and apply without intentional and deliberate training or preparation. This can be done through the household chores or tasks that an adult learns during childhood to help them with employability skills. Yet, caregivers and parents are often focused on so many goals for improvement with their autistic loved one that the prioritization of daily living skills and soft skills required for independence can be overlooked.

In research of college students with ASD there have been best practice, recommendations provided to help prepare these transitioning adults (Anderson & Butt, 2017). They are as follows:

- Choosing a smaller institution and one that is closer to home yields better results, including fewer reported mental health issues.
- Taking a slower approach or pace to degree completion can lead to decreased anxiety and easier adjustment to college life.
- Finding an institution whose culture accepts different abilities can increase flexibility and individualization of student needs.

Given that there are specific challenges that some autistic adults may experience in traditional college or university settings, it's important to have a resource that can point to the latest educational programs that exist and provide additional support for students who need it. At the time of writing, there are between 60 (ASD) to 260 (ASD+) college programs that have specifically designed supports for students with autism and other diagnoses (College Autism Spectrum and Think College). Therefore, sorting through the list of autism-friendly programs that families can choose from is an important part of the process.

One way to help identify programs that are a good fit is to consider the bullet points above about size, location, and the kinds of support made available to students with ASD. Identifying college and university programs that are accredited regionally or nationally is another helpful tip to obtaining a competitive degree. Lastly, working with the adult themselves to identify what characteristics they are looking for in a college will be important. These characteristics could range from their interest in degrees to the kind of food they serve on campus. Assisting them in doing the research about schools that meet these needs will engage them in the process. Since sorting through the post-secondary education options is daunting, here are a few resources that can aid in the process:

- College Autism Spectrum, https://collegeautismspectrum.com
- Navigating College, The Autistic Self Advocacy Network e-book: http://navigatingcollege.org/download.php
- Think College, https://thinkcollege.net
- Florida Atlantic University's Academy for Community Inclusion, www.fau.edu/education/academicdepartments/ese/aci

Living and Residential Options

Adults with autism across the spectrum tend to struggle in obtaining independent living arrangements. This isn't for lack of interest or attempts in many cases. Our clients will often have a variety of living options they either have experienced or will experience throughout adulthood. By most accounts, living or housing arrangements are dictated by income and resources; with financial stability comes predictability in one's housing. The educational and employment status of a person typically informs what kind of residential options are available to them. Since independence is based on these critical elements and adults with autism report major problems in these areas, living options are limited.

The primary residential arrangements that people with autism experience include living at home (with family members as roommates and/or care-givers), supported living programs (group homes or apartment options), roommate arrangements or living alone (Autism Housing Network, 2017). These living arrangements vary in levels of support and will need to be decided on based on an individual needs and family's resources. The range of supported living scenarios includes residing with parents or other family members and professional residential programming with different levels of care.

Living with Family

We know the landscape of how many autistic adults live with caregivers or other family members. This is often the "first choice" for family members of their adult children because other options require more financial resources. It is not often the first choice of the autistic adult themselves. In fact, even though 87 percent of adults live with their parents only 22 percent want to live this way (Autism Housing Network, 2017).

Aside from the family home being the most cost-effective option, many caregivers are hesitant to explore other living arrangements due to the quality of existing housing services and lack of trust in care taking staff. Mistrust in adult, residential facilities for adults with disabilities is well founded when looking at investigative reports of abuse and neglect that have been published across national news outlets and research publications. In one study, up to 70 percent of adults with autism were abused while living in residential programs (Baladerian, Coleman & Stream, 2013). It's understandable that families who have spent 18 or more years taking care of their adult child would not be able, due to financial constraints, or hesitate, due to fear, to utilize housing or residential programs.

Parents who are over the age of 65 face the daunting reality of planning for housing arrangements with their autistic adult child after their deaths. Once parents are no longer able to residentially or financially support their loved one, this responsibility is often passed on to other family members. This primarily becomes the role of siblings. Siblings can take on a primary care-giving role for their autistic brothers and sisters in many family dynamics due to the likelihood that they share similar lifespans and are less likely to outlive one another significantly (Tomeny, Ellis, Rankin, & Barry, 2017). Therefore, some autistic adults move from living in one family home to another throughout their lifespan.

If an adult with autism is living with parents or other family members, there are some best practice recommendations for promoting independence within this environment. One of those is to help the person establish and increase financial responsibility. A potential risk of living with family members is that clients with autism don't get an opportunity to learn about the value nor costs associated with housing.

For example, if someone has lived in their family home since childhood and transitions to adulthood without understanding how much it costs, this can cultivate issues that lead to an unrealistic view of housing and adds to tension for caregivers who continue to provide a residence without compensation. Compensation includes the acknowledgment of both the financial and psychological value their family provides them. Without some reciprocity between the ASD adult and their family members, negative emotions and exchanges in the home will likely build and fester; this can endure throughout all of the person's adult years. The accompanying distress associated with this negatively impacts our client's mental health and opportunity for independence.

A model for compensation, at a small or large value, can be established and lessen the emotional and financial burden that impacts both parties. In some cases, families arrange an informal or formal rental agreement. These agreements are typically individualized and built on several factors that take the family member and autistic adult into consideration. The factors that can be at play when initially planning for this kind of arrangement includes the ASD adult's income, cost of living in the geographical area and tasks completed in the home. This includes how much income the person can contribute financially to the household, how this compares to other housing costs nearby and other forms of compensation via cleaning or maintaining the living space. Many families use these considerations to help determine how to compensate for living with the caregiver. In applying for benefits from the state and federal government, having documented housing costs that the adult contributes to directly can be helpful in getting the maximum compensation (Social Security Administration, 2018).

An example of how costs can be determined is how the Johnson family decided that their daughter, Robin, would compensate for living at their house. By working part-time at a horse stable, Robin makes about $800 per month. Her parents ask her to research the cost of one-bedroom apartments or roommate arrangements online to see how much they would cost. This provides her with the opportunity to see how expensive it would be to live on her own, even though this is not the family's current plan. The cost of living with a roommate, the most affordable option, would cost her at least $600 monthly. Robin realizes it would be difficult, if not impossible, to pay for rent and other living expenses given her current income.

Together, with Robin, the family can assess how much she will contribute to the house. She is proficient at doing laundry and agrees not only to do her own but offers to do so for her whole family, which include her parents and younger brother. They calculate that value at about $15 per week. Given that the average suggested percentage of income that should be dedicated to housing be less than 30 percent, the family and Robin decide that $250 a month is a realistic amount for her to pay given that she is also contributing an extra $60 in value for laundry duties.

Creating this kind of arrangement with a family member can seem unnatural or awkward when it first begins. Yet, it can be a critical step in promoting independence in one of the living arrangement options that has the potential to encourage a more dependent dynamic. Therefore, when families have an autistic loved one living in their home, financial, practical responsibility and other contributions can aid in promoting independence.

In addition to promoting independence, another result of these arrangements can include improved reciprocity and social support. Through learning the value of contributing to the home and family members, our clients gain the experience of not only getting something out of the exchange but also giving back (Baker, 2006). When they have the opportunity to give in practical and financial ways, through household tasks and reasonable "rent", there is a better chance that they may learn to provide emotional or social support to their loved one. Living with others is not only about the exchange of money and goods, but also an experience of cultivating a healthy and stable living environment. If reciprocity can extend to conversations and lending a hand when their family member is distressed or unwell, this will ultimately enhance the quality of those relationships and contribute positively to the home dynamic.

Supported Living Programs

If living with family members is not the best fit for an adult with autism, there are supported living programs that some can take advantage of. The quality of supported living programs varies depending on the funding source. Government-funded group homes face a common issue among publicly-funded programs, they are resourced enough to meet standard or, by some definitions, sub-standard living conditions. This is not only an issue for group homes, but most government affordable housing options are under-resourced and mismanaged (Baladerian, Coleman, & Stream, 2013). Privately funded supported living programs, from group homes to apartment options, provide for higher quality living facilities and programming to accompany the shelter offered. But private programs require family members to pay a lot of money to benefit from these services. The costs associated with residential accommodations for autistic adults in the United Kingdom and United States ranged from $18,000 to $41,000 annually (Buescher et al., 2014). The economic disparity in housing for adults with autism is typically based on how well resourced their families are and what they can afford.

Although supported living programs for adults with autism are out of reach for many families who cannot afford private options, there are some nationally recognized services worth mentioning. The Madison House Foundation began its housing and residential services, and has now grown into an enormous network via Autism Housing Network, because of a family member's emergence into adulthood (Autism Housing Network, 2017). Their model of housing through a farm program aims to integrate therapeutic, social and recreational services into a rural, residential community.

Cutting edge models of apartment community living have emerged as well, with one of these being First Place in Phoenix, Arizona. This program is a result of decades of research in a collaboration between academia, municipal government and private corporations. In this residential design, there are apartments and a suite of supports that help enrich residents' personal and community lives.

Please visit these resources to learn more about supported living programs available for adults with autism:

- Autism Housing Network, www.autismhousingnetwork.org
- National Association of Residential Providers for Adults with Autism, www.narpa.org
- Independent Living Research Utilization, www.ilru.org/projects/cil-net/cil-center-and-association-directory

Social and Recreational Programs

Between 10 and 40 percent of autistic adults who participated in research report having a sedentary life without regular daytime activities for engagement or enrichment (Farley et al., 2009; Gray et al., 2014; Taylor & Seltzer, 2012; Barneveld et al., 2014; Cederlund, Hagberg, Billstedt, Gillberg, & Gillberg, 2008; Gillespie-Lynch et al., 2012; Osada, Tachimori, Koyama, & Kurita, 2012). This problem in adulthood translates to the above stated issues they face in employment, because if they are not actively going to work, it leaves for a lot of empty time. This also translates to a lack of involvement in social and recreational opportunities depending on where the person lives. Clients in supported living arrangements can be exposed to, and in some cases strongly encouraged into, social relationships with housemates, roommates and others in a program. Yet, clients with autism who live at home, can be more socially isolated without social programming built into daily or weekly structured or forced events. In order to provide people with autism with these opportunities, options exist for structured and semi-structured services that can be helpful to connect them to.

As has been highlighted in previous chapters of this book, because adults with autism struggle with the initiation and maintenance of social relationships, interventions to help address these are provided through social programs. Most residential and educational services offered for those with autism have created related services that include social outings, get-togethers, and hangouts. Social and recreational programs do exist within other wrap-around services and on their own to help adults with autism connect socially and engage in recreational activities that aim to improve their quality of life.

A popular option for social programming is the development of support groups for ASD adults. Support groups are a therapeutic service with the goal of processing common challenges and seeking solutions from others. For a population who are typically isolated and lonely, connecting with others in a group setting to promote social connects and skill building can help improve life satisfaction (Farley et al., 2009).

Other social and recreational programs for adults with autism include organized opportunities to engage in common interests and activities. Organizing an outing to local sporting events, playing miniature golf, going to the movies and more can offer the adult with autism a chance to engage in an activity they might otherwise not join and to facilitate the initiation of friendship. Even when this isn't the aim of the group, enjoying time with others and connecting with like-minded people can positively contribute to overall quality of life (Howlin, Moss, Savage, & Rutter, 2013).

Healthcare and Transportation Services

The above domains of independence are important for success but are not the only elements necessary to living a happy and healthy life. In fact, other key health and mobility factors need to be in place in order for these others to be possible. For example, access to healthcare, public and private transportation, and nutritional options often dictate how possible it is to be well-educated, employed, and mentally healthy (Slack et al., 2014). Without the foundation of physical health and transportation, any of the other components of independence in adulthood can be significantly challenged. Therefore, the other services we'll focus on in this section that help promote independence are healthcare and transportation services.

Adults with autism report a higher prevalence of physical health problems and medical costs associated with getting these treated (Vohra, Madhavan, & Sambamoorthi, 2017; Croen et al., 2015). In studies across various states, adults with autism averaged approximately $13,000 dollars in healthcare costs per year, while their non-ASD counterparts spent around $9000. Myriad health problems result from biological vulnerabilities, sedentary lifestyle and poor food choices, and some of these include nutritional deficiencies, gastrointestinal problems and metabolic issues such as diabetes (Vohra et al., 2017).

People typically have three primary categories of transportation to choose from when they need to get around: personal, private, and public transportation options. Personal transportation includes motor vehicles that require driver licensing, and other modes such as bicycles or scooters. Private transportation services are available through technological apps, limousines or taxi services. Public transportation is most readily available in urban and suburban areas where systems for buses, trains, or underground rail exist.

Barriers to transportation have decreased in recent years with the advent of affordable and accessible driving services such as Lyft and Uber. Before these options, adults with autism who did not have personal transportation options had to rely on public transportation. Public transportation options vary greatly based on one's geographic location, and in some areas are not available at all. Those who live in rural areas face transportation barriers and often times have to explore alternatives that are not always convenient, reliable or affordable.

This includes options such as getting rides with family members or friends and using other modes such as bicycles or scooters that have inherent challenges when dealing with inclement weather.

For those who live in suburban and urban areas, some public transportation options are available and tailored for individuals with medical and other transportation needs. Many cities or counties have both typical and specialized train and bus systems that autistic adults can take advantage of and be funded to do so. For example, after completing an application many people who meet medical criteria can get a discounted, specialized bus to provide door-to-door transportation services for specific activities or appointments. In each state, these services will vary, but in Florida each county arranges such services and allows those who are eligible to ride to get to and from doctors' appointments, educational and training facilities and structured social group outings at a better cost than private options.

With more access to private options and some public transportation, depending on location, the barrier of transportation is one that is easier to overcome. It's no longer necessary for adults, with or without autism, to rely solely on family members or obtain their own driver's license across different areas of the United States. As counselors, we need to be willing to explore different personal, public and private transportation options with our clients in order to help manage the challenges that getting from one place to another can create.

Note

1. Commonly available resources provided in this book will include examples of services offered throughout most of the United States, with the understanding that some regions, states and cities are under-resourced and may not always include all service options mentioned here. Rural communities have fewer resources than urban areas.

References

Advancing the Future for Adults with Autism. (2018). Retrieved from: www.aafa-us.org.

American Psychiatric Association. (2013). *Diagnostic & statistics manual of mental disorders* (5th ed.). Arlington, VA: American Psychiatric Association.

Americans with Disabilities Act. (1990). Retrieved from: www.eeoc.gov/eeoc/history/35th/1990s/ada.html.

Anderson, C., & Butt, C. (2017). Young adults on the autism spectrum at college: Successes and stumbling blocks. *Journal of Autism and Developmental Disorders, 47*, 3029–3039.

Auerbach, R.P., Mortier, P., Bruffaerts, R., Alonso, J., Benjet, C., Cuijpers, P., … WHO WMH-ICS Collaborators (2018). WHO world mental health surveys international college student project: Prevalence and distribution of mental disorders. *Journal of Abnormal Psychology, 127*, 623–638. doi:10/1037/abn0000362.

Autism Housing Network. (2017). *Madison House Autism Foundation gives major support for its unique Autism Housing Network connecting families with project starters.* Retrieved from: www.autismhousingnetwork.org.

Autism Speaks (2018). Adults with autism. Retrieved from: www.autismspeaks.org/adults-autism.

Autistic Self Advocacy Network (ASAN). (2013). *Navigating college: A handbook on self- advocacy written for autistic students from autistic adults.* Retrieved from: http://autistic advocacy.org.

Baker, J. (2006). *Preparing for life: The complete guide for transitioning to adulthood for those with autism & Asperger's syndrome.* Arlington, TX: Future Horizons.

Baladerian, N.J., Coleman, T.F., & Stream, J. (2013). A report on 2012 national survey on abuse of people with disabilities. *Disability & Abuse Project.* Retrieved from: http://disabilityandabuse.org/survey/survey-report.pdf.

Barneveld, P.S., Swaab, H., Fagel, S., van Engeland, H., & de Sonneville, L.M.J. (2014). Quality of life: A case-controlled long-term follow-up study, comparing young high-functioning adults with autism spectrum disorders with adults with other psychiatric disorders diagnosed in childhood. *Comprehensive Psychiatry, 55*(2), 302–310. doi:10.1016/j.comppsych.2013.08..001.

Buescher, A.V., Cidav, Z., Knapp, M., & Mandell, D.S. (2014). Costs of autism spectrum disorders in the United Kingdom and the United States. *Journal of American Medical Academy Pediatrics, 168*, 721–728. doi:10.1001/jamapediatrics.2014.210.

Cederlund, M., Hagberg, B., Billstedt, E., Gillberg, I.C., & Gillberg, C. (2008). Asperger syndrome and autism: A comparative longitudinal follow-up study more than 5 years after original diagnosis. *Journal of Autism and Developmental Disorders, 38*, 72–85.

College Autism Spectrum. (2018). Retrieved from: https://collegeautismspectrum.com.

Croen, L.A., Zerbo, O., Qian, Y., Massolo, M.L., Rich, S., Sidney, S., & Kripke, C. (2015). The health status of adults on the autism spectrum. *Autism: The International Journal of Research and Practice, 19*, 814–823.

Farley, M.A., McMahon, W.M., Fombonne, E., Jenson, W.R., Miller, J., Gardner, M., … Coon, H. (2009). Twenty-year outcome for individuals with autism and average or near-average cognitive abilities. *Autism Research, 2*, 109–118.

Fleming, A.R., Del Valle, R., Kim, M., & Leahy, M.J. (2012). Best practice models of effective vocational rehabilitation service delivery in the public rehabilitation program: A review and synthesis of the empirical literature. *Rehabilitation Counseling Bulletin, 56*(3), 146–159. doi:10.1177/0034355212459661.

Gerhardt, P.F., & Lainer, I. (2011) Addressing the needs of adolescents and adults with autism: A crisis on the horizon. *Journal of Contemporary Psychotherapy, 41*, 37–45.

Gill, M. (2005). The myth of transition: Contractualizing disabilities in the sheltered workshop. *Disability & Society, 6*, 613–623. doi:10.1080/09687590500248399.

Gillespie-Lynch, K., Sepeta, L., Wang, Y., Marshall, S., Gomez, L., Sigman, M., & Hutman, T. (2012). Early childhood predictors of social competence of adults with autism. *Journal of Autism and Developmental Disorders, 42*, 161–174.

Grandin, T., & Duffy, K. (2008). *Developing talents: Careers for individuals with Asperger syndrome and high-functioning autism.* Shawnee Mission, KS: Autism Asperger Publishing.

Gray, K.M., Keating, C.M., Taffe, J.R., Brereton, A.V., Einfield, S.L., Reardon, T.C., & Tonge, B.J. (2014). Adult outcomes in autism: Community inclusion and living skills. *Journal of Autism and Developmental Disorders, 44*, 3006–3015.

Howlin, P., & Moss, P. (2012). Adults with autism spectrum disorders. *Canadian Journal of Psychiatry, 57*, 275–283.

Howlin, P., Moss, P., Savage, S., & Rutter, M. (2013). Social outcomes in mid to later adulthood among individuals diagnosed with autism and average nonverbal IQ as children. *Journal of the Academy of Child and Adolescent Psychiatry*, *52*, 572–581.

Interagency Autism Coordinating Committee (IACC). (2018). Retrieved from: https://iaac.hhs.gov.

Kins, E., & Beyers, W. (2010). Failure to launch, failure to meet criteria for adulthood? *Journal of Adolescent Research*, *25*, 743–777. doi:10.1177/0743558410371126.

Lavelle, T.A., Weinstein, M.C., Newhouse, J.P., Munir, K., Kuhlthau, K.A., & Prosser, L.A. (2014). Economic burden of childhood autism spectrum disorders. *Pediatrics*, *133*, 520–529. doi:10.1542/peds.2013-0763.

Lounds, J., Seltzer, M.M., Greenberg, J.S., & Shattuck, P.T. (2007). Transition and change in adolescents and young adults with autism: Longitudinal effects on maternal well-being. *American Journal of Mental Retardation*, *112*, 401–417.

Mandell, D.J., & Ward, S.E. (2011). Building the blocks of executive functioning: Different early developing processes contributing to executive functioning skills. *Developmental Psychobiology*, *53*, 796–805. doi:10.1002/dev.20552.

Maslow, A.H. (1970). *Motivation and personality*. New York: Harper & Row.

Morris, E.A., Brooks, P.R., & May, J.L. (2003). The relationship between achievement goal orientation and coping style: traditional versus nontraditional college students. *College Student Journal*, *37*, 3+.

Newman, D.S., & Ingraham, C.L. (2017). Consultee-centered consultation: Contemporary perspectives and a framework for the future. *Journal of Educational and Psychological Consultation*, *27*, 1–12. doi:10/1080/10474412.2016.1175307.

Office of Special Education and Rehabilitative Services. (2017). Retrieved from: www2.ed.gov.

Osada, H., Tachimori, H., Koyama, T., & Kurita, H. (2012). Longitudinal developmental courses in Japanese children with autism spectrum disorder. *Child Psychiatry and Human Development*, *43*, 895–908.

Roux, A.M., Rast, J.E., Anderson, K.A., & Shattuck, P.T. (2015). *National autism indicators report: Transition into young adulthood*. Philadelphia, PA: Life Course Outcomes Program, A.J. Drexel Autism Institute, Drexel University.

Roux, A.M., Rast, J.E., Anderson, K.A., & Shattuck, P.T. (2017). *National autism indicators report: Developmental disability services and outcomes in adulthood*. Philadelphia, PA: Life Course Outcomes Program, A.J. Drexel Autism Institute, Drexel University.

Roux, A.M., Shattuck, P.T., Cooper, B.P., Anderson, K.A., Wagner, M., & Narendorf, S.C. (2013). Postsecondary employment experiences among young adults with an autism spectrum disorder. *Journal of the American Academy of Child and Adolescent Psychiatry*, *52*, 931–939.

Rutkowski, S., Daston, M., Van Kuiken, D., & Reihle, E. (2006). Project SEARCH: A demand-side model of high school transition. *Journal of Vocational Rehabilitation*, *25*, 85–96.

Rutter, M. (2011). Progress in understanding autism: 2007–2010. *Journal of Autism and Developmental Disorders*, *41*, 395–404.

Slack, K.S., Holl, J.L., Yoo, J., Amsden, L.B., Collins, E., & Bolger, K. (2014). Welfare, work and health care access predictors of low-income children's physical health outcomes. *Children and Youth Services Review*, *29*, 782–801.

Smith, L.E., Greenberg, J.S. & Mailick, M.R. (2012). Adults with autism: Outcomes, family effects and the multi-family group psychoeducation model. *Current Psychiatry Reports*, *14*, 732–738. doi:10.1007/s11920-012-0328-1.

Smith, L.E., Maenner, M.J., & Seltzer, M.M. (2012). Developmental trajectories in adolescents and adults with autism: The case of daily living skills. *Journal of the American Academy of Child and Adolescent Psychiatry*, *51*, 622–631.

Social Security Administration. (2018). Spotlight on living arrangements – 2018 edition. Retrieved from www.ssa.gov/ssi/spotlights/spot-living-arrangements.htm.

Sosnowy, C., Silverman, C., & Shattuck, P. (2018). Parents' and young adults' perspectives on transition outcomes for young adults with autism. *Autism*, *22*(1), 29–39. doi:10.1177/1362361317699585.

Strickland, D.C., Coles, C.D., & Southern, L.B. (2013). JobTIPS: A transition of employment program for individuals with autism spectrum disorders. *Journal of Autism & Developmental Disorders*, *10*, 2472–2483. doi:10.1007/s10803-013-1800-1804.

Sue, D.W. & Sue, D. (2016). *Counseling the culturally diverse: Theory and practice.* Hoboken, NJ: Wiley.

Taylor, J.L., & Seltzer, M.M. (2012). Developing a vocational index for adults with autism spectrum disorders. *Journal of Autism and Developmental Disorders*, *42*, 2669–2679.

TEACCH Supported Employment Program. (2013). Retrieved from: http://teach.com/clcc.

Think College. (2018). Retrieved from: http://thinkcollege.net.

Tomeny, T.S., Ellis, B.M., Rankin, J.A., & Barry, T.D. (2017). Sibling relationship quality and psychosocial outcomes among adult siblings of individuals with autism spectrum disorder and individuals with intellectual disability without autism. *Research in Developmental Disabilities*, *62*, 104–114. doi:10.1016/j.ridd.2017.01.008.

Vohra, R., Madhavan, S., & Sambamoorthi, U. (2017) Comorbidity prevalence, healthcare utilization, and expenditures of Medicaid enrolled adults with autism spectrum disorders. *Autism*, *21*, 995–1009. doi:10.1177/1362361316665222.

White, S.W., Elias, R., Salinas, C.E., Capriola, N., Conner, C.M., Asselin, S.B., … Getzel, E.E. (2016). Students with autism spectrum disorder in college: Results from a preliminary mixed methods needs analysis. *Research in Developmental Disabilities*, *56*, 29–40.

Index

Page numbers in **bold** denote tables, those in *italics* denote figures.